Contemporary Cultural Theory

Contemporary Cultural Theory

THIRD EDITION

Andrew Milner
Jeff Browitt

RAWAT PUBLICATIONS
Jaipur • New Delhi • Bangalore • Guwahati • Kolkata

ISBN 978-81-7033-770-6

Indian Reprint, 2018

First published by
Allen & Unwin, 83 Alexander Street, Crows Nest NSW 2065, Australia.
This edition published by arrangement with Allen & Unwin, Australia.

Published by
Prem Rawat for **Rawat Publications**
Satyam Apts., Sector 3, Jawahar Nagar, Jaipur - 302 004 (India)
Phone: 0141 265 1748 / 7006 Fax: 0141 265 1748
E-mail : info@rawatbooks.com
Website: rawatbooks.com

New Delhi Office
4858/24, Ansari Road, Daryaganj, New Delhi 110 002
Phone: 011-23263290

Also at *Bangalore, Guwahati* and *Kolkata*

Printed at Nice Printing Press, New Delhi.

For our partners, Verity Burgmann and Nidia Castrillón,
and our children, David, James and Robert Milner
and Helen Browitt.

Acknowledgements

We are indebted to our respective partners, Verity Burgmann and Nidia Castrillón, and to our children, David, James and Robert Milner and Helen Browitt, for all the important things. We are indebted too to friends, colleagues and students in the Centre for Comparative Literature and Cultural Studies at Monash University and to staff at the Monash University Library. Comparisons are always invidious, but special thanks are due to Richard Clarke, Claire Colebrook, Rob Cover, Anthony Elliott, Kathleen Ferguson, Kevin Hart, Hélène Pouliquen, Kate Rigby, David Roberts, Philip Thomson, Gail Ward and Chris Worth. We are also grateful to John Iremonger and Elizabeth Weiss at Allen & Unwin for the enthusiasm with which they supported various stages of the project. Acknowledgement is due to the Faculty of Arts at Monash University, which provided us each with completion grants of A$5000.

Contents

Reader's note: Where emphasis occurs in quoted material, this is as it appears in the original except where we indicate otherwise.

1

Cultural studies and cultural theory

Cultural studies emerged as one of the more significant academic growth industries during the last quarter of the twentieth century, especially in its last decade. It now has separate courses or departments in every continent but Antarctica. If not quite the 'genuinely global movement' Simon During describes (During, 1999, p. 11), cultural studies has nonetheless grown into a putatively international discipline, with a serious intellectual presence, stretching beyond Europe, the Americas and Australia, into India, Taiwan and South Korea (see Appendix). For all this apparent ubiquity, the term 'cultural studies' remains an unusually 'polysemic' sign. At one level, of course, its meaning is obvious: cultural studies is the academic study of culture. The problem, however, is that there is absolutely no agreement as to what exactly we mean by 'culture'. The latter is one of the most widely used abstract nouns in the lexicon. People worry about the independence of their 'national culture', but also about whether they are sufficiently 'cultured' as individuals to 'get on' in life. They worry about the possibility and desirability of living in a 'multicultural' society. Economists and politicians wonder about the 'culture industries' and the prospects of 'culture-led' economic recovery. In our own profession as university teachers, we worry about culture whenever we worry about the administrative organisation of cultural studies in our university.

The odd thing about these worries, however, is that each is

worryingly ambiguous. When people think of an independent national culture, they might well have in mind distinctive arts, as embodied both in individual works and in institutions such as art galleries and opera houses. But they might also be thinking more generally about their distinctively national ways of doing things: their cuisine and their eating habits, their religion and their sports. To be 'cultured' might mean the ability to spot intertextual references to T.S. Eliot; but it might also mean the capacity to affect an 'upper-class' accent. 'Multiculturalism' might mean more 'immigrant' literature in schools or more foreign films on public television; but it might also mean significant modifications to those distinctively national ways of doing things—curry as well as fish and chips in England, or soccer instead of American or Australian football. A 'culture-led' economic recovery probably would have something to do with theatres, film production or higher education; but it might also mean that people would be persuaded to sell their way of life as a drawcard for the tourist industry. As for cultural studies, for some it clearly means the classics, fine arts and the high literary canon; for others it might mean the sociology of adolescent gang warfare and the anthropology of kinship. The problem is that we all mean a great deal more than we know.

DEFINING CULTURE

Raymond Williams, the Welsh cultural theorist and late Professor of Drama at Cambridge University, famously described 'culture' as 'one of the two or three most complicated words in the English language' (Williams, 1976, p. 76). That complexity is nowhere more apparent than in his own attempts to define its usage. In his first major work, *Culture and Society 1780–1950*, he drew attention to four important kinds of meaning that attach to the word: an individual habit of mind; the state of intellectual development of a whole society; the arts; and the whole way of life of a group or people (Williams, 1963, p. 16). In the later *Keywords*, only the latter three usages remained in play (Williams, 1976, p. 80). Later still, his sociology textbook, *Culture*, reintroduced the first usage, grouping it together with the second and third as 'general', and contrasting these with the fourth, more specifically 'anthropological' meaning (Williams, 1981, p. 11). Williams distinguished between the word's physical and human applications; its positive and negative connotations; its use as a noun of process and as a noun of configuration; its politically radical and politically reactionary applications; and so on. He was clear, however, that these confusions and complications belonged to our 'culture' itself, rather than to any fault either in his analysis or in the term: 'These variations . . . necessarily involve alternative views of the activities, relationships and processes which this complex word indicates. The complexity, that is to say, is not finally in the word but in the problems which its variations of use significantly indicate' (Williams, 1976, p. 81). The range and the overlap of meanings, the distinctions simultaneously elided and insisted upon, are all in themselves 'significant' (p. 80).

More recently, Geoffrey Hartman, Professor of English and Comparative Literature at Yale University, has observed that culture is 'an inflammatory word', which in some circumstances can even kindle 'actual wars' (Hartman, 1997, p. 14). Culture is a good thing, then, but also a dangerous thing. Hartman notes the same complexity that Williams observed, and the way the word's use proliferates—'camera culture, gun culture, service culture, museum culture, deaf culture, football culture'—so that it becomes a kind of 'linguistic weed' (p. 30).

Both Williams and Hartman attempted to trace the intellectual history of the concept. In its earliest meanings, in English and in French, it had referred to the tending of natural growth, either in animals or in plants. Williams dated the word's extension to include human development from the early sixteenth century in English usage; and its earliest use as an independent noun, to refer to an abstract process, from the mid-seventeenth century (Williams, 1976, pp. 77–8). His version of this history remained overwhelmingly English in focus, leading to Eliot, F.R. Leavis, Orwell and, by implication, himself. Hartman's version (which includes Williams) is more cosmopolitan and leads to Spengler, Benda, Nazism and Heiner Müller. For Williams, the idea of culture held out the promise of emancipation; for Hartman, 'the fateful question' as to whether a truly 'generous' idea of culture is possible remains only 'precariously' open (Williams, 1963, pp. 322–3; Hartman, 1997, pp. 192–3).

For Hartman, the most crucial of the various distinctions in the term's meaning is that between 'culture' as a general ideal, 'a "republic of letters" in which ideas can be freely exchanged', and '*a* culture' as 'a specific form of embodiment or solidarity'; he believes there is a crucial need to protect the former against the latter (Hartman, 1997, pp. 36, 41). For Williams, the most crucial distinction was that between the term's use in the humanities and in the social sciences. The concept of 'culture', he explained:

> became a noun of 'inner' process, specialized to its presumed agencies in 'intellectual life' and 'the arts'. It became also a noun of general process, specialized to its presumed configurations in 'whole ways of life'. It played a crucial role in definitions of 'the arts' and 'the humanities', from the first sense. It played an equally crucial role in definitions of the 'human sciences' and the 'social sciences', in the second sense (Williams, 1977, p. 17).

Culture, then, may be counterposed to society, as 'art'; but the two words may also be defined nearly coextensively, as everything that is left over after politics and economics. There is a clear parallel between Hartman and Williams here, since 'culture' is to 'a culture' as 'arts' is to 'a whole way of life'. But where for Hartman the key distinction runs between a generality and a particular, a general public sphere and a singular subculture, for Williams it ran between two generalities, the arts and the whole way of life. Note the wider significance of this: while for Williams society still remained a generality, or a commonality, for Hartman it has already become a multicultural plurality of particulars. We shall return to the competing claims of what Williams termed the 'common culture' and politico-social multiculturalism in the chapters that follow. For the moment, however, suffice it to note that this is an issue of quite fundamental significance, not simply for academic cultural studies, but also for the future of our society and our culture.

The available definitions of the term 'culture' are many and various then, and we shall have cause to consider them in more detail in later chapters. But let us now offer our own working 'non-definition' of 'culture' as referring to that entire range of institutions, artefacts and practices that make up our symbolic universe. In one or another of its meanings, the term will thus embrace: art and religion, science and sport, education and leisure. By convention, however, it does not embrace the range of activities normally deemed either 'economic' or 'political'. This threefold distinction, between the economics of the market, the politics of the state and the culture of what is sometimes referred to as civil society, has been a recurrent motif in modern social theory: it occurred, for example, in Karl Marx as the distinction between mode of production, political superstructure and social consciousness (Marx, 1975, p. 425) and in Max Weber as that between class, party and status (Weber, 1948). But it is clear that in each case, as in a whole range of parallel instances, consciousness/status/culture (ideology/discourse etc.) are largely residual categories, defined as much as anything by their negative property of not being economics or politics. As that which is neither work/class/exploitation nor war/power/oppression, culture becomes 'the heart of a heartless world', to borrow Marx's description of religion (Marx, 1975, p. 244). But just as religion in the abstract translates in practice into religions in the bitterly contested plural, so too culture readily translates into cultures. Hence its almost talismanic status during the so-called 'culture wars' of late twentieth-century United States, where it could denote simultaneously both the canonical high 'culture' of established academic tradition and the ethnic, sexual, generational and gendered 'counter-cultures' of the 'new social movements'.

DEFINING CULTURAL STUDIES

The culture wars provide a suitable occasion to proceed from culture to cultural studies, since part of what was at stake in their still unresolved outcome is precisely the status of the new 'proto-discipline' in American higher education. As currently constructed, cultural studies still remains deeply indebted to the pioneering work of the Birmingham Centre. Founded in 1964, as a graduate research unit under the directorship of Richard Hoggart, then Professor of English Literature at Birmingham, the Centre became the intellectually pre-eminent institutional location for cultural studies, both in Britain and internationally, for most of the 1970s and 1980s. Anthony Easthope, late Professor of English and Cultural Studies at Manchester Metropolitan University, judged the Birmingham Centre's work the most important 'intervention in cultural studies in Britain' (Easthope, 1988, p. 74). Lawrence Grossberg, now Professor of Communication and Cultural Studies at North Carolina, agreed that: 'there remains something like a center—to be precise, the tradition of British cultural studies, especially the work of the Centre for Contemporary Cultural Studies' (Grossberg et al., 1988, p. 8). Graeme Turner, founding editor of the *Australian Journal of Cultural Studies* and now Director of the Centre for Critical and Cultural Studies in Queensland, echoed this view: 'the Birmingham Centre . . . can justifiably claim to be the key institution in the history of the field' (Turner, 1996, p. 70). It is tempting, then, to look to Birmingham for a model of what is meant by 'cultural studies'. Once again, however, the sign appears radically polysemic, for there was never a single Birmingham model, but rather an inescapable plurality of competing and often contradictory models.

The unusually polysemic quality of 'cultural studies' attaches as much to the term 'studies' as to 'culture' or 'cultural': not only is there no clear consensus over what to study, but also none over how to organise this study. The various senses of 'cultural studies' seem to cluster around four main sets of meaning: as inter- or post-disciplinary; as a political intervention into the existing academic disciplines; as an entirely new discipline, defined in terms of an entirely new subject matter; and as a new discipline, defined in terms of a new theoretical paradigm. Cultural studies was clearly intended by Hoggart, in the initial proposal to establish the Centre, as essentially interdisciplinary in character, but with literary studies as its single 'most important' element (Hoggart, 1970, p. 255). A quarter of a century later, this continued to be his view: 'the student should have an initial discipline outside Cultural Studies,' he would write, 'an academic and intellectual training, and a severe one' (Hoggart, 1995, p. 173). The modish notion of a 'post-disciplinary' cultural studies, canvassed in the early issues of the *International Journal of Cultural Studies*, appears to differ only very slightly from Hoggart's sense of the interdisciplinary (cf. Hartley, 1998, pp. 5–8). There is a real difference, however, in the conception of cultural studies as a kind of political intervention, associated above all with Hall, Hoggart's immediate successor as Director at Birmingham. For Hall, the 'seriousness' of cultural studies was inscribed in its 'political' aspect: 'there is something *at stake* in cultural studies,' he insisted, 'in a way that . . . is not exactly true of many other . . . intellectual . . . practices' (Hall, 1992, p. 278). Similarly 'political' conceptions recur throughout the cultural studies literature. According to During, this politically 'engaged form of analysis' constitutes one of the discipline's most obviously distinguishing features (During, 1999, p. 2).

The third conception sees cultural studies as an entirely new discipline defined in terms of a new subject matter: that is, the study of popular culture. America's culture wars were substantially matters of race and ethnicity, gender and sexuality, but insofar as they also brought cultural elitism into conflict with cultural populism, they clearly touched on this issue. For cultural elitists such as Harold Bloom, Professor of Humanities at Yale University, cultural studies has threatened to substitute '*Batman* comics, Mormon theme parks, television, movies, and rock' for 'Chaucer, Shakespeare, Milton, Wordsworth and Wallace Stevens' (Bloom, 1994, p. 519). For cultural populists like Grossberg, this is precisely its promise. There can be little doubt that cultural studies did indeed emerge by way of a quasi-populist reaction against the elitism of older forms of literary study. All three of the discipline's widely acknowledged British 'founding fathers'—Hoggart himself, E.P. Thompson and Williams—were clearly committed to the study of popular or working-class culture. Nonetheless, none of them actually imagined cultural studies as in any sense coextensive with the study of the 'popular arts'. The growing sense of cultural studies as a sociology of mass media consumption, nicely symbolised in Hall's appointment to the chair of sociology at the British Open University, is a subsequent development, and one that ran against the grain of Birmingham's founding moment. It is also misconceived, it seems to us, if only because the binary organisation of 'elite' and 'popular' cultures is in the process of being replaced by a large number of cultural niche markets, each dominated by the same international media conglomerates and subject to variously critical or uncritical commentary from the same academic and media institutions.

Francis Mulhern uses the German word *Kulturkritik* to denote the elitist position in this debate, 'Cultural Studies' to denote the populist. There is obvious justification for this usage. Both Hartman and Williams attached a crucial significance, in the history of the term 'culture', to the legacy of German Romanticism, where German *Kultur* was troped against French *civilisation*, as human nature in opposition to mechanical artifice (Hartman, 1997, pp. 205–7, 210; Williams, 1976, pp. 78–80). It is this legacy that Mulhern acknowledges in his use of *Kulturkritik* to denote not only the German tradition proper, but also the English tradition of Matthew Arnold, Eliot and Leavis (Mulhern, 2000, pp. xv–xvi). Where *Kulturkritik* valorises high art, what Mulhern calls Cultural Studies valorises mass civilisation. But the two positions are by no means as antithetical as they appear, he continues, since Cultural Studies actually reproduces the same 'metacultural' discursive form as that of traditional *Kulturkritik* (p. 156). In either mode, he writes, metacultural discourse 'invents an authoritative subject, "good" culture, be it minority or popular, whose function is to mediate a symbolic metapolitical resolution of the contradictions of capitalist modernity' (p. 169).

There is much to be said for the argument, but Mulhern's categories are by no means as inclusive as he suggests. As he acknowledges, Williams' work was an important exception to this observation, insofar as it set out to establish a distinctive 'politics of culture' (p. 72) in opposition to both elitist *Kulturkritik* and populist Cultural Studies. We would add, however, that quite apart from these specifically political issues, there has always been a fourth option in play, where cultural studies is seen as deliberately connecting the study of the popular with that of the 'literary'. In this definition, it represents a shift not so much in empirical subject matter as in theoretical paradigm. This conception was important for Williams, whose 'empirical' work quite systematically transgressed the boundaries between elite and popular cultures. But it is also present, for example, in Easthope's understanding of 'literary study' as 'increasingly indistinguishable from cultural studies' (Easthope, 1991, p. 65); in Tony Bennett's sense of cultural studies as fundamentally concerned with 'the relations of culture and power' (Bennett, 1998, p. 53); or in Stephen Greenblatt's description of his own work on Renaissance literature as 'the new historicism in cultural studies' (Greenblatt, 1990, p. 158).

No doubt, there is something to be said for all four senses of the term: they each register important aspects of different phases in the development of cultural studies. But there is a cumulative logic, nonetheless, which suggests to us that the greater promise lies with this fourth conception: not in the discovery of a new subject matter, nor even in the 'deconstruction' of the disciplinary boundaries that demarcated literature from fiction, art from culture, elite from popular; but rather in the development of new methods of analysis for both. Andrew Milner half-seriously 'defines' cultural studies as the 'social science of the study of the production, distribution, exchange and reception of textualised meaning' (Milner, 2002, p. 5) and this will serve as our definition here. We use the term 'social science', as he does, to denote a discipline the primary purposes of which are description and explanation rather than judgement or 'canonisation'. We use the term 'textualised meaning' to denote a concern with signifying practices in general rather than literature and art or the mass media in particular. And we use the phrase 'production, distribution, exchange and reception' to denote an interest in how texts are produced, circulated and received in determinate social contexts, as well as in texts considered 'in their own right'. If this is indeed what we mean by cultural studies, then it follows that its intellectual novelty is primarily theoretical, rather than substantive. Which leads us to the central subject matter of this book: not so much cultural studies in general as cultural theory in particular.

CULTURAL STUDIES AND CULTURAL THEORY

Cultural theory, or 'Theory' with a capital 'T', as it is sometimes written in the United States, is different from either philosophy or discipline-specific theories such as sociological theory. Some see it as a new and distinctly 'postmodern' type of transdisciplinary theorising. Fredric Jameson cites Michel Foucault as providing the exemplary instance of this kind of 'undecidable' genre, which takes as its object not so much a particular class of phenomena as the textualisation of the phenomenal in general (Jameson, 1998, p. 3). For Jameson, Theory is very specifically post-structuralist: he uses the terms more or less interchangeably to denote 'very precisely a postmodernist phenomenon' in which 'depth is replaced by surface'. Thus understood, Theory is characterised by an in principle opposition to depth models, be they hermeneutic (inside/outside), dialectical (appearance/essence), psychoanalytic (latent/manifest), existential (authenticity/inauthenticity) or semiotic (signifier/signified) (Jameson, 1991, p. 12). But if contemporary Theory is indeed both transdisciplinary and textual, in our view it need not necessarily be post-structuralist. Jameson himself writes Theory of a distinctly transdisciplinary and textual character, while nonetheless maintaining a clear distance from what remains of post-structuralism (however we define that term).

Ironically, this use of 'Theory' as more or less identical to post-structuralism replicates an earlier trope from British cultural studies, where theory was understood as essentially structuralist. During the 1970s, the Birmingham Centre witnessed a sustained encounter between an earlier English tradition of 'literary' cultural criticism and a variety of French structuralist and more generally continental 'western Marxist' (and sociological) traditions. The encounter was theorised as that between 'structuralism' and 'culturalism' by two successive directors, Hall himself and Richard Johnson (Hall, 1980; Johnson, R., 1979). In each case, an empiricist culturalism was contrasted with a theoreticist structuralism. We shall return to this matter in the chapter that follows. For the moment, note only that for Hall, structuralism's superiority over culturalism derived precisely from its recognition 'not only of the necessity for abstraction as the instrument of thought through which "real relations" are appropriated, but also of the presence . . . of a continuous and complex movement *between different levels of abstraction*' (Hall, 1980, p. 67). Whatever the merits of Hall's wider argument, it seems to us that he clearly misconstrued the situation insofar as his stress fell on the supposedly atheoretical nature of British culturalism. Indeed, Hall had himself observed of Williams' *The Long Revolution*, one of the seminal 'culturalist' texts, that: 'It attempted to graft on to an idiom and mode of discourse irredeemably particular, empirical and moral in emphasis, its own . . . kind of "theorizing" . . . The difficult, somewhat abstract quality of the writing . . . can largely be ascribed to its status as a "text of the break"' (Hall, 1980a, p. 19).

Moreover, Hall seriously underestimated the properly 'theoretical' content of the culturalist tradition as it had evolved before Williams. If the mode of exposition of Leavisite literary criticism (perhaps the single most important instance of British culturalist thought) was indeed irredeemably particular, its intellectual content—as, for example, in the debate about industrialisation and cultural decline or that about the 'dissociation of sensibility'—remained highly theoretical. There is nothing especially particular nor even especially empirical about Leavis' insistence that the disintegration of the pre-industrial organic community was 'the most important fact of recent history' (Leavis & Thompson, 1960, p. 87). In truth, the various discourses about culture, which developed in Britain and Germany, France and Italy, Russia and the United States, essentially as a series of sustained reflections on the nature of cultural modernisation and, later, postmodernisation, have *all* been irretrievably 'theoretical' in nature, no matter how apparently 'empirical' their particular reference points. Hence, the invariable accompaniment of courses in cultural studies by parallel courses in cultural theory. Hence, too, the subject matter of this book.

Our point here is neither to celebrate nor to bemoan the significance of cultural theory for cultural studies, but merely to note its general significance. Almost everyone who worked in the humanities and social sciences, whether in western Europe, the

Americas or Australasia, at any time during the last three decades of the twentieth century, would have encountered transdisciplinary 'Theory' of this kind. Whether appalled by its poverty, like Thompson, or attracted to its glamour, like Terry Eagleton, there is no doubting its cultural salience (Thompson, 1978; Eagleton, 1996, pp. 191–2). Even Hoggart, as unlikely a theoretician as any, would admit that 'one does not wish to undervalue the importance of theory and the need for theoretic languages' (Hoggart, 1995, p. 177). For our part, we concede to Hoggart that theory 'must not be made into a charm, or a prop; or a waffle-iron to be banged on top of the material' (p. 178); in short, it must be about something. But we would want to insist that many of the older disciplines Hoggart imagined as contributing to an interdisciplinary cultural studies, and their attendant theories, have in fact become increasingly irrelevant to contemporary culture. To take the obvious example, the postmodern cultures of the late twentieth and early twenty-first centuries are now so thoroughly mediatised, commodified and relativised as to demand very different modes of analysis from those Hoggart learnt from English Literature. This is not to suggest that we are now somehow able to move beyond 'disciplinarity'. Quite the contrary, this latest version of transdisciplinary Theory seems likely to be a transitional form—like its predecessors—by which older disciplines are recomposed into new ones more appropriate to a changed and changing culture. As Jameson himself notes, contemporary Theory is already confronted by a renewed impetus towards disciplinary re-differentiation: 'philosophy and its branches are back in force' (Jameson, 1998, p. 94). We might add that cultural studies itself is also increasingly subject to calls for 'disciplinisation' (Bennett, 1998).

CULTURE AND SOCIETY: ANTI-UTILITARIANISM AND MODERNITY

What, then, is the occasion for these recurrent bouts of theorising? Discourses become self-consciously theoretical, which is another way of saying that they become self-reflexive, as a general rule only when their subject matters become in some significant sense problematic. And it is only in the modern and postmodern periods that 'culture', however defined, has become such. Pre-modern societies, like the feudalisms of medieval Europe or the hunting and gathering communities of tribalism, clearly exhibit behaviours we can easily recognise as 'cultural', whether religious or artistic, educational or 'scientific'—as Lévi-Strauss reminds us, 'primitive' knowledge can indeed be understood as a kind of science (Lévi-Strauss, 1966, pp. 13–16). But this is our retrospective understanding, not their own. Precisely because culture, and especially religion, remained central to the life of feudal or tribal societies, they typically possessed no sense of the cultural as 'different' or residual, such as is conveyed by contemporary western usage. In short, culture has become a theoretical problem for the West only because it is already socially problematic. Cultural theory is not, then, simply a particular, specialist academic discourse, the guiding hand behind a particular set of empirical, substantive, research problems; it is also, and more interestingly, the repressed 'other' of a society the official rhetoric of which is provided almost entirely by economics and politics. Cultural theory is, in fact, one of the central discontents of our civilisation.

But if culture has indeed become so problematic, why has this been so? The short answer lies in the nature of socio-cultural modernisation itself, and in particular in the rise to dominance of a distinctively capitalist system of economic organisation, in which goods and services are produced primarily for sale in a more or less competitive market. This is as true of modern *cultural* production as of any other kind of production. Indeed, a strong case can be made for the view that the book trade was the first modern capitalist industry: as Febvre and Martin observe, 'the printer and the bookseller worked above all and from the beginning for profit' (Febvre & Martin, 1976, p. 249). This historically novel mode of cultural production required, for its eventual success, not only the general development of capitalist forms of organisation, but also a number of factors quite specific to cultural production itself, such as copyright laws and techniques of 'mechanical reproduction' (cf. Benjamin, 1973). This unprecedented commercialisation of cultural production brought about an equally unprecedented transformation in the social position and status of cultural producers, such as writers, artists, priests and teachers, those whom we might today designate as, collectively, 'the intelligentsia'. Earlier forms of cultural 'patronage' had guaranteed the material security of cultural producers at the price of a radical subordination of intellectual life to the church, the aristocracy and the royal court. Such cultures required no specifically cultural theory, but only a theology or a politics. In capitalist society, however, what Peter Bürger terms 'the separation of art from the praxis of life' becomes the decisive characteristic of 'the autonomy of bourgeois art' (Bürger, 1984, p. 49).

The term 'autonomy' here denotes both relative freedom from social control and a corresponding social irrelevance (cf. Marcuse, 1968). These autonomies have never appeared either unproblematic or uncontestable, either to the cultural producers themselves or to others. Hence the various forms of political and religious intervention in the cultural commodity market—for example censorship, subsidy and education. The cultural conflicts thereby instigated are evidence, according to Williams, 'of the most significant modern form of asymmetry' (Williams, 1981, p. 102), between capitalist mechanical reproduction and the older established institutions of cultural and social reproduction. As one consequence among many, such asymmetries have prompted the emergence of contemporary cultural theory, not as a single body of authoritative discourse, but as a set of competing, often mutually exclusive, often internally contradictory, almost always deeply troubled, narrative paradigms. Cultural theory is thus the discursive articulation of a set of characteristically modern social contradictions, which structure the lived experiences of characteristically modern kinds of intellectuals. In a society as thoroughly encultured as is ours, such theories become, by turn, the property not only of specialist intellectuals, but also of the collective lives of whole communities. They are, then, matters of no small consequence.

UTILITARIANISM AND ITS OTHERS

By a strange irony, most university courses in cultural theory carefully manage to ignore what is almost certainly the single most influential such theory available to our culture: utilitarianism. Historically, this was the first of all modern cultural theories, chronologically prior to the whole range of competing successor paradigms. But it almost certainly still represents the preferred paradigm of the vast majority of members of the contemporary business and political elite—as distinct from the cultural elites—and, as such, exercises an enduring influence over a great deal of cultural policy formation. We use the term 'utilitarianism' to denote a view of the social world as consisting, ideally or factually, in a plurality of discrete, separate, rational individuals, each of whom is motivated, to all intents and purposes exclusively, by the pursuit of pleasure (or 'utility') and the avoidance of pain. The good society is thus one organised so as to least inhibit the individual in pursuit of his or her pleasures, one in which markets are as freely competitive as possible, and in which governments exist only to establish the legal framework within which such markets can freely function. It is a view that has its origins in seventeenth-century England. Its evolution can be traced from the social contract theories of politics propounded by Thomas Hobbes (1588–1679) and John Locke (1632–1704), and the empiricist philosophical systems of David Hume (1711–76), through to the political economy of Adam Smith (1723–90) and David Ricardo (1772–1823), and on to the self-proclaimed utilitarianism of Jeremy Bentham (1748–1832) and John Stuart Mill (1806–73).

This is an overwhelmingly British intellectual tradition, but one that certainly found echoes in eighteenth-century French thought. Its political correlate is liberalism, in the nineteenth-century sense of the term (which is how the term still tends to be used in contemporary French and German discourse). Utilitarianism provided the single most powerful justification for the forms of social organisation characteristic of modern capitalist society: that they guarantee the greatest happiness of the greatest number. It provided the intellectual underpinnings for the discipline of economics, especially as it is practised in the

English-speaking world. In its most recent manifestation, as 'neo-liberalism' or 'economic liberalism'—what in Britain was known as 'Thatcherism'; in the United States, 'Reaganism'; in Australia, bizarrely enough, 'economic rationalism'—it has provided the major analytical framework for the policy-making of governments both of the Left and of the Right. For the substance of economic Reaganism continued under Clinton, and that of economic Thatcherism under Blair. As a Conservative member of the British House of Lords, updating Milton for the twenty-first century, observed shortly after the 2001 general election: 'New Labour was but old Thatcherism writ large' (Gilmour, 2001, p. 16). Both in Australia and in New Zealand, this shift towards neo-liberalism was actually initiated by the Labor Party.

There is in utilitarianism, moreover, not only a theory of the market and of the state, but also a quite explicit theory of culture. The Canadian political philosopher C.B. Macpherson described utilitarianism as a 'theory of possessive individualism', and argued that from Hobbes onwards it had presupposed a model of 'possessive market society'. In such a society, Macpherson explained, 'individuals are free to expend their energies, skills and goods as they will'; they 'are not given or guaranteed, by the state or the community, rewards appropriate to their social functions'; and they 'seek to get the most satisfaction they can for a given expenditure' (Macpherson, 1962, p. 51). It requires only the further postulate that objects of cultural preference, be they literary genres or religious doctrines, can be treated as commodities for sale in the marketplace to lead us to the conclusion that every individual is entitled to whatever cultural pleasures they might please, for so long as they are practically procurable in the cultural marketplace. Thus each person becomes their own church or court. Or as Bentham had it: 'push-pin is of equal value with . . . poetry' (Bentham, 1962, p. 253).

Such strictly Benthamite utilitarianisms implicitly endorse the reduction of cultural values to the level of the marketable commodity. But if this is the logical terminus of any consistent cultural utilitarianism, it is not easily arrived at by those who believe in notions of traditional cultural value such as are typically sustained by the churches, the education system, and so on. Nor is it one many utilitarian philosophers chose to embrace with any great enthusiasm. Hume, for example, hurriedly proceeded to the qualification that: 'Whoever would assert an equality of genius and elegance between Ogilby and Milton . . . it appears an extravagant paradox, or rather a palpable absurdity, where objects so disproportioned are compared together' (Hume, 1965, p. 7). While John Stuart Mill insisted that: 'It is better to be . . . Socrates dissatisfied than a fool satisfied' (Mill, 1962, pp. 258, 260). Williams' asymmetry between capitalist production for profit and cultural and social reproduction is clearly inscribed in both texts. Hume and Mill sought to resolve the problem by an appeal to the notion that particular individuals might not be properly fit to judge in matters of 'taste'. Proper judgement between two pleasures, Mill concludes, can be made only 'by those who are competently acquainted with both' (p. 259). Commendable though the implied preference for poetry over push-pin might seem to those who value poetry (or philosophy), it remains intellectually incoherent. Qualitative definitions of experiential value, such as those Mill experiments with, are quite fundamentally incompatible with the utilitarian schema's initial starting point in the so-called 'felicific calculus' (or calculation of happiness): the utility maximisation principle remains workable only as long as happiness is understood as providing a single, quantitative measure of human well-being.

Which is not to suggest that Mill's preferences are mistaken, only that he cannot justify them in consistently utilitarian terms. The case against utilitarianism itself, which Mill refuses to make, is essentially sociological in character. The doyen of mid-twentieth century American sociology, Professor Talcott Parsons of Harvard, summarised the central argument as early as 1937. The peculiarity of the utilitarian schema, he observed, was that it proceeded as if people's goals were random and their ways of knowing the world, and so of identifying those goals, essentially indistinguishable from those of rational-scientific knowledge (Parsons, 1949, pp. 60–61). In reality, however, human goals are very clearly structured or patterned. In reality, moreover, human actors know the world in ways other than that of positive science: their goals are patterned as much by systems of religious, political, ethical and aesthetic value as by any kind of cognitive knowledge, scientific or otherwise. Hence the importance for Parsons of 'a common system of ultimate values as a vital element in concrete social life' (p. 469). It is precisely such systems of ultimate value, he argued, that organise, integrate and de-randomise the ends of individual social actors. Whatever the strengths or weaknesses of Parsons' general sociology, he was surely right to identify in utilitarianism this fundamental incapacity to understand the significance for action of human values, whether religious, political, ethical or aesthetic. For economists such sins are merely venial, but for the cultural theorist they become irreparably mortal.

The enduring appeal of utilitarianism owes a great deal more, however, to a happy coincidence between its thematics and those of powerful business interests than to whatever inherent intellectual power it might possess. This was obviously so during the 1980s, when Thatcherism and Reaganism were simultaneously at their most hegemonic and most radical. But the immense institutional and intellectual prestige that still attaches to university economics departments also seems to owe far less to the discipline's supposed 'scientificity' than to its effectiveness as political and social propaganda. As the German sociologist Max Horkheimer observed, the consonance between 'theory' and 'fact', in intellectual thought as much as in commonsense, is 'conditioned by the fact that the world of objects to be judged is in large measure produced by an activity that is itself determined by the very ideas which help the individual to recognise that world and to grasp it conceptually' (Horkheimer, 1972, p. 202). In our view, utilitarianism functions in precisely such a fashion in contemporary western societies. It will figure in what follows, then, not as an alternative solution to the cultural problems of capitalism, but rather as importantly constitutive of those very problems, as part of the socio-cultural context against which other cultural theories have been obliged to define themselves.

In chapters 2 to 6, we chart the development of five versions of non-utilitarian cultural theory, which we term, very loosely: culturalism, critical theory, semiology, difference theory and postmodernism. We use the term 'culturalism' to denote an intellectual tradition that deliberately counterposed the value of culture to the claims of utility. This is a tradition that typically conceived culture in radically anti-individualist fashion, as an organic whole, and in radically anti-utilitarian fashion, as a repository of values superior to those of material civilisation. It has been an essentially literary tradition, but one that provided important inspiration to two contemporary movements—cultural studies and cultural materialism—each of which has sought to problematise the boundaries between literature and non-literature. By 'critical theory' we refer above all to the *Kulturkritik* of the 'Frankfurt School', but also to the key thinkers from whom the School derived inspiration, notably Marx, Weber and Freud, and to other contemporary critics who have derived their own inspiration from these or related sources. This is a tradition that combined a culturalist sense of the antithesis between culture and civilisation with a utilitarian sense of the importance of material interests. It has been a largely sociological tradition, the key concepts of which include notions such as ideology, legitimation and hegemony.

We use the term 'semiology' to refer to the intellectual tradition prompted either directly or indirectly by Ferdinand de Saussure's anticipation of a science of the study of signs. In its opening 'structuralist' phase, this tradition was characterised by a search for underlying and constraining patterns and structures, especially patterns analogous to those that occur in language. In its later 'post-structuralist' phase, the emphasis shifted towards the plurality and indeterminacy of meaning, but remained fundamentally 'linguistic' nonetheless. In this tradition, cultural artefacts are best understood as elements within systems of signification. By 'difference theory', we mean the whole range of late twentieth-century cultural theories inspired in whole or in part by the politics of difference associated with the 'new social movements'. Here we explore how socio-historical differences, such as those between genders and sexualities, nationalities and ethnicities, have been theorised in relation to the non-immediacy, the différance, as Derrida has it, of language and culture. The key concepts here will include identity and, of course, difference itself.

By 'postmodernism', we refer to the kind of cultural theory that has sought to represent such differences as testimony to the peculiar novelty of a contemporary 'postmodern condition'. Where utilitarianism, culturalism, critical theory, semiology and even difference theory each represent a distinctive type of cultural theory, each with its own characteristic core concepts—utility, culture, ideology, signification, difference—postmodernism, by contrast, remains not so much a kind of theory as a particular question posed to each of the other kinds. The question, of course, is whether contemporary western society has undergone a transformation in its culture and political economy so far-reaching as to mark the end of modernity as such, and the beginning of something that might properly be deemed 'post-modern'. Stated thus, the postmodern question radically reproblematises the whole of contemporary cultural theory, for each of these other traditions is, in some significant sense, a characteristically modern cultural construct. Utilitarianism and culturalism, Marxism and sociology, structuralism and psychoanalysis, equality feminism and anti-imperialist nationalism are all obviously such. And insofar as structuralism remains implicated in post-structuralism, equality feminism in difference feminism, anti-imperialism in postcolonialism, these too might turn out to be less postmodern than they at first appear. In chapters 6 and 7 we move to a discussion, not simply of what cultural theory has been to date, but of what it might need to become for the future. The book's concluding chapter is devoted to a particularly important aspect of this debate: the argument over whether or not there remains a proper place for any kind of cultural critique, as distinct from cultural policy advice, in a society and culture increasingly saturated by market ideologies.

The first Australian edition of *Contemporary Cultural Theory* was published in 1991, a second (British) edition in 1994, a Korean translation of the British edition in 1996. Both earlier editions were written by Andrew Milner. This third international edition has been fully revised and rewritten by Andrew Milner and Jeff Browitt. Chapters 1, 5 and 7 are almost entirely new; chapters 2, 3, 4 and 6 have been very extensively revised.

2

Literature and society: from culturalism to cultural materialism

The term 'culturalism' is of relatively recent origin and has typically been defined in opposition to structuralism. Moreover, it has sometimes been accorded a quite distinctly Marxist inflection. Writing in the 1970s, Richard Johnson saw the new discipline of cultural studies as founded upon a theoretical terrain demarcated between, on the one hand, a kind of Anglo-Marxist culturalism best represented by the work of historian E.P. Thompson and literary critic Raymond Williams and, on the other, the type of Francophone structuralist Marxism established by the philosopher Louis Althusser (Johnson, R., 1979, pp. 51–2). We propose to use the term rather differently: to denote that type of anti-utilitarianism that became incorporated within a largely 'literary-humanist' tradition of speculation about the relationship between culture and society, variants of which recur within both German and British intellectual life. In both versions, the concept of culture is understood as combining a specifically 'literary' sense of culture as 'art' with an 'anthropological' sense of culture as a 'way of life'. In each case, the claims of culture are counterposed to those of material civilisation. Hence Shelley's famous dictum that: 'Poets are the unacknowledged legislators of the world' (Shelley, 1931, p. 109). The most sophisticated 'culturalist' theorisations tend to derive from Germany, however, rather than from England, and it is with this German tradition, then, that we begin.

GERMAN CULTURALISM: HERMENEUTICS AND HISTORICISM

In its German formation, what we have termed 'culturalism' has three relatively distinct aspects: Romanticism, historicism and hermeneutics. All three developed by way of reaction against the variously rationalist, mechanistic and neo-classicist ideals that had characterised the eighteenth-century European Enlightenment and its political articulation in the American and French Revolutions. The term 'Romanticism' refers very generally to this broad international movement against the Enlightenment, as it appeared in the arts and in philosophy. For our purposes, its most important thematics were a view of the artist as a uniquely creative individual, a genius and visionary, and a belief in the superiority of art, as *Kultur*, over the mechanism of everyday civilisation. The key figures in German Romanticism included Friedrich Schiller (1759–1805), Novalis (1772–1801) and, most important of all, Johann Wolfgang Goethe (1749–1832).

Historicism

The term 'historicism' originally referred to the view that historical events can properly be understood only in the immediate context of their occurrence, rather than as instances of some kind of universal, abstract theory, such as that propounded by the Enlightenment. This stress on the specificity of human historical contexts echoes the more generally Romantic preoccupation with human individuality. Moreover, these immediate contexts were often seen as distinctly 'national', so that historicism often seemed readily compatible with cultural nationalism. In principle, Romanticism need be neither historicist nor nationalist: Goethe himself hoped that the 'increasing communication between nations' would produce a 'world literature', *Weltliteratur*, capable of superseding individual national literatures (Goethe, 1973, p. 7). But German culturalism tended, nonetheless, to connect cultural specificity and uniqueness with the native language, and with notions of nationality. The key figure here was almost certainly Johann Gottfried Herder (1744–1803), who sought to define and legitimise the autonomy and individuality of German culture as 'lived experience' by grounding experience and value judgements in the nation, rather than in the abstract ideals of reason and law. For Herder, 'The cultivation of its mother tongue alone can lift a nation out of a state of barbarism' (Herder, 1968, p. 328).

After Herder, the most important German 'historicist' is almost certainly G.W.F. Hegel (1770–1831). Hegel's was a historicism of a very different kind, however: it attempted to effect a theoretical synthesis between culturalist Romanticism and Enlightenment rationalism. For Hegel, as for the earlier historicists, history was essentially the history of 'world-historical' nations. So in the *Philosophy of History* (Hegel, 1956), for example, the nation is the medium through which the 'World Spirit' is consciously realised. But for Hegel an appreciation of the cultural specificity of each age could also be subsumed within a wider understanding of historical development as possessing an overall rationality and direction. Hegelian philosophy would later exercise a very real fascination for the twentieth-century Anglo-American culturalist poet and critic T.S. Eliot. But in Germany itself, Hegel's 'historicism' opened up an intellectual space from within which much emerged: a great deal of the modern discipline of history; Marx's Marxism, or 'historical materialism', as he would term it; and, finally, that set of responses to Marx, both positive and negative, which provided the founding moment and much of the continuing momentum behind German sociology. We shall return to these matters in the chapter that follows.

Hermeneutics

The third aspect of German culturalism is 'hermeneutics', a term normally used to refer to those theories of 'interpretation' that take as their central problem how to understand the more or less intended meanings of others. Historically, the origins of hermeneutics can be traced to the Reformation and to the Protestant insistence on the believer's right to interpret the Bible free from the authoritative dictates of the Catholic church. In the first instance, then, what was to be interpreted was the religious canon itself, and for no less a purpose than to understand God's own intended meaning. This is obviously no small matter: if God speaks only the truth, as by definition He does, then the intended authorial meaning of His own texts must take an absolute priority over any subsequent readings. For modern literary and philosophical hermeneutics, which begins with Friedrich Schleiermacher (1768–1834), the relevant meanings were those intended, consciously or unconsciously, by the author of the text. In Schleiermacher's famous phrase, the task was: 'to understand the text at first as well as and then even better than its author' (Schleiermacher, 1985, p. 83). For historical and sociological hermeneutics, by contrast, the relevant meaning would be that intended, again either consciously or unconsciously, by the historical or social actor. So Max Weber's distinction between the natural and social sciences would devolve precisely upon the latter's concern with 'the empathic understanding' of 'psychological and intellectual (*geistig*) phenomena' (Weber, 1949, p. 74).

During the twentieth century, the hermeneutic tradition was refined and further developed by the existentialism of Martin Heidegger (1889–1976), reaching its most sophisticated contemporary articulation in the work of Hans-Georg Gadamer (1900–2002). A former student of Heidegger, Gadamer was concerned with the differences between truth in the humanities and in the natural sciences. His point of departure is provided by the way our pre-understandings, or 'prejudices', not only condition our understanding and interpretation, but also provide the conditions without which understanding cannot take place. For Gadamer, as for Heidegger, both the interpreter and that which is to be interpreted are necessarily historically situated. This led Gadamer himself to a theoretical rehabilitation of the notion of 'tradition'. Historical consciousness is only possible, he concludes, insofar as historical tradition connects our 'horizon' with that of those we seek to understand: 'Our own past and that other past towards which our historical consciousness is directed help to shape this moving horizon out of which human life always lives and which determines it as heritage and tradition' (Gadamer, 1990, p. 304).

The hermeneutic tradition represents German culturalism at its most theoretically sophisticated. As such, it has been a powerful influence on the discipline of comparative literature; much less so, however, on either English literature or cultural studies. For English literature this has been—in part, no doubt—an effect of the discipline's notorious insularity. But it remains surprising, if only because hermeneutics reproduces so many of English literature's characteristic tropes in more theoretically articulate form. This is so precisely because they are each literary humanisms. Noting the parallels between Gadamer and Eliot, Eagleton has argued that both exhibit 'a grossly complacent theory of history', in which 'the alien is always secretly familiar' (Eagleton, 1996, p. 73). Thus the affinity between English literature and German hermeneutics seems almost to have forewarned and forearmed British cultural studies against the latter. But the German tradition is neither so fixated on the author nor so insistently elitist as British cultural studies has sometimes supposed. Hans Robert Jauss (1922–97), for example, developed a post-Gadamerian 'aesthetic of reception' able to theorise the role of the reader as well as that of the author (Jauss, 1982). And though Jauss himself remained preoccupied with 'high' literature, his methods are applicable to popular texts, at least in principle. Indeed, there is no necessary connection between hermeneutics and high culture. If the texts of popular culture have meaning, as clearly they do, then they can be made available to hermeneutic analysis.

BRITISH CULTURALISM: FROM ARNOLD TO LEAVIS

In its British formation—or perhaps more properly its English formation—culturalism remains similarly indebted to Romanticism and historicism, but not to hermeneutics. The classic account of the historical evolution of this British culturalist tradition is Raymond Williams' *Culture and Society 1780–1950*. As we have seen, a central motif in culturalist theory is the necessary antithesis between culture and civilisation. In *Culture and Society*, Williams traces the history of the concept 'culture' as it developed in British intellectual life from Edmund Burke (1729–97) to George Orwell (1903–50). At its inception, this 'culture and society' tradition was very obviously indebted to its German counterpart: at least two of the central figures in Williams' lineage, Thomas Carlyle

(1795–1881) and Samuel Taylor Coleridge (1772–1834), were intimately familiar with the German debates. In Britain, as in Germany, the concept of culture increasingly emerged as what Williams terms 'an abstraction and an absolute', merging two distinct responses: 'first, the recognition of the practical separation of certain moral and intellectual activities from the driven impetus of the new kind of society; second, the emphasis of these activities, as a court of human appeal, to be set over the process of practical social judgement and yet to offer itself as a mitigating and rallying alternative' (Williams, 1963, p. 17). Here, the antithesis between culture and civilisation, as also that between the authenticity of natural, lived experience and the mechanistic imperatives of industrialisation, clearly attest to the pain and the trauma of the very first industrial revolution, that which occurred in Britain itself. This is a tradition that clearly embraced both a radically conservative reaction against capitalist modernity and a radically progressive aspiration to go beyond that modernity. Whatever the register, however, culturalism remained irretrievably adversarial in its relations both to capitalist industrialisation and to utilitarian intellectual culture. We do not intend to repeat here Williams' account of the culturalist tradition as a whole; we will instead concentrate on what seem three representative figures: Matthew Arnold (1822–88), T.S. Eliot (1885–1965) and F.R. Leavis (1895–1978).

Matthew Arnold

Arnold is indisputably one of the central figures in the English culturalist tradition. He is, both theoretically and practically, perhaps the single most important nineteenth-century progenitor of contemporary English literature studies. The key text for our purposes is almost certainly *Culture and Anarchy*, first published in 1869. Arnold's definitions of 'culture' are various: it is sweetness and light, it is the best that has been thought and said, it is essentially disinterested, it is the study of perfection, it is internal to the human mind and general to the whole community, it is a harmony of all the powers that make for the beauty and worth of human nature. But, however it is defined, culture stands in opposition to mechanical civilisation: 'culture . . . has a very important function to fulfil for mankind. And this function is particularly important in our modern world, of which the whole civilization is . . . mechanical and external, and tends constantly to become more so' (Arnold, 1966, pp. 48–9).

Culture is thus for Arnold a social force in opposition to material civilisation, the equivalent, at the societal level, to his own individual role as inspector of schools. As such, it clearly requires embodiment in some social group or another. But Arnold firmly rejected the pretensions to the title of guarantor of culture of each of the three major social classes: the Barbarian aristocracy suffers from a 'natural inaccessibility, as children of the established fact, to ideas'; the Philistine middle class is so preoccupied with external civilisation that 'not only do they not pursue sweetness and light, but . . . even prefer . . . that sort of machinery of business . . . which makes up [their] dismal and illiberal life'; and the working-class Populace either aspires to follow the middle class, or is merely degraded, 'raw and half-developed . . . half-hidden amidst its poverty and squalor' (pp. 101–5). No class, but rather the 'remnant' of the cultured within each class, what today we might perhaps term 'an intelligentsia', sustains the continued development of human culture: 'persons who are mainly led, not by their class spirit, but by a general *humane* spirit, by the love of human perfection' (p. 109). This group is by no means necessarily fixed in size. Quite the contrary: it can be expanded through state-sponsored education.

For Arnold, the state becomes, in effect, the institutional corollary of the concept of culture. Hence the title of the book, in which culture is counterposed not to material civilisation, but to anarchy. If the preservation and extension of culture is a task that devolves essentially upon the state, then it must follow that any threat of 'anarchy and disorder' will be directed as much at culture as at the state itself: 'without order there can be no society, and without society there can be no human perfection' (p. 203). And anarchy, Arnold is clear, emanates from the 'working class . . . beginning to assert and put into practice an Englishman's right to do what he likes' (p. 76). Arnold's defence of culture is conceived in organicist and anti-individualist terms suggestive of a rejection of middle-class utilitarianism—closely parallel, as we shall see, to the defences attempted by both classical sociology and classical Marxism. But the critique of utilitarian culture becomes displaced, through a similarly organicist and anti-individualist conception of the state, into a fear of anarchy, and a corresponding faith in the remnant, both of which are much more reminiscent of sociology, especially French sociological positivism, than of Marxism. The Arnoldian programme becomes, then, a programme of liberal, but not thereby individualist, social reform.

Williams argues that the key weakness in Arnold is his inability to explain how it is that the state might be influenced by the remnant, rather than by the classes, so as to make it possible for it to fulfil the cultural role allocated it. In short, Arnold can offer no institutional mechanism by which the remnant might be organised. Thus the case for the ideal state collapses into a defence of an actual state that is in reality far from ideal (Williams, 1963, p. 133). There is one obvious reply to this charge, though it is not one of which Arnold could have availed himself. It could be argued that Arnold's remnant is better understood as a social class in its own right, rather than as an aggregate 'number of *aliens*' (p. 109), and that it should therefore prove at least as capable of directing the state, at least in particular directions, as are the Barbarians, the Philistines and the Populace. Neither Arnold nor Williams contemplate this prospect. But had either done so, it might well have provided them with an explanation for the transparently educative role of much of the business of the modern state. A problem remains, however: understood thus—that is, as an intellectual class—the remnant would in all probability be motivated, not by a general humane spirit, but by their own class spirit. Such a class spirit would, of course, prove unusually sympathetic to the business of intellectual work. But there is no reason at all to imagine that it would be inspired by the love of human perfection.

T.S. Eliot

If Arnold was the central nineteenth-century figure in the development of the culturalist tradition, then the equivalent status for the period since the First World War, at least insofar as the general intellectual culture is concerned, is almost certainly that occupied by the poet T.S. Eliot. Eliot was born and brought up in the United States and became English only by an act of conversion, which came to embrace not only British naturalisation, but also High Tory politics, High Anglican religion and High Royalist monarchism. A deeply learned man, greatly influenced by Hegelian philosophy, his prose writings include a very serious attempt to fashion a specifically Christian social theory. For Eliot, as for Arnold, culture came to be understood in an essentially totalistic and organicist fashion: thus a specifically 'literary' culture evolves, not as the creation of an aggregate of individual writers, but rather, in characteristically Hegelian fashion, as that of 'the mind of Europe . . . which abandons nothing *en route*' (Eliot, 1963, p. 16). Eliot's most celebrated discussion of the concept of culture, in his *Notes Towards the Definition of Culture*, draws on Arnold's insistence on the connectedness of the literary and the non-literary, but expands upon it so as to develop a much more contemporary, anthropological sense of the term. 'By "culture"', Eliot writes, 'I mean first of all . . . the way of life of a particular people living together in one place. That culture is made visible in their arts, in their social system, in their habits and customs, in their religion' (Eliot, 1962, p. 120).

A culture, in Eliot's sense of the term, is only properly such insofar as it is shared in by a whole people. But a common culture is not, however, one in which all participate equally: it will be consciously understood only by the cultural elites of the society, but can nonetheless be embodied in the unconscious texture of the everyday lives of the non-elite groups. In principle, culture is not a minority resource to be disseminated through education, but is rather already (more or less consciously) present in the lives of all classes. But if this is so for a 'healthy' society, such as Eliot imagined medieval Europe to have been, then it is much less so for the increasingly non-Christian society conjured into being largely by industrialisation. There is an important sense, then, in which Eliot's social theory becomes simply inoperable: if the good society is one modelled as closely as possible on those of the European Middle Ages, then in truth the good society is no longer attainable. For whatever the deleterious social and cultural consequences of the rise of capitalism (and there can be little doubt that Eliot is here often very acute), industrialisation itself appears an essentially irreversible process. Stripped of its peculiar Christian medievalism, and rendered compatible, if not with secularism, then at least with Nonconformist Protestantism, Eliot's social theory might easily have proven much less pessimistic in its general import. It is precisely such a transformation in the culturalist paradigm, requiring a partial rehabilitation, at least, of Arnold's earlier reformism, that we find in the work of Dr Leavis of Cambridge.

F.R. Leavis

The journal *Scrutiny*, and the group around it—F.R. Leavis himself, his wife Q.D. Leavis, Denys Thompson, L.C. Knights—inherited from Eliot a number of their characteristic themes, especially a clearly organicist conception of culture, and a correspondingly pessimistic understanding of recent historical process as cultural decline. Leavis' own organicism is at its most apparent in his sense of literature itself 'as essentially something more than an accumulation of separate works: it has an organic form, or constitutes an organic order in relation to which the individual writer has his significance' (Leavis, 1962, p. 184). The centre of Leavis' intellectual effort consists of an attempt to map out the tradition of the English novel on the one hand, the tradition of English poetry on the other, each imagined in exactly such organicist terms, and imagined, moreover, as bearing important moral truths—in particular, as bearers of the value of 'life', by which Leavis means, in short, non-determined, spontaneous creativity (Leavis, 1972, p. 15). For Leavis, as for Eliot, literary and non-literary culture are thus inextricably connected: in a healthy culture, there is 'behind the literature, a social culture and an art of living' (Leavis, 1962, p. 190). And for Leavis, again as for Eliot, such cultural health must entail some kind of unity of sophisticated and popular cultures. But Leavis nonetheless privileges elite culture—or 'minority culture', to use his own phrase—much more than did Eliot. The essential value of a common culture, for Leavis, is its capacity to sustain a culturally superior minority: 'In their keeping . . . is the language, the changing idiom, upon which fine living depends, and without which distinction of spirit is thwarted and incoherent. By "culture" I mean the use of such a language' (Leavis, 1948, p. 145).

Like Eliot, Leavis subscribed to a theory of cultural decline. In his version, however, the problem arises quite specifically as a result of industrialisation and the techniques of mass production that unavoidably accompany it. Together these generate a 'technologico-Benthamite' civilisation, the defining characteristics of which are cultural levelling and standardisation. Hence the remarkably bleak conclusion to *New Bearings in English Poetry*: 'the finer values are ceasing to be a matter of even conventional concern for any except the minority . . . Elsewhere below, a process of standardization, mass production and levelling down goes forward . . . So that poetry, in the future, if there is poetry, seems likely to matter even less in the world' (Leavis, 1938, pp. 213–14). Such pessimism echoes that of Eliot, though the weight accorded to material factors is, perhaps, more reminiscent of 1930s Marxism. And yet Leavis also insisted that: 'enormously . . . as material conditions count, there is a certain measure of spiritual autonomy in human affairs . . . human intelligence, choice and will do really and effectively operate' (Leavis, 1962, p. 184). It was through the discipline of English, through the University English School, and through the English teachers that it would train, that such intelligence, choice and will were to become operative. So Leavis recovered for the culturalist tradition both the general cultural evangelism and the more specifically pedagogical strategic orientation first broached by Arnold.

As with Arnold and Eliot, so too with Leavis—a common culture, that of the pre-industrial organic community, and its continuing echo in the legacy of the English language, are pitted against modern industrial civilisation. Here, though, there can be no compromise with the existing class structure, such as Eliot was clearly prepared on occasion to countenance. Rather, the literary intelligentsia was to be mobilised against the developing mass society. In itself, this almost certainly represents a much more plausible programme of action than any in either Arnold or Eliot.

What Leavis recognised, in a way that Arnold could not, was the capacity for collective self-organisation latent within the intellectual class. He failed, however, to confront its obvious likely corollary: that the intelligentsia might prove as incapable of Arnoldian 'disinterestedness' as the establishment itself. In that failure is surely to be found the source of much of the bitterness and rancour that so soured Leavis' later years.

THE NEW LEFT: THOMPSON, HOGGART AND WILLIAMS

It should be clear that Leavis' culturalism was both culturally elitist and politically reactionary. As such, it was unlikely to appeal to those of a more egalitarian political persuasion. During the 1950s the more independently minded left-wing British intellectuals began to forge their own 'third way' both in practical politics and in cultural theory, between Leavisism on the one hand and Marxian socialism on the other. The politics eventually became that of the 'New Left'; the theory became what would be represented in structuralist restrospect as 'culturalism', but is surely more accurately described as 'left culturalism'. The founding theoretical moment of left culturalism can be located fairly precisely in the early writings of three key figures: E.P. Thompson (1924–93), Richard Hoggart and Raymond Williams (1921–88).

E.P. Thompson and Richard Hoggart

Something of what would become 'left culturalism' had first been explored in Thompson's first book (Thompson, 1955), which discovered in William Morris much of the strength of the earlier Romantic critique of utilitarianism. Thompson's best-known work, *The Making of the English Working Class*, would later quite explicitly compare working-class and Romantic anti-utilitarianism. The 'heroic culture' of the early English working class, he argued, had 'nourished, for fifty years, and with incomparable fortitude, the Liberty Tree'. 'After William Blake', he concludes, 'no mind was at home in both cultures, nor had the genius to interpret the two traditions to each other. In the failure of the two traditions to come to a point of junction, something was lost. How much we cannot be sure, for we are among the losers' (Thompson, 1963, p. 832).

Less directly political in intent, Hoggart's *The Uses of Literacy* marked the point at which post-Leavisite culturalism decisively shifted emphasis from 'literature' to 'culture'. Hoggart combined an ethnographic account of Yorkshire working-class culture with Leavisite practical criticism of mass media texts. His central theme was that of the damage done to the older, inter-war working-class culture by the new print media: 'The old forms of class culture are in danger of being replaced by a poorer kind of classless . . . culture . . . and this is to be regretted' (Hoggart, 1958, p. 343). Like Leavis, Hoggart was arguing a theory of cultural decline. But for Hoggart it was working-class culture, rather than that of the 'sensitive minority', that needed to be valorised, if only so as, in turn, to be elegised. Hoggart's achievement was thus to divest Leavisism of much of its cultural elitism, if not perhaps of its nostalgia; Thompson's was to divest British socialism of its Marxian economic determinism, and to make explicit what had previously only ever been an implicit—and barely acknowledged—Romanticism.

Raymond Williams

The full analytical range of this left culturalism only became apparent, however, in Williams. His originality in relation to the culturalist tradition, as he had encountered it in the work of Eliot and Leavis, was to effect a dramatic reversal of socio-cultural evaluation, such that a distinctly working-class cultural achievement came to be valorised positively rather than negatively. Quite centrally, Williams insisted that 'culture is ordinary'; and, more famously, that 'a culture is not only a body of intellectual and imaginative work; it is also and essentially a whole way of life' (Williams, 1989; Williams, 1963, p. 311). In principle this is little different from Eliot. But in the practical application of that principle, Williams so expanded its range as to include within 'culture' the 'collective democratic institution', by which he meant the trade union, the co-operative and the working-class political party (Williams, 1963, p. 313). Thus redefined, the notion of a single common culture becomes supplemented, and importantly qualified, by that of a plurality of class cultures: 'The basis of a distinction between bourgeois and working-class culture . . . is to be sought in the whole way of life . . . The crucial distinction is between alternative ideas of the nature of social relationships' (p. 311). For Williams, the antithesis of middle-class individualism was no longer the minority culture of the intelligentsia—it was proletarian solidarity.

If the common culture is not yet properly common, then it follows also that the literary tradition must be seen not so much as the unfolding of a group mind, but as the outcome, in part at least, of a set of selections made necessarily in the present: 'selection will be governed by many kinds of special interest, including class interests . . . The traditional culture of a society will always tend to correspond to its *contemporary* system of interests and values' (Williams, 1965, p. 68). Despite such qualification, the ideal of a common culture remains of quite fundamental importance to Williams. In a characteristically radical move, he relocates the common culture from the historical past to the not too distant future. And insofar as any of the elements of such a culture can indeed be found in the present, then they occur primarily within the culture of the working class itself: 'In its definition of the common interest as true self-interest, in its finding of individual verification primarily in the community, the idea of solidarity is potentially the real basis of society' (Williams, 1963, p. 318). Where Eliot and Leavis diagnosed cultural decline, Williams, by contrast, discerned a 'long revolution' leading towards, rather than away from, the eventual realisation of a socialistic, common culture.

There is, however, an important second sense in which Williams makes use of the concept of a common culture. For even as he insisted on the importance of class cultures, Williams was careful also to note the extent to which such distinctions of class are complicated, especially in the field of intellectual and imaginative work, by 'the common elements resting on a common language' (p. 311). For Williams, any direct reduction of art to class, such as is canvassed in certain 'leftist' versions of Marxism, remained entirely unacceptable. In studying literature, and other cultural artefacts, Williams developed the key concept of 'structure of feeling'. 'In one sense', he writes, 'this structure of feeling is the culture of a period: it is the particular living result of all the elements in the general organization' (Williams, 1965, p. 64). He continues: 'in this respect . . . the arts of a period . . . are of major importance . . . here . . . the actual living sense, the deep community that makes the communication possible, is naturally drawn upon' (pp. 64–5). So, for example, the English novel from Dickens to Lawrence becomes, for Williams, one medium among many by which people seek to master and absorb new experience through the articulation of a structure of feeling, the key problem of which is that of the 'knowable community' (Williams, 1974). Such deep community must, of course, transcend class; and yet it remains irredeemably marked by it. For the early, 'left culturalist' Raymond Williams this remained a circle that stubbornly refused to be squared. Only in the course of a later encounter with 'western Marxism' did it finally become possible for him to explain, to his own satisfaction at least, how it is that structures of feeling can be common to different classes, and yet represent the interests of some particular class.

CULTURAL MATERIALISM

Between the publication of *The Long Revolution* in 1961 and *Marxism and Literature* in 1977, Williams' work proceeded by way of a series of often radically innovative encounters with an extremely diverse set of substantive issues, ranging across the whole field of literary and cultural studies and including pioneering analyses of both the mass media and the literary canon. His most powerful work of literary criticism, *The Country and the City*, dates from this period. Here he argued, against the weight of contemporary academic interpretation, for a critique, based on 'questions of historical fact' (Williams, 1973, p. 12), of such mythologising misrepresentations of rural life as those in the tradition of English country-house poetry. The cumulative effect of these diverse lines of inquiry finally registered in *Marxism and Literature*, where the theoretical contours of Williams' later 'cultural materialism' are elaborated at length. Despite its title, this book is not the 'extraordinary theoretical "coming out"', where 'Williams finally admits the usefulness of Marxism' (Turner, 1996, p. 60) that Graeme Turner takes it to be. To the contrary, Williams' argument displays a theoretical novelty and originality best represented not as a kind of Marxism, but rather as a quite distinctive 'post-culturalism' (Milner, 2002, p. 170).

Williams' cultural materialism

Williams coined the term 'cultural materialism' to describe the theoretical synthesis he effected between what we have been terming 'left culturalism' and 'western Marxism'. Cultural materialism, he explained, 'is a theory of culture as a (social and material) productive process and of specific practices, of "arts", as social uses of material means of production (from language as material "practical consciousness" to the specific technologies of writing and forms of writing, through to mechanical and electronic communications systems)' (Williams, 1980, p. 243). He then sought to circumvent what he saw as the false opposition between 'idealist' accounts of culture as consciousness and 'materialist' accounts of culture as the 'superstructural' effect of an economic base, by insisting that culture is itself both real and material. 'From castles and palaces and churches to prisons and workhouses and schools . . .', he wrote, 'from weapons of war to a controlled press . . . These are never superstructural activities. They are necessarily material production' (Williams, 1977, p. 93). Williams' cultural materialism was thus part of a wider movement, begun in the 1960s and 1970s, towards new theoretical paradigms that acknowledged the necessary materiality of cultural texts and institutions.

Though Williams' later work was less Marxist than is sometimes claimed, its emergence was significantly conditioned, nonetheless, by the encounter with Marxism. A detailed consideration of Marxist cultural theory can be found in the chapter that follows. For the moment, note only that Williams was primarily interested in 'western Marxism', that is, the tradition of 'critical' Marxism that developed in Germany, Italy and France, as distinct from official Communist Marxism. Initially, this meant little more than the discovery of theoretical preoccupations similar to his own in the work of individual western Marxist writers. But in the work of Antonio Gramsci, the Italian theorist of 'hegemony', he found occasion for a much more positive redefinition of his own theoretical stance. Two chapters of the first part of *Marxism and Literature* are devoted to two key concepts, and two keywords, deriving respectively from Leavisism and Marxism: 'Culture' (the first chapter) and 'Ideology' (the last chapter). In a subsequent chapter, Williams argues for the theoretical superiority of the Gramscian notion of hegemony over each of these: '"Hegemony" goes beyond "culture" . . . in its insistence on relating the "whole social process" to specific distributions of power and influence' (pp. 108–9). For Williams, Gramsci's central achievement consisted of the articulation of a culturalist sense of the wholeness of culture with a more typically Marxist sense of the interestedness of ideology. Culture is therefore neither 'superstructural' nor 'ideological', but rather 'among the basic processes of the formation' (p. 111). Tradition now becomes not only selective, but also decisively important in the effective operation of hegemony, and dependent on identifiably material institutions and 'formations' (pp. 115, 117–20).

Like Gramsci, Williams was concerned with the problem of counter-hegemony. The alternatives to hegemony include both the 'emergent' and the 'residual', he observed, but it was the former that most interested him. By 'emergent', he meant those genuinely new meanings and values, practices, relationships and kinds of relationship that are substantially alternative or oppositional to the dominant culture; by 'residual' he meant those cultural elements, external to the dominant culture, that nonetheless continue to be lived and practised as an active part of the present 'on the basis of the residue . . . of some previous social and cultural institution or formation' (pp. 122–3). An emergent culture, he argues, will require not only distinct kinds of immediate cultural practice, but also—and crucially—'new forms or adaptations of forms'. Such innovation at the level of form, he continues, 'is in effect a *pre-emergence*, active and pressing but not yet fully articulated' (p. 126). The concept of structure of feeling is brought back into play at this point: these 'can be defined as social experiences *in solution*, as distinct from other social semantic formations which have been *precipitated*' (pp. 133–4). In short, structures of feeling are quite specifically counter-hegemonic. Williams remained insistent, moreover, that there is much in any lived culture that cannot be reduced to the dominant: '*no dominant culture*', he wrote, '*ever in reality includes or exhausts all human practice, human energy, and human intention*' (p. 125). As Higgins rightly observes, this stress on human agency is part of the 'clearly defined conceptual content' of Williams' cultural materialism (Higgins, 1999, p. 172). It is also very distinctively 'culturalist' in character.

Dollimore and Sinfield

Cultural materialism has been widely influential in literary and cultural studies. It has influenced the recognisably feminist cultural materialism of Terry Lovell, for example, or Janet Wolff (Lovell, 1987; Wolff, 1990; Wolff, 1993). It informs the work of Nicholas Garnham and his colleagues at the University of Westminster, who co-edit the journal *Media, Culture and Society*. Garnham himself has explicitly identified his work with 'what is coming to be called . . . cultural materialism' (Garnham, 1983, p. 321; cf. Garnham, 1988). In literary studies, Jonathan Dollimore and Alan Sinfield are both self-proclaimed 'cultural materialists'. Dollimore and Sinfield's *Political Shakespeare*, significantly subtitled *Essays in Cultural Materialism* (Dollimore & Sinfield, 1994), has proven so influential in Shakespeare studies as to prompt the large claim that 'cultural materialism in Britain and New Historicism in America . . . now constitute the new academic order . . . in Renaissance studies' (Wilson, 1995, p. viii). As we shall see, this American 'New Historicism' is rather different from what Williams meant by 'cultural materialism'. Their linking by Wilson might, then, be read as indicative of how little Dollimore and Sinfield actually owe to Williams. The claims of these rival cultural materialisms have been much canvassed, with opinion ranging from Dollimore's own view that his work derives from 'the considerable output of Williams himself' (Dollimore & Sinfield, 1994, p. 2) to Gorak's observation that writers like Dollimore 'have reduced Williams's program to little more than a slogan' (Gorak, 1988, p. 90). While Dollimore and Sinfield clearly subscribe to a much looser sense of the term than Williams uses, their insistence on their own indebtedness suggests something at least of the continuing relevance of his work.

Terry Eagleton

The most significant contemporary figure in the cultural materialist line, however, is surely Terry Eagleton, Professor of Cultural Theory at the University of Manchester. Though Eagleton clearly occupies a less representative position in relation to literary studies than does, say, Stuart Hall in relation to cultural studies, the trajectory of his intellectual career nevertheless nicely traces the varying impact on literary studies of Williams' work. Eagleton's early work was written very much in the shadow of *Culture and Society* (Eagleton, 1968) and as late as 1975, his book-length study of the Brontës managed to combine a continuing debt to Williams with an emergent sympathy for Althusser's structural Marxism (Eagleton, 1975). Only a year later, however, would come *Criticism and Ideology*, and with it, not only a fairly full-fledged 'Althusserianism', but also a pointedly trenchant critique of Williams. Eagleton's Althusserianism consisted of two things: a highly formalist elaboration of 'the major constituents of a Marxist theory of literature', which centred around the twin concepts of 'mode of production' and 'ideology'; and the proposal for a structuralist 'science of the text', concerned with how literature 'produces', in the sense of 'performs', ideology (Eagleton, 1976).

The critique of Williams found his work guilty of an 'idealist epistemology, organicist aesthetics and corporatist sociology', all three of which have their roots in 'Romantic populism' (p. 27). The defining characteristic of that Romanticism, as of the very notion of 'culture' itself, was, for Eagleton, a radical 'over-subjectivising' of the social formation by which structure is reduced to experience (p. 26). In short, Williams had failed to understand how working-class subjectivity is determined by bourgeois ideology; structure of feeling was thus an essentially inadequate conceptualisation of ideology, misreading structure as pattern (pp. 33–4); and even Williams' use of the Gramscian notion of hegemony was wrongly predicated on its experiential primacy and was, therefore, necessarily 'structurally undifferentiated' (p. 42). We can concede something to the power of Eagleton's critique of Williams' earlier culturalism, while still insisting on its markedly retrospective quality: Williams' later cultural materialism, which was substantially formed by 1976, was much less susceptible to these charges. Moreover, insofar as real differences did indeed persist, it was Eagleton's position, rather than Williams', which was the more 'idealist and academicist' (p. 25). Eagleton's Althusserian insistence on the determining power of ideology over the human subject led almost unavoidably to an enormous condescension towards popular activity, whether political or cultural. His defence of the notion of aesthetic value, coupled as it was with a substantive acceptance of the content of the literary canon and a passing sneer at the 'abstract egalitarianism' of cultural studies (pp. 162–3), seem similarly academicist.

The intent of these remarks is not to take Eagleton to task for views he would in any case soon abandon, but to emphasise the extent to which structuralism and cultural materialism offered alternative, very different and, in some ways, opposed ways out of the theoretical deadlock between idealist humanism and determinist Marxism. These differences revolved around their respective concepts of structure, agency and subjectivity: for structuralism, as we shall see, structure was all-determining, agency an illusion and subjectivity the ideological effect of structure; for cultural materialism, structure sets limits and exerts pressures, agency takes place within those limits and pressures, though taking the form of an unavoidably material production, and subjectivity, though socially produced and shared, is both real and active. The analytical logic of structuralism pointed towards a perennial search for the ideology concealed within the deep structures of the text. Thus the substantive focus remained the business as usual of the interpretation of the literary-critical canon. By contrast, the analytical logic of cultural materialism points towards a necessary decentring of texts into the contexts of their production, reproduction and consumption, of Literature into culture, of literary studies into cultural studies. If Williams' politico-theoretical rhetoric was a great deal less 'revolutionary' than Althusser's, the substantive case at issue was much more so. Certainly, this was to prove Eagleton's own eventual assessment.

Back to the future

By the end of the 1970s, Eagleton had turned to the materialist aesthetics of Walter Benjamin and begun his long march back to Williams. *Walter Benjamin* and *The Rape of Clarissa*, published in 1981 and 1982 respectively, represent the moments in his work where a repudiation of Althusserianism coincides with a horrified fascination for post-structuralism and a developing respect for cultural materialism. Though this combination of repudiation, fascination and respect was actually announced in *Walter Benjamin*, it is much more properly constitutive of the argument in *The Rape of Clarissa*, where a kind of feminist deconstruction goes hand in hand with what Eagleton terms 'historical materialism', but is actually cultural materialist in its stress on 'literary modes of production' (Eagleton, 1982, p. viii). Following Habermas (Habermas, 1989), Eagleton proposed to understand this eighteenth-century mode of literary production as formed within the context of the new bourgeois 'public sphere' (Eagleton, 1982, pp. 6–7). *The Rape of Clarissa* thus inaugurated an 'institutional' analysis of the social functions of literature and criticism; this provided the central organising theme for Eagleton's most fully cultural materialist books to date, *Literary Theory* and *The Function of Criticism*.

The first of these was, of course, a textbook, though the apparent conventionality of its form is belied by the subversive intent of its argument. Its critical and often hostile accounts of various contemporary schools of literary theory are predicated on an institutional history of the development of English studies as a discipline, which itself culminates in the polemical call for a kind of 'political criticism' that will go beyond the limits of the institution (Eagleton, 1996). This argument is resumed in *The Function of Criticism*. In both books, the stress falls on the institutional production of criticism, as it had for Williams. In both, too, the category of 'Literature' is radically decentred (pp. 16, 197; Eagleton, 1996a, pp. 107–8), as it also had been for Williams. In the latter book, moreover, Eagleton specifically invoked Williams as 'the most important critic of post-war Britain', whose concept of 'structure of feeling' he deemed 'vital' in 'examining the *articulations* between different sign-systems and practices' (Eagleton, 1996a, pp. 108–10).

Eagleton's writing of the 1990s can be seen as redeploying and reapplying a whole set of essentially Williamsite categories to distinctly un-English contexts. *The Ideology of the Aesthetic* is an attempt at a critical history of the concept of the aesthetic, as it has evolved in modern, mainly German thought, from Baumgarten to Habermas. The central purpose of Eagleton's argument here was to recover both the negative and the positive moments within the 'aesthetic' tradition. The obvious, but little remarked upon, point of comparison is with Williams' own account of the English 'culturalist' tradition in *Culture and Society*: as Eagleton notes, and as we have suggested in our own account, 'the Anglophone tradition is in fact derivative of German philosophy' (Eagleton, 1990, p. 11). Eagleton's *Heathcliff and the Great Hunger* can also be read as a reworking of *Culture and Society*, taking Irish literature rather than German philosophy as its primary object. So Eagleton traces the differences between English and Irish writing, showing how Williams' own keyword, 'Culture', has been differently troped against 'Nature'; and, more specifically, how Irishness itself has been troped as Nature to English Culture. So too he re-places many of the thinkers from Williams' 'culture and society tradition'—Burke, Shaw and Wilde—in relation to the quite different Irish 'tradition' running from Swift to Joyce and Yeats. These studies in Irish culture build on Williams' work in at least two respects: first, in their understanding of how Englishness and Irishness have been defined and constructed, in relation to and against each other, through the processes and projects of hegemony; and second, in their insistence that cultural representations can and should be measured against the historical referents to which they really do sometimes bear some relation. In the opening chapter of *Heathcliff and the Great Hunger*, for example, Eagleton moves between the text of *Wuthering Heights*, the historical reality of the Irish Famine and its representation and non-representation in subsequent historiographical and literary texts (Eagleton, 1995).

This substantial body of work suggests the uses to which cultural materialism can be put in hands as creative as Eagleton's. The latter's own judgement warrants repetition here: 'the notion of cultural materialism is . . . of considerable value . . . it extends and completes Marx's own struggle against idealism, carrying it forcefully into that realm ("culture") always most ideologically resistant to materialist redefinition'. Though Eagleton still insisted on the general priority of historical materialism, he nonetheless conceded that a 'cultural materialist concern for . . . social and material conditions . . . carried into the academic institutions, would make the most profound difference to what actually got done there' (Eagleton, 1989, p. 169). Moreover, Eagleton now sees Williams' stress on the institutional prerequisites of a properly common culture as one of the latter's most powerful insights. 'Whereas for Eliot the culture is common in content', he writes, 'its commonness for Williams lies chiefly in its political form'. The power and the paradox of Williams' position, Eagleton argues, is in its recognition that cultural diversity actually requires for its achievement the kind of common belief and action necessary for the creation of common institutions. 'To establish genuine cultural pluralism', he continues, 'requires concerted socialist action. It is precisely this that contemporary pluralism fails to see. Williams' position would no doubt seem to it quaintly residual, not to say positively archaic; the problem in fact is that we have yet to catch up with it' (Eagleton, 2000, p. 122).

NEW HISTORICISM

New historicism shares with cultural materialism a conception of culture as material practice. As we have noted, the two are often regarded as essentially cognate theoretical positions: so Felperin describes cultural materialism as the 'counterpart in Britain' of new historicism (Felperin, 1990, p. 1), while Wilson treats new historicism as 'the bastard offspring of . . . cultural materialism' (Wilson, 1995, p. 55). Certainly, there are grounds for Wilson's claim.

Gallagher and Greenblatt

The founding text of a distinctively 'new historicist' critical practice is generally held to be Stephen Greenblatt's *Renaissance Self-Fashioning* (Greenblatt, 1980), although the term itself wasn't used until his 'Introduction' to *The Power of Forms in the English Renaissance* (Greenblatt, 1982, p. 5). Now Professor of English at Harvard University and general editor of the Norton Shakespeare, Greenblatt had studied at Cambridge and cheerfully admits that his work in Renaissance studies was inspired in part by Williams (Greenblatt, 1990, pp. 2–3). Though associated above all with Greenblatt, other new historicist writers include Catherine Gallagher, Walter Benn Michaels and Louis Montrose. The title of Greenblatt's 1982 volume is indicative of the general character of the new historicist enterprise—both its debt to Michel Foucault, whose work on knowledge and power we will examine in chapter 4, and in its intention to explain the literary text's imbrication in the workings of Renaissance social structures. As Greenblatt explains, Foucault's extended visits to Berkeley 'helped to shape' their literary-critical practice (pp. 146–7).

New historicism's starting point is something very like Clifford Geertz's 'thick description'—that is, the close analysis of the social, cultural and historical milieu in which a text is produced and received (Geertz, 1973; Gallagher & Greenblatt, 2000, pp. 20–2). New historicist analyses typically bring both literary and non-literary discourse into creative juxtaposition, so as to show how social power and historical conflict permeate the textuality of a society's literature. So, for example, Greenblatt sets the 'eucharistic anxiety' in *Hamlet* against the rhetoric of Protestant opposition to the Catholic Mass (Gallagher and Greenblatt, 2000, pp. 151–62). As Greenblatt himself describes it, he is preoccupied with 'the embeddedness of cultural objects in the contingencies of history' (Greenblatt, 1990, p. 164). Individual authors and texts are thus in no sense autonomous. Rather, the work of art is a product of the 'negotiation between a creator or class of creators, equipped with a complex, communally shared repertoire of conventions, and the institutions and practices of society'. These negotiations take place, Greenblatt continues, through the 'circulation of materials and discourses' in the 'hidden places of negotiation and exchange' (pp. 158–9).

New historicism and cultural materialism

New historicism clearly shares many of its methodologies and assumptions with cultural materialism. According to Ryan, they 'are united by their compulsion to relate literature to history, to treat texts as indivisible from contexts, and to do so from a politically charged perspective forged in the present' (Ryan, 1996, p. xi). New historicism could, in a sense, be considered as cultural materialism in a postmodern register, preoccupied with historicising texts and with the workings of power through culture, but focused on issues of individual subjectivity construction, gender and the workings of patriarchy, rather than on class and nation. Where Williams' cultural materialism had been concerned with the connections between social class and collective emancipatory politics, new historicism tends to exhibit the characteristic preoccupations of the officially sanctioned forms of political radicalism within the North American academy: subjectivity formation, desire, race, gender, queer theory, and so on. These latter are also analysable in more strictly cultural materialist terms, however, as Dollimore and Sinfield's work clearly suggests (Dollimore, 1991; Sinfield, 1994; Sinfield, 1994a). The more fundamental differences between cultural materialism and the new historicism are threefold: first, the theoretical question, concerning the subversive potential of apparently subversive texts; second, the political question, concerning the competing claims of academic professionalism and subordinate subcultures; and third, the epistemological question, concerning the status of the 'referent' to which texts refer.

As to the first, the issue hinges on how to read and apply Foucault (as a theorist of incorporation or of disruption), and on how to understand in/subordination (as always already necessarily contained or as at least potentially resistive). Just as for Foucault the apparently autonomous self had been a socio-discursive effect of quite specific forms of social power, so for the Greenblatt of *Renaissance Self-Fashioning* the texts and performances of Renaissance literature and drama are actively productive of the new forms of self. In new historicism, as in Foucault, this simultaneous stress on the discursivity of power and on the power of discourse easily leads to an overly 'functional' understanding of the self as effectively subordinated to and integrated within the social formation. So in much of Greenblatt's work the apparently subversive moment in apparently subversive texts is read as ultimately affirmative of and complicit with the dominant discursive formation. The obvious instance here is the essay included in *Political Shakespeare*, and much reprinted elsewhere, which reads the subversive perceptions in Shakespeare's history plays as ultimately supportive of the kingly authority they appear to question (Greenblatt, 1994).

For Sinfield, this new historicist insistence on the affirmative properties of apparently subversive texts amounts to an 'entrapment model' of ideology and power. Entrapment is indeed important, he concedes, as a way of theorising the dominant ideology, but it is much more important to theorise the scope for effective dissidence: 'This, centrally, is what Raymond Williams was concerned with in his later work' (Sinfield, 1994a, p. 24). Hence Sinfield's interest in Williams' accounts of the alternative and the oppositional, the residual and the emergent. For cultural materialism, Sinfield continues to argue that 'dissident potential derives . . . from conflict and contradiction that the social order inevitably produces within itself, even as it attempts to sustain itself' (Sinfield, 1992, p. 41). Gallagher argues that cultural materialist readings of the literary text as disruptive actually replicate the literary-critical consensus as to the disturbing, destabilising and estranging functions of art. New historicism's break with that consensus is thus 'an attempt to de-moralize our relationship to literature, to interrupt the moral narrative of literature's benign disruptions' (Gallagher, 1996, p. 53). The lines of disagreement can be overdrawn: musing on whether sites of resistance are ultimately cooptable, Greenblatt comments simply that 'Some are, some aren't' (Greenblatt, 1990, p. 165); confronting much the same issue, Sinfield concludes that 'there is no simple way through, but every reason to go on trying' (Sinfield, 1994a, p. 27). They are agreed, in short, that entrapment and dissidence are both theoretically possible. The difference is one of relative probabilities, then, but also of intent and purpose and hence, necessarily, of politics.

Which takes us to our second difference. New historicism has generally been much more reticent than cultural materialism as to its politics. So where Dollimore and Sinfield insisted on cultural materialism's commitment to the 'transformation' of the entire 'social order', Gallagher describes the new historicism as 'a criticism whose politics are . . . difficult to specify' (Gallagher, 1996, p. 45). Greenblatt himself famously defined the 'function of the new historicism' as 'to renew the marvelous at the heart of the resonant'—a nice turn of phrase, to be sure, but hardly a political manifesto (Greenblatt, 1990, p. 181). As Wilson has observed: 'In the many maps New Historicists drew of themselves . . . "cultural materialism" was noticed and noted as a . . . more outspoken, more political, . . . in "scholarly" terms less sophisticated, version of the same thing' (Wilson, 1995, p. 55). He might well have added that Sinfield's maps tend to return the favour. So for Sinfield, the new historicist fascination with ideological entrapment is not so much a profound insight as 'tellingly homologous with its own professional entrapment' in the higher reaches of the American university system (Sinfield, 1992, p. 290). Citing Williams' unease at the communal cost of individual upward social mobility, Sinfield's 'preferred alternative' to academic professionalism has been to 'work intellectually . . . in dissident subcultures' of 'class, ethnicity, gender and sexuality' (p. 294). The 'best chance for literary and leftist intellectuals to make themselves useful', he writes, is to commit themselves to 'a subcultural constituency' (Sinfield, 1997, p. xxiv).

The third of our major differences between cultural materialism and new historicism is over the epistemological status of the referent. As Ryan observes, new historicism consciously defined itself in opposition to older historicisms, which claimed to 'ground their accounts of literature in a factual historical reality that can be recovered and related to the poems, plays and novels that reflect it' (Ryan, 1996, p. xiii). So Greenblatt insists that: 'methodological self-consciousness is one of the distinguishing marks of the new historicism in cultural studies as opposed to a historicism based upon faith in the transparency of signs and interpretive procedures' (Greenblatt, 1990, p. 158). Neither Dollimore nor Sinfield—nor Williams nor Eagleton—ever believed in the transparency of either signs or interpretive procedures. Nor did they believe anything so foolish as that literature either does or should 'reflect' reality. But all four agree that signs do sometimes have referents and that texts can be used both to represent and misrepresent other extra-textual 'realities'. The kind of analysis conducted by Williams in *The Country and the City*, or by Eagleton in *Heathcliff and the Great Hunger*, where literary text and historical context are productively compared, in part so as to test the extent to which the texts misrepresent their contexts, tends to be precluded by the remorseless 'textualism' of new historicist criticism. This isn't so much a matter of judging the truth or falsity of the textual representation—although this is by no means entirely irrelevant—as of understanding how textuality performs ideology. Such strategies are much less readily available to a theoretical position as determinedly post-structuralist as the new historicism. For, as Ryan observes, 'new historicism turns history into a text and treats all texts as literary texts susceptible to the same interpretive techniques . . . The post-structuralist price of the return to history is the evaporation of the world that produced all these words' (Ryan, 1996, p. xiv).

CULTURAL STUDIES: FROM HOGGART TO HALL

While cultural materialism and new historicism were mainly concerned to apply 'post-culturalist' forms of analysis to literary studies, the roughly equivalent approach to the study of popular culture was that developed, in the first place, as 'Cultural Studies' at the University of Birmingham. Excluded from 'English' by Leavisism, 'the popular' had become the subject matter of the new proto-discipline of cultural studies largely at the instigation of Williams and Hoggart themselves. In 1962, Hoggart was appointed Professor of Modern English Literature at Birmingham. Two years later he became director of the new Centre for Contemporary Cultural Studies. For Hoggart, Williams' 'interesting work' was to be one source of intellectual inspiration for the Centre (Hoggart, 1970, p. 255). Williams reciprocated, judging this 'an excellent pioneering example' of institutional innovation (Williams, 1976a, p. 149). Moreover, Williams' own work sketched out much of the subject matter of the new discipline. In two books on the media, *Communications* and *Television: Technology and Cultural Form* (Williams, 1962; Williams, 1974a), he was able to develop a critique of existing mass media institutions and texts that avoided the disabling cultural elitism of Leavisite criticism. Both books sought to identify the institutional forms that could sustain a properly democratic communications system. Thus the new televisual technologies were, in Williams' opinion, 'the contemporary tools of the long revolution towards an educated and participatory democracy' (Williams, 1974a, p. 151).

Stuart Hall

When Hoggart left Birmingham in 1968, he was succeeded by Stuart Hall, then still very much under the influence of the left culturalist argument. Hall himself had previously co-authored *The Popular Arts* with Paddy Whannel, a study that dealt directly with problems of 'value and evaluation' in the study of popular culture. Like Williams and Hoggart, Hall and Whannel were concerned to rescue what was valuable and creative in 'popular art' from its denigration as 'mass' culture. Their intention to develop a method for discriminating between 'good' and 'bad' popular culture, and so to educate popular taste, was in some respects clearly residually Leavisite. As Storey sees it: '[Hall and Whannel] seem to suggest that because most school students do not have access . . . to the best that has been thought and said, they can instead be given critical access to the best . . . within the popular arts of the new mass media: jazz and good films make up for the absence of Beethoven and Shakespeare' (Storey, 1997, p. 69). This kind of theoretical culturalism continued to remain in play at the Birmingham Centre. It is particularly evident, for example, in the Centre's work on youth subcultures, where an ethnographic focus inspired by *The Uses of Literacy* was combined with an emphasis on generation and class deriving in part from Williams in order to produce accounts of subcultural resistance to the dominant culture (Hall & Jefferson, 1976).

Hall was director of the Birmingham Centre until 1979, when he took up the chair of sociology at the Open University, which he held until his retirement. At Birmingham, he left behind a rich tradition of critical cultural inquiry, which has subsequently been exported to North America, Australia, Korea, Taiwan and elsewhere. One of its most important legacies is, as Turner observes, the 'strategy of "reading" cultural products, social practices, even institutions, as "texts"' (Turner, 1996, p. 81). During Hall's directorship, the Centre became increasingly involved with the 'new' issues of gender, race and ethnicity. Paul Gilroy and feminists such as Angela McRobbie firmly placed the issues of racism and sexism on the Centre's agenda, a move initially resisted by Hall himself. These questions will be explored in much greater detail in chapter 5. For the moment, let us note only that the development of British cultural studies under Hall's guidance was, as he himself has observed, in part a reflection of his coming to terms with a personal trajectory as outsider—a black Jamaican emigré working and living in the heart of white, high British academic culture.

The Centre's shift in substantive focus was accompanied by a theoretical shift towards the kinds of semiology that will provide our major concern in chapter 4. Substantively, Hall's own work tended to focus on the mass media, especially on how these construct public opinion and, in effect, police those popular subcultural practices and subversions that might threaten the state's legitimacy; theoretically, it became fascinated by structuralist and later post-structuralist thematics. This turn towards semiotic and structuralist methodologies is definitively marked by Hall's important article, 'Encoding and Decoding in Television Discourse', first published as a CCCS stencilled paper in 1973 (Hall, 1999). For Hall, such meaning-making practices as those arising out of conflicts over rival interpretations of social reality and history are linked to 'a struggle over a particular kind of power—cultural power: the power to define, to "make things mean"' (Hall, 1982, p. 12). Moreover, the Centre's interest in semiology was often combined with various Marxist thematics, especially those deriving from Gramsci and Althusser. These various structuralisms and Marxisms will be considered in more detail in the chapters that follow. Suffice it to note that the combined impact of structuralist semiology and structural Marxism was to establish a considerable distance between Hall and the earlier culturalist arguments

Structuralism versus culturalism

The precise point at which these divergences constitute a difference is difficult to document. By 1980, however, when Hall published the seminal essay, 'Cultural studies: two paradigms' (Hall, 1980), 'culturalism' was no longer the obviously available starting point for the would-be discipline, but rather only one of two competing paradigms, each with its attendant strengths and weaknesses. For Hall, 'culture' in Williams and 'experience' in Thompson were seen as performing fundamentally analogous theoretical functions, that is, they denoted simultaneously, and thereby elided the distinction between, active consciousness and relatively 'given', determinate conditions. The result was a theoretical humanism, with two distinguishing characteristics: first, a general 'experiential pull', and second, an 'emphasis on the creative' (p. 63). Hall's response to this 'empiricism' was to insist that: 'Analysis must deconstruct . . . "lived wholeness" in order to be able to think its determinate conditions' (p. 62). The scene was set, then, for a structuralist 'interruption' as theoretical salvation. Formally, of course, Hall aspired not to any thoroughgoing structuralism, but to a synthesis of culturalist and structuralist paradigms: 'between them . . . they address what must be the *core problem* of Cultural Studies' (p. 72). The logic of the argument, however, leaves culturalism with remarkably little to do. In truth, Hall's was an anti-culturalist argument, its effects all the more damaging because of its professed evenhandedness.

The crucial difference here was between Williams' and Hall's respective readings of Gramsci. If hegemony is a culture, in a recognisably culturalist sense, as Williams supposed, then it is materially produced by the practices of conscious agents, and may be countered by alternative, counter-hegemonic, practices. If hegemony is a structure of ideology, as Hall came to believe, then it will determine the subjectivity of its subjects in ways that radically diminish the prospects for counter-hegemonic practice. Hegemony as culture is a matter of material production, reproduction and consumption; hegemony as structure is a matter for textual decoding. While Williams' interpretation of Gramsci remained resolutely 'post-culturalist', Hall progressively assimilated it to a developing structuralist—and post-structuralist—paradigm. These theoretical differences increasingly devolved, moreover, on a particular substantive issue: how to read the political successes of the Anglo-American New Right during the 1980s and 1990s.

Postmodern 'New Times'

Defined originally in exclusively British terms as 'Thatcherism', but later generalised as 'New Times', Hall and his co-workers directly addressed the cultural politics of what we would now recognise as the 'postmodern' late twentieth century. The issues at stake were claimed for cultural studies, rather than political science, precisely insofar as they appeared to pertain to the social construction of consent: 'What is particularly significant for our purposes', wrote Hall, 'is Thatcherism's capacity to become popular, especially among those sectors of society whose interests it cannot possibly be said to represent in any conventional sense of the term' (Hall, 1988, p. 41).

Hall's analyses commenced from the assumption that Thatcherism was substantially different from earlier forms of Conservatism, and that this difference centred on the particular ways in which hegemony was established and maintained.

What was at issue, he argued, was the 'move toward "authoritarian populism"—an exceptional form of the capitalist state which . . . has been able to construct around itself an active popular consent' (Hall, 1983, pp. 22–3). Strongly influenced by the 'post-Marxism' of Ernesto Laclau and Chantal Mouffe (Laclau & Mouffe, 1985; Laclau & Mouffe, 1987), whose work he would describe as 'seminal' and 'extraordinarily rich' (Grossberg, 1996, p. 145), Hall's central contention was that this popular consent had been secured through the effective 'articulation' of Thatcherism with key elements in traditional working-class culture. According to Hall, Thatcherism operated directly 'on popular elements in the traditional philosophies and practical ideologies of the *dominated* classes'. This was possible, he explained, because such elements 'have no intrinsic, necessary or fixed class meaning' and can therefore be recomposed in new ways, so as 'to construct the people into a populist political subject: *with*, not against, the power bloc' (Hall, 1983, p. 30). In subsequent reformulations, Hall sought to 'disarticulate' the politics of the Anglo-American New Right from economic and cultural postmodernity: Thatcherism, he insisted, 'represents . . . an attempt . . . to harness and bend to its political project circumstances . . . which do not necessarily have a "New Right" political agenda inscribed in them' (Hall, 1989, pp. 116–17).

No doubt Hall was right to insist that the Left could neither revive nor survive if 'wholly cut off from the landscapes of popular pleasures, however contradictory and "commodified"' (pp. 128–9). But some critical distance, some continuing sense of the 'classed' nature of capitalism, was surely necessary were the Left to go on being left. There were good empirical reasons, moreover, to treat Hall's approach with some caution. Alternative explanations were available: Williams himself had suggested that the scale of Conservative electoral victory was more plausibly explained by the 'first-past-the-post' electoral system than by a successfully Thatcherite ideological mobilisation (Williams, 1989, p. 163); he had shown that pro-Labour loyalties persisted among union members, the unemployed and manual workers (Williams, 1983, pp. 156–7); and that the fall in the Labour vote was as much a consequence of the splits in the Party as of any direct transfer to the Conservatives (p. 155). Moreover, Williams was concerned at the political risk entailed in any such 'block diagnosis of Thatcherism': that it 'taught despair and political disarmament in a social situation which was always more diverse, more volatile and more temporary' (Williams, 1989a, p. 175).

Culture as experience versus culture as text

We might note that Williams was dealing here with precisely the kind of 'objective coordinates' or 'structural determinants' that culturalism is often alleged to ignore. Indeed, it was Williams' explanation, rather than Hall's, that seemed the more readily compatible with mainstream empirical sociology. As Britain's leading expert in the empirical study of class inequalities, J.H. Goldthorpe would observe of Hall: 'Not only is no evidence provided of the supposed "hegemony" at work, but the argument for it involves ignoring the . . . quite substantial findings to indicate that Thatcherism *cannot* be linked with any very significant belief and value changes within British society, and that many Conservative policies are well out of line with prevailing opinion' (Goldthorpe, 1990, p. 431). Certainly, the accumulating empirical data on the continuing resilience of the connections between class identity and politics, both in Britain and internationally (cf. Wright, 1997), calls into question some of Hall's work on the New Right.

Theoretically, we need to ask why Williams was able to read Thatcherism more accurately than Hall. At one level, the answer must rest with the legitimacy he accorded the proper claims of experience. Like Thompson, Williams had persisted in a long-standing commitment, inherited from Leavisism, not to experience *per se*, but to the analysis of the connections between being, consciousness and experience. By contrast, Hall progressively abandoned all three, initially in favour of the notion of ideology as structure, later still in favour of the even more 'immaterial' notion of discursive formation. Hence the increasing preoccupation with 'cultural representations and signifying practices', the subtitle to his *Representation* (1997). The focus here is on how the dynamic relationship between representation, fantasy and pleasure functions in the visual imagery of the popular media and how that imagery produces and perpetuates stereotypes of identity and otherness: the construction of national cultural identity through photography; the ideology of exhibition in ethnographic museums; stereotypes and fantasies of the 'racialised Other', especially blacks, in film, advertising and other popular media; the construction of male identity in consumer advertising; and the gendering of social roles in television soaps. Important though this work undoubtedly is, its weaknesses are also apparent. Even the Leavises had known that historical reality could never simply be deduced from a close reading of texts. But as Sparks observes, contemporary cultural studies has increasingly regressed 'beyond Hoggart and Williams, beyond the Leavises and the British marxists, to an essentially textualist account of culture'. If this has been Hall's achievement, then it is surely, as Sparks concludes, quite 'fundamentally regressive' (Sparks, 1996, p. 98).

What we have termed 'culturalism' emerged from out of a heady combination of Romantic humanism and historicism. Its most generally defining features were a stress on human agency and creativity and a commitment to the positive value of a 'common culture', often understood as both national in character and reaching its highest form in 'art'. During the 1950s and 1960s, the 'left culturalist' challenge to literary studies sought to radically decentre high art in favour of a much more properly common understanding of culture, from out of which there developed what eventually became 'cultural studies'. But from the 1970s on, this left culturalism was itself increasingly challenged and apparently out-radicalised by theoretical perspectives associated with western Marxism and structuralist or post-structuralist semiology. It is to these other intellectual traditions, whose impress we have already registered in the new historicism and in the work of Stuart Hall, that we turn in the chapters that immediately follow. This is not to suggest, however, that the theoretical and practical questions typically posed by culturalism were somehow either resolved or transcended. Quite the contrary—the matters at issue in these older debates over community and culture, class and nation, have repeatedly returned to haunt both literary and cultural studies. The pretensions to theoretical and practical adequacy variously advanced for Marxism, structuralism and post-structuralism will thus be adjudicated, in part at least, precisely by how well they each propose new answers to these older culturalist questions.

3

Critical theory: from ideology critique to the sociology of culture

The term 'critical theory' was coined by the Institute for Social Research at the University of Frankfurt, to distinguish their own kind of 'critical' sociology from what they saw as the 'traditional theory' of mainstream social science. Founded in 1923, the 'Frankfurt School', as it became known, included such figures as Theodor Adorno (1903–69), Max Horkheimer (1895–1973), Walter Benjamin (1892–1940), Herbert Marcuse (1898–1979) and, more recently, Jürgen Habermas and Axel Honneth. In a 1937 essay entitled 'Traditional and Critical Theory', Horkheimer had argued that where traditional theory conceived of itself as 'stored-up knowledge', that is, a condensed description of 'the actual facts' of the present, critical theory sought to understand the social world as changeable, thereby stripping reality of its character as 'pure factuality' (Horkheimer, 1972, pp. 188, 209). In a postscript to the main body of the essay, he spelt out the position more forcefully: 'critical theory . . . never aims simply at an increase of knowledge as such. Its goal is man's emancipation from slavery' (p. 246). Committed to such radical goals, it is hardly surprising that their work is often characterised as 'Marxist'. And they were indeed indebted to Marx in many significant respects, not least their shared sense of mass culture as ideology. But the Frankfurt School writers were inspired as much by the subtitle as the main title of Marx's masterpiece: *Capital: A Critique of Political Economy*. Moreover, Horkheimer stressed the School's and Marx's indebtedness to the entire critical tradition in German idealist philosophy—especially Kant and Hegel—and to 'philosophy as such' (p. 245). We might add that they also owed much to Weber, the 'founding father' of German sociology, and to Freud, the founder of psychoanalysis. It is to these three key precursors—Marx, Weber and Freud—that we turn initially. Thereafter, we will proceed to accounts both of the Frankfurt School itself and of the wider 'critical' tradition inspired by these selfsame sources.

MARX, WEBER AND FREUD

Karl Marx (1818–83) was the co-founder, with Frederick Engels (1820–95), of what they termed 'historical materialism', but has since come to be known as 'Marxism'. A committed socialist excluded by political repression from the academic career to which he had originally aspired, Marx sought to fashion a self-consciously progressive social theory that would be of political value to the infant labour movement. His own academic training in Hegelian philosophy profoundly affected the shape of this theory. What emerged was a synthesis between German Hegelianism and British utilitarian political economy, in which a culturalist antithesis between culture and civilisation was combined with a utilitarian sense of the power of material interest, and incorporated into an overall Hegelian understanding of history as process. Marx's use of the culture/civilisation trope is at its most apparent in the theory of 'alienation' outlined in the *Economic and Philosophical Manuscripts* of 1844. These *Manuscripts* were organised around a conceptual dichotomy between actually existing alienated labour, where labour power is transformed into a commodity and the worker reduced to a mere thing, and the ideal of a non-alienated labour represented in the notion of 'species-being' (Marx, 1975, pp. 327–30). By the latter Marx meant simply the humanness of humanity, constituted in his view by our capacity for conscious, collective, creative production (p. 328). Insofar as it was present in reality, unalienated labour was best exemplified by art and intellectual culture: 'Animals produce only according to the standards and needs of the species to which they belong, while man is capable of producing according to the standards of every species . . . hence man also produces in accordance with the laws of beauty' (p. 329). Marx also argued that capitalist civilisation tended to substitute alienated for unalienated labour: 'The bourgeoisie has stripped of its halo every occupation hitherto honoured and looked up to with reverent awe', he wrote: 'It has converted the physician, the lawyer, the priest, the poet, the man of science, into its paid wage-labourers' (Marx & Engels, 1967, p. 82).

In Volume I of what is widely regarded as his masterwork, *Capital*, we find a further development of this notion of alienation in the concept of 'commodity fetishism', a term used to describe the way human relations take on the appearance, in a market economy, of relations between things, that is, between commodities. Capitalist culture is therefore a fetishistic culture, in which 'a definite social relation between men . . . assumes, in their eyes, the fantastic form of a relation between things' (Marx, 1970, p. 72). The Arnoldian antithesis between culture and civilisation was thus transposed into Marx's, between unalienated labour and capitalist commodification. Furthermore, for Marx, as for Arnold, this fetishised culture 'tends constantly to become more so'. The crucial difference, however, is in Marx's stress on production as distinct from Arnold's on cultural consumption. It was precisely this difference that propelled Marx away from a pedagogical solution to the cultural crises of capitalism—which could only ever aspire to reform the habits of 'taste'—and towards the alternative of a revolutionary transformation in the system of production itself

Marx on ideology

Insofar as cultural theory has been concerned, the most important idea from Marx is not so much alienation as 'ideology', an entirely original notion (though not an original term) with no counterpart in Arnold, designed to express the inner connectedness of culture and economy (or class). In its most general form, Marx's theory of ideology maintained simply that: 'Life is not determined by consciousness, but consciousness by life' (Marx & Engels, 1970, p. 47). But this later gave way to two much more specific theses: that the ideas of the ruling class are the ruling ideas; and that the economic 'base' in some sense 'determines' the cultural 'superstructures'. The first is argued in *The German Ideology*: 'The ideas of the ruling class are in every epoch the ruling ideas: i.e. the class which is the ruling *material* force of society, is at the same time its ruling *intellectual* force' (p. 64). Culturally dominant ideas thus became, for Marx, the ideal expression of the dominant material relations, produced in the interests of the ruling class, and by that class's own specialist ideologists. Though the ruling ideas might be dominant, they are not thereby uncontested. Rather, rival classes produce rival ideas in the struggle for social leadership, and historically these become increasingly more abstract and universal in form. Like the class struggle itself, this struggle for intellectual and cultural mastery will come to an end only in the future classless society, which will be ushered into being by the proletarian revolution.

The base/superstructure model appeared initially in the 1859 'Preface' to *A Contribution to the Critique of Political Economy*. Marx's formulation is so succinct that it is as well to quote it at length:

> The totality of . . . relations of production constitutes the economic structure of society, the real foundation, on which arises a legal and political superstructure and to which correspond definite forms of social consciousness. The mode of production of material life conditions the general process of social, political and intellectual life (Marx, 1975, p. 425).

Marx adds, in an important qualification, that a distinction should always be made 'between the material transformation of the economic conditions of production, which can be determined with the precision of natural science, and the legal, political, religious, artistic or philosophic—in short, ideological forms in which men become conscious of this conflict and fight it out' (p. 426).

There is no necessary incompatibility between the two arguments. Neither directly denied the sense of an antithesis between cultural creativity and the commodity fetishism of capitalist civilisation. Both insisted that culture was also always ideology; that is, that it is conditioned by material reality. The first laid much greater stress on the significance of class, as distinct from that of economy. But this was partly a matter of semantics: the 'relations of production' referred to in the 1859 'Preface' were, for Marx, invariably relations of class. The second made use of a peculiar analogy with construction (foundation/superstructure), combined with a powerfully evocative reference to the precision of natural science, so as to suggest a process of mechanical causation, where the economy is the cause, culture the effect. But much of that suggestion is denied both by the carefully qualifying verbs—'rises/correspond/conditions', but *not* 'causes', nor even 'determines', in the sense of causation—and by the clear implication that cultural transformation, unlike material transformation, *cannot* be determined (that is, known) with the precision of natural science. There has been a clear incompatibility between the rival systems of interpretation subsequently attached to each. In general, supposedly 'scientific' Marxisms opted for strongly determinist versions of the base/superstructure model, 'critical' Marxisms for versions of the ruling ideas thesis in which economy and culture were theorised as different aspects of the 'totality', rather than as cause and effect. The difference has been described as that between 'mechanical' and 'expressive' causality (Althusser & Balibar, 1970, pp. 186–7).

This difference between scientific and critical Marxisms raises the interesting question of the epistemological status of Marx's work, as either science or ideology. There is no doubt that Marx imagined it to be in some significant sense scientific. On the other hand, he understood it also as political, as a means by which the socialist movement would become conscious of itself in the class struggle. As such it is a superstructure, and presumably, therefore, subject to the same processes of material conditioning that operate on all other superstructures, processes that might be interpreted as denying to Marxism the extra-social objectivity implied by the term 'science'. In short, Marxism's pretensions to scientificity might run contrary to its claims to political efficacy. For Marx himself this does not appear to have been a problem. Subsequent Marxisms have found it much less easy, however, to reconcile the two notions. Marxism has often appeared in the guise of an objective science, dispensed by a proletarian, or supposedly proletarian, political party; sometimes as proletarian consciousness, or ideology, whether that of party or union; and sometimes as the critical consciousness of oppositional intellectuals. But these have rarely been combined so effectively or so apparently unproblematically as in Marx.

Weber on rationality and legitimation

Classical German sociology was conceived substantially in reaction to the challenge of Marxism. Max Weber (1864–1920), the German 'bourgeois Marx', became a sociologist, Albert Salomon famously observed, 'in a long and intense debate with the ghost of Marx' (Salomon, 1945, p. 596). This debate, in turn, decisively shaped the subsequent history of German sociology; and also of what is often termed 'western Marxism', a phrase coined by the French philosopher Maurice Merleau-Ponty to describe the tradition of critical Marxism that developed in western Europe, especially in Germany, in more or less deliberate opposition to official, Soviet, 'scientific' Marxism (Merleau-Ponty, 1974). It is common in the Anglophone literature to link Weber with Emile Durkheim as the 'founding fathers' of sociology, and to contrast the classical sociology thereby constructed with the classical Marxism of Marx and Engels. But this exaggerates the affinities between Weber and Durkheim, and also overlooks the extent to which Marx and Weber can both be situated within a specifically German tradition of debate about culture and society. Weber's stress on the causal efficacy of culture, it seems to us, is better understood as an important corrective to the overemphasis on material factors in scientific Marxism than as embodying an outright rejection of materialism *per se*. This was certainly Weber's own view: 'it is . . . not my aim to substitute for a one-sided materialistic an equally one-sided spiritualistic causal interpretation of culture and of history' (Weber, 1930, p. 183).

Critical theory would learn three things from Weber: that ideas mattered a great deal more than scientific Marxism had imagined, and significantly more than Marx; that the capitalist system remained subject to a developmental logic of rationalisation; and that social order depended substantially on political legitimacy. The first such lesson is asserted most effectively in *The Protestant Ethic and the Spirit of Capitalism*. Weber clearly accepted, and indeed became fascinated by, the type of correlation between social stratification and cultural belief that Marx analysed in terms of ideology. Between Marx (or, at least, Engels) and Weber there is no real disagreement as to the correlation between Calvinism and capitalism. What Weber insisted on, however, was the view that Protestant beliefs played an active, energising role in the social process by which capitalism came into being. Thus *The Protestant Ethic* is designed to demonstrate the extent to which 'religious forces have taken part in the qualitative formation and the quantitative expansion' (p. 91) of the spirit of capitalism.

The rationalisation thesis is central to Weber's account both of modernity and of modernisation: he sees capitalism as a system of rational economic calculation; bureaucracy as the distinctly modern form of rational organisation; Protestantism as a system of religious belief peculiarly conducive to a radical rationalisation of individual ethical conduct; and even occidental music and its system of notation as distinctively and characteristically rationalised (Weber, 1964, p. 279; Weber, 1930, pp. 153–4; Weber, 1958). In some respects this notion runs parallel to Marx's theory of alienation, and especially so in its negative moment, as in the characterisation of modernity as an 'iron cage' of reason (Weber, 1930, p. 181). It is sometimes suggested that the rationalisation thesis implies a more benign vision of capitalism than that in Marx. This seems doubtful, however, for Weber feared the negative moment in rationalisation, just as Marx had acknowledged the positive in capitalism. Paradoxically, the fundamental difference between Marx and Weber is, as Giddens recognised, over whether history itself has a rationality: Marx, following Hegel, thought that it had; Weber, following Kant, that it hadn't (Giddens, 1971, p. 193). Hence Weber's suspicion that socialism, far from providing a solution to the problems of bureaucratisation, might only exacerbate them (Weber, 1968, pp. 1401–2). This understanding of the modern world as an iron cage of disenchantment is yet another instance of the culturalist antithesis between culture and civilisation, or, to use Weber's own roughly equivalent terms, *Wertrationalität* and *Zweckrationalität* (Weber, 1964, p. 115).

Weber's theory of legitimation provides an especially important instance of this general stress on the social effectivity of belief. Despite the recognition in *The German Ideology* of the significance of ruling ideas, both Marx and most immediately subsequent Marxists tended to explain social order, insofar as it could be said to exist at all, as a consequence either of the mode of production or of the state. Weber, by contrast, stressed legitimate authority, that is, a type of imperative control based on the acceptance by subordinates of the right of superordinates to give orders. Weber sketched out an ideal typology of three main kinds of legitimation, but by far the most significant for modernity was the rational/legal type, which rests 'on a belief in the "legality" of patterns of normative rules and the right of those elevated to authority under such rules to issue commands' (p. 328). In effect, this is little more than a restatement of the 'ruling ideas' version of Marx's theory of ideology, but with the extremely important qualification that such ideas are conceived not simply as ruling, but as ruling effectively. Insofar as legitimate authority does exist, it is uncontested. Moreover, there was for Weber no necessary succession of different types of class rule, and hence of ruling ideas, as there had been for Marx. In principle, at least, a legitimate authority might last indefinitely.

Freud and the unconscious

Sigmund Freud (1856–1939) is best known for his development of the psychoanalytic concept of the 'unconscious'. The relevance of this work for critical theory lay in the promise that it might explain how individual subjectivity is articulated with social structure. Though not the first to believe in the existence of an unconscious, Freud's signal contribution was to link it to the notion of psychic repression. The human psyche, he argued, was constituted by energy flows, or 'instincts' and 'drives' as he would come to term them. Much of this desire is narcissistic and destructive and must therefore be repressed if social cohesion is to exist. Desires that cannot be fulfilled are thus channelled into socially useful activities, in a process he termed 'sublimation'. Indeed, civilisation itself is founded upon a necessary repression of these unconscious drives and desires. If the sexual drives are too strong, Freud suggests, they might manifest themselves in such 'perverse' activity as homosexuality or sadomasochism. If they can be neither expressed in perversion nor sublimated into such acceptable cultural activities as work, sport, art or intellectuality, then they manifest themselves as neurosis.

In his first major work, *The Interpretation of Dreams*, Freud outlined the methods he had used to understand hysteria and neurosis in his own patients. The central technique was to persuade them to describe their dreams and to talk about the possible connections between these and their childhood experiences, especially traumatic events related to sexuality and conflict with their parents. Through his work on dream analysis, Freud refined a progressively more complex model of early childhood psychic development. He argued that both males and females are bisexual and polymorphously 'perverse' during what he termed the 'oral' and 'anal' stages of early childhood development. Their sexuality is dispersed, uninhibited and not yet centred on genitality: 'it spreads in all directions and can embrace all objects and bodily parts, it is purely and simply about *pleasure* with no thought for propriety or procreation' (Frosh, 1999, p. 46). When the pan-sexuality underlying these pleasure-seeking instincts, the so-called 'pleasure principle', enters into conflict with the social order, or the 'reality principle', it undergoes transformation through repression, displacement and sublimation. The period of sublimation begins during the 'phallic stage', the precursor to adult sexuality, when both boys and girls become fascinated by their genitalia and when the presence or absence of a penis becomes the primary marker of sexual difference.

Freud hypothesised that in the latter part of the phallic stage, children enter into society and culture through a process he named the 'Oedipal phase', after Sophocles' tragedy, *Oedipus Rex*. He explained the continuing power of this play by the fact that Oedipus' destiny 'might have been ours . . . It is the fate of all of us . . . to direct our first sexual impulse towards our mother and our first hatred and our first murderous wish against our father' (Freud, 1976, p. 364). This is the most fundamental of repressed desires for both boys and girls, he argued, though it is resolved differently in the two sexes. Eventually, the male child is driven through fear of castration to identify with the authoritarian father figure, so that his desire for the mother effectively disappears. Lacking a penis, the female child can never identify so completely with the father and therefore redirects her desire from mother to father. She nonetheless continues to suffer from 'penis envy', which can only find resolution in giving birth to a baby, as a replacement object for the initial constitutive lack. Later, Freud famously reformulated this theory in terms of the tripartite distinction between id, ego and super-ego, where the ego was the self, the super-ego the social part of the self, and the id a new term for what he had meant by the unconscious. The id, Freud explained, 'is the dark, inaccessible part of our personality . . . we call it chaos, a cauldron full of seething excitations . . . It is filled with energy reaching it from the instincts, but it has no organization . . . only a striving to bring about the satisfaction of instinctual needs . . . The id . . . knows no judgements of value: no good and evil, no morality' (Freud, 1973, pp. 105–7).

But what has all this to do with culture? The short answer is everything, since culture is simultaneously the source of psychic repression and fuelled by that repression. It thus becomes quite fundamentally a matter of the regulation and control of desire. In *Totem and Taboo*, Freud's excursion into anthropology, he even went so far as to argue that 'the beginnings of religion, morals, society and art converge in the Oedipus complex' (Freud, 1985, p. 219). In *The Future of an Illusion*, he identified two distinguishing features of human civilisation: the control and exploitation of nature and the rational organisation of relations among people. The latter is achieved by coercion and the suppression of libidinal instincts. Human beings do not readily accept such social control, since it requires so much in the way of instinctual renunciation, but it remains necessary, to overcome the 'destructive, and therefore anti-social and anti-cultural, trends' present 'in all men' (Freud, 1985a, p. 185). Historically, Freud observes, religion has played the major role in securing the necessary renunciation of instinctual desires. Though religious beliefs can be examined rationally, they are not themselves rational, but rather reflect 'illusions, fulfilments of the oldest, strongest and most urgent wishes of mankind' (p. 212); that is, they are a symbolic representation of the protection offered by the father after the Oedipal phase (p. 226).

Unlike Marx, Freud could imagine no utopian exit from this state of affairs. Hence his dismissal of investment in radical social change as merely a search for 'consolation': 'at bottom that is what they are all demanding—the wildest revolutionaries no less passionately than most virtuous believers' (p. 339). Freud's legacy remains highly controversial, but even his harshest critics tend to admit to the reality of both the unconscious and psychic repression. The precise degree to which these influence our thoughts and actions or underpin the edifice of civilisation remains in dispute. The Frankfurt School saw Freud's work as pointing towards an emancipatory politics, despite his own pessimistic appraisal of the possibilities for radical social change, and made use of this account of rational and irrational individual behaviour in their studies of repressive domination. Before we proceed to their work, however, we also need to consider the more obviously cognate theorisations of cultural modernity developed in the western Marxism of Georg Lukács and Antonio Gramsci.

LUKÁCS, GRAMSCI AND THE ORIGINS OF WESTERN MARXISM

The Frankfurt School was part of the much larger intellectual movement Merleau-Ponty and others have dubbed western Marxism. This was itself a radically culturalist version of the Marxian tradition, which, in Anderson's phrase, 'came to concentrate overwhelmingly on study of *superstructures* . . . It was culture that held the central focus of its attention' (Anderson, 1976, pp. 75–6). The characteristic thematics were human agency, subjective consciousness, and hence also culture. This was true of Georg Lukács (1885–1917), the Hungarian-born but German-speaking and German-educated philosopher; of his

Franco-Rumanian disciple, the sociologist of literature, Lucien Goldmann (1913–70); and of Lukács' heirs in the Budapest School, notably Agnes Heller and Ferenc Fehér (1933–94). It was true also of the Italian revolutionary leader Antonio Gramsci (1891–1937), and of the French existential Marxist Jean-Paul Sartre (1905–80) (cf. Goldmann, 1964; Heller & Fehér, 1986; Sartre, 1976). At its origin in the early 1920s, this stress on agency and consciousness provided both Lukács and Gramsci with the means to underwrite a leftist rejection of the political fatalism implicit in economic determinism, in favour of the immediate possibilities of revolution. As Gramsci observed of the Bolshevik Revolution of 1917, it was a revolution against *Capital* (Gramsci, 1977, pp. 34–7). But as the moment of revolutionary optimism failed, as Lukács came to terms with Stalinist Communism and Gramsci struggled to produce the *Prison Notebooks* in an Italian Fascist prison, so the emphasis shifted towards an analysis of the system-supportive nature of cultural legitimations.

Georg Lukács

Where scientific socialism theorised the relationship between culture and society in terms of the base/superstructure model, western Marxism sought to understand both base and superstructure as particular moments within a contradictory totality. Thus for Lukács, the revolutionary principle in Marx, as in Hegel, was that of the dialectic, 'the concept of totality, the subordination of every part to the whole unity of history and thought' (Lukács, 1971, pp. 27–8). For the Lukács of *History and Class Consciousness*, this notion of totality provided the positive pole against which to develop the central, critical concept of reification. Here Lukács expanded upon the discussion of commodity fetishism in *Capital*, reading it in the light both of Hegel and of Weber's rationalisation thesis (but not that of the still unpublished *Economic and Philosophical Manuscripts*), to develop what was, in effect, a version of the theory of alienation. By 'reification' Lukács meant something similar to what Marx had meant by 'commodity fetishism'. But Lukács generalised the notion beyond the commodity relation, insisting that capitalism was itself a system of reification. Human reality is necessarily detotalised under capitalism, he argued, both by commodity fetishism and by other reified forms of consciousness, the most important of which is, in fact, science (pp. 6–7).

For the young Lukács, reified thought could be overcome only by the proletariat's coming to consciousness of itself as the identical subject and object of history (p. 20). In the early 1920s Lukács clearly viewed the prospects for such development as fairly imminent: the 'imputed' class consciousness (p. 51) embodied in Marxism was to be actualised in the empirical consciousness of a working class led by the revolutionary party. But as Lukács recoiled from both Nazism and Stalinism, this revolutionary optimism gave way to an increasing reliance on the realist novel as the principal totalising instance in our culture (Lukács, 1963). While Anderson is mistaken seeing western Marxism as *born* from a moment of failure (quite the contrary—it was born from a moment of high revolutionary optimism)—it would eventually be characterised by 'a common and latent *pessimism*' (Anderson, 1976, pp. 92, 88). Hence the preoccupation with how culture as ideology functions to legitimate the capitalist system, and so too the growing scepticism as to the possibilities for successful working-class opposition.

Antonio Gramsci

Such pessimism is typically Weberian, but paradoxically it was Gramsci, perhaps the western Marxist thinker least influenced by Weber, who produced by far the most theoretically persuasive, and indeed influential, Marxist theory of legitimation. As is well known, Gramsci substituted, for the more orthodox base/superstructure model, a civil society/political society model, which derived from both Hegel and Marx, but which had commanded relatively little attention among Marxists. Political society here denoted the coercive elements within the wider social totality, civil society the non-coercive. Where most Marxists had previously stressed politico-economic coercion, and where Weber had stressed legitimation, Gramsci chose to point towards both, and towards their inextricable interconnection in the maintenance of social stability. Hence the famous formula: 'State = political society + civil society, in other words hegemony protected by the armour of coercion' (Gramsci, 1971, p. 263). The term 'hegemony' here refers to something very similar to Weber's legitimate authority: to the permeation throughout the whole of society of a system of values and beliefs supportive of the existing ruling class. This is, in effect, a value consensus, and one very often embodied in commonsense, but constructed, however, in the interests of the ruling class.

'The intellectuals', Gramsci argued, 'are the dominant group's "deputies" exercising the subaltern functions of social hegemony and political government' (p. 12). They are not in themselves an autonomous and independent social class, but rather, the 'functionaries' of the superstructures. Gramsci distinguished between 'organic' intellectuals, that is, the type of intellectual that each major social class creates for itself so as to 'give it homogeneity and an awareness of its own function' (p. 5), and 'traditional' intellectuals, that is, 'categories of intellectuals already in existence . . . which seem to represent . . . historical continuity' (p. 7). Intellectuals of the latter type, most importantly the clergy, but also administrators, scholars and scientists, theorists and philosophers affect a certain autonomy from the dominant social classes, but it is an autonomy that is ultimately illusory. For Gramsci himself, the central political problem was that of the creation of a layer of organic working-class intellectuals capable of leading their class in the battle for counter-hegemony. But in his own work, and even more so in that of subsequent Gramscians, the substantive focus very easily slides towards the explanation of an apparently impregnable bourgeois hegemony. If hegemony is never in principle either uncontested or indefinite, it can quite often come to appear both.

THE FRANKFURT SCHOOL

From Marx, the Frankfurt School inherited the theory of ideology and a model of capitalism as exploitative and oppressive; from Weber, a suspicion of rationalism and a diagnosis of contemporary science and culture as (over) rationalised; from Freud, the theory of the unconscious and the notion that social order functions in part by way of psychic repression. These influences would shape the general trajectory of the School's theoretical development. In his inaugural address as director, Horkheimer had defined the Institute's central focus as:

> The connection between the economic life of society, the psychological development of its individuals and the changes within specific areas of culture to which belong not only the intellectual legacy of the sciences, art, and religion, but also law, customs, fashion, public opinion, sports, entertainment, lifestyles, and so on (Horkheimer, 1989, p. 31).

They shared with Lukács a stress on the notion of totality, a rejection of science and scientific socialism as partial and detotalising, and a sense of the truth value of theory as related to its social role, initially as theoretical companion to the working class, always as in itself emancipatory. But they soon came to reject the notion of the working class as revolutionary subject, so that, as early as 1937, Horkheimer declared that 'even the situation of the proletariat is in this society, no guarantee of correct knowledge' (Horkheimer, 1972, p. 213). This in turn marked a shift away from a celebration of the emancipatory potential of culture as human self-activity, and towards a recognition of the debilitating and disabling power of culture as ideology.

Adorno and Horkheimer

For the Adorno and Horkheimer of *Dialectic of Enlightenment*, written while in exile in America during the Nazi period, capitalism was already a fully rationalised system of domination, the inherent logic of which tended towards fascism. Fascism was thus a culmination of the dehumanised and positivistic science and society unleashed by the Enlightenment: 'Enlightenment behaves toward things as a dictator toward men. He knows them in so far as he can manipulate them' (Adorno & Horkheimer, 1979, p. 9). *Dialectic of Enlightenment* is at the same time a critique of instrumental reason, a history of bourgeois society and a history of western civilisation. Adorno and Horkheimer locate the contradictions of class society in relation to a more fundamental and prior contradiction, that of the struggle between man and nature. Human 'progress'—self-actualisation, the development of social complexity and reason—thus goes hand in hand with the subjugation and manipulation of nature: 'A philosophical conception of history', they insist, 'would have to show how the rational domination of nature comes increasingly to win the day, in spite of all deviations and resistance, and integrates all human characteristics' (p. ix). The will to domination over nature is based on 'fear of the unknown', they argue, and it not only alienates humankind from nature, but also turns inward, repressing the natural drives and instincts. As in Freud, the history of western civilisation is read as a 'history of renunciation' (p. 55). In a radical reading of the *Odyssey*, Adorno and Horkheimer interpreted the eponymous hero of Homer's epic as the prototype of the bourgeois subject. Civilisation, administered society and bourgeois subjectivity were thus set in opposition to nature, spontaneity and imagination.

The mass media or 'the culture industries', as they described them, became central targets for this critique. Authentic art, they argued, involves a necessary confrontation with already established traditional styles; 'inferior' work is merely the practice of imitation. 'In the culture industry', they conclude, 'imitation finally becomes absolute. Having ceased to be anything but style, it reveals the latter's secret: obedience to social hierarchy' (p. 131). In short, the central function of the mass media is ideological manipulation in the interests of profit. Adorno and Horkheimer describe the technologies of the culture industries, noting how these involve the combination of a few production centres with many dispersed consumption points. The technological rationale for such an organisation, they argue, is the rationale of domination (p. 121), where the cultural 'consumer' is made passive and manipulated. 'There is nothing left . . . to classify', they write: 'Producers have done it for [us]' (p. 125). The culture industries' products are thus increasingly standardised, and are characterised by a predominance of 'effect' over 'idea', so that the technical perfection of effects permits the ideological illusion that reality is as it is represented in the media. Hence their startling observation that:

> Real life is becoming indistinguishable from the movies . . . The . . . film . . . leaves no room for imagination or reflection on the part of the audience . . . hence the film forces its victims to equate it directly with reality . . . They are so designed that quickness, powers of observation, and experience are undeniably needed to apprehend them . . . yet sustained thought is out of the question if the spectator is not to miss the relentless rush of facts (pp. 126–7).

Walter Benjamin

For most of the Frankfurt School writers, avant-garde modernist art and music represented the key sites of resistance to such cultural manipulation. The obvious exception is Benjamin, close friend of the Communist playwright Bertolt Brecht and author of a magisterial study of the urban cultures of Paris (Benjamin, 1973; Benjamin, 1999). In a famous essay on 'The Work of Art in the Age of Mechanical Reproduction', Benjamin sought to forge connections between the cultural avant-garde and the new popular media, pitting the emancipatory potential of both against the traditional myth of the 'autonomous' artwork. He coined the term 'mechanical reproduction' to refer to any form of cultural production characterised by the relatively large-scale replication of cultural artefacts by means of machine technologies, where each replica is neither any more nor any less 'original' than any other. This was more than a simple matter of technology, since mechanical reproduction transformed the nature of aesthetic experience itself. Benjamin argued that much of the aesthetic power of the traditional work of art had derived from its status as a unique object, using the term 'aura' to refer to this combination of uniqueness, authenticity and authority, all of which he viewed as inextricably interconnected. For Benjamin, aura derived from the artwork's embeddedness in cultural tradition, which in turn had its historical origins in the religious cult: the sacredness of art is thus derivative of the sacredness of magical and religious ritual (Benjamin, 1973a, p. 225). It is this aura that 'withers in the age of mechanical reproduction' (p. 223).

The paradigmatic Frankfurt School response to the decline of aura was a gloomy cultural pessimism, as in Adorno and Horkheimer. For Benjamin, however, mechanical reproduction and non-auratic art provided the initial preconditions, at least, for the creation of something that could become a cultural democracy. 'It is inherent in the techniques of the film', he wrote, 'that everybody who witnesses its accomplishments is somewhat of an expert' (p. 233). This might well represent the end of western civilisation as the high bourgeois intelligentsia had known it, but that might not be an altogether bad thing. As Benjamin observed: 'The film makes the cult value recede into the background not only by putting the public in the position of critic, but also by the fact that at the movies this position requires attention. The public is an examiner, but an absent-minded one' (pp. 242–3).

Adorno shared many of Benjamin's concerns, but viewed his antipathy to traditional art and corresponding enthusiasm for mass culture as essentially one-sided (Adorno, 1980, pp. 122–3). Adorno was himself neither simply a high modernist nor simply hostile to mass culture. But it is very clear that modernism seemed to him an adversarial culture of quite fundamental importance, and that he could therefore have little sympathy for either Benjaminian celebrations of the new media or Lukácsian nostalgia for literary realism (Adorno, 1980a). The dispute between Lukács' anti-modernism, Benjamin's enthusiastic popular modernism and Adorno's tortured and tortuously pro-modernist dialectic is perhaps the single most intellectually intriguing incident in the history of western Marxism. For all the acrimony with which it was conducted, especially between Lukács and Adorno, the entire debate rested upon the shared assumption of an antithesis between culture (whether realist or modernist) and mechanical (rationalised, reified and detotalised) civilisation. But where Marx had linked that antithesis to the critique of ideology, and had aspired to its transcendence through revolution, both the later Lukács and Adorno remained content with its reproduction in essentially unamended form. Benjamin, alone of the three, continued to hope for a cultural politics that could be at once popular and avant-garde. His eventual suicide in 1940, after an unsuccessful attempt to escape into Spain from Nazi-occupied France, tells us much about the destinies of both western Marxism and critical theory.

Herbert Marcuse

There is a similarly redemptive cast to the work of Marcuse, a member of the Institute from as early as 1932, who, like Adorno and Horkheimer, took refuge in the United States, but unlike them, never permanently returned to Germany. An outspoken opponent of the Vietnam War, Marcuse emerged as a somewhat improbable counter-cultural hero for the American student New Left. Like Adorno and Horkheimer, his work remained heavily indebted to Freud and to the Marx of the *Economic and Philosophical Manuscripts*. In *Eros and Civilisation*, he would try to account for the apparently 'self-defeating' nature of emancipatory struggles through a Freudian analysis of guilt. Guilt feeling, he wrote, 'introjects into individuals, and thus sustains, the principal prohibitions, constraints, and delays in gratification upon which civilisation depends' (Marcuse, 1966, p. 63). While conceding the force of Freud's general theory of repression, Marcuse would insist nonetheless that class societies produce levels of 'surplus repression' far in excess of those necessary to the creation of social life *per se*. Moreover, the internalisation of guilt becomes ever more pronounced under modern capitalist relations: 'The political economy of advanced capitalism', he declared, 'is also a "psychological economy": it produces and administers the needs demanded by the system—even the instinctive needs' (Marcuse, 1967, p. 6). The liberation of individual psychology from repressive guilt, he argued, could be achieved only by a turn to *Eros* and the freeing of sensual desire under the sign of the pleasure principle. This apparently utopian ambition was attainable, Marcuse hoped, insofar as the overcoming of scarcity makes the need for the surplus repression largely redundant.

While the pleasure principle provided Marcuse—and

eventually much of the student Left—with a sense of redemptive purpose, *One-Dimensional Man* defined the shape of their opponents. For Marcuse, as for Adorno and Horkheimer, 'technological society' was above all 'a system of domination' (Marcuse, 1972, p. 14). For Marcuse, as for Adorno and Horkheimer, a combination of mass affluence and mass media had delivered the working class into the arms of the bourgeoisie:

> If the worker and his boss enjoy the same television programme and visit the same resort places . . . then this assimilation indicates not the disappearance of classes, but the extent to which the needs and satisfactions that serve the preservation of the Establishment are shared by the underlying population (p. 21).

The working class in one-dimensional society had thus become 'a prop of the established way of life', whose triumph could only ever 'prolong this way in a different setting' (p. 197). For Marcuse, as for Adorno and Horkheimer, Marx's dialectic was thereby reduced to a theory bereft of practice: 'Dialectical theory', he concluded, 'defines the historical possibilities . . . but their realization can only be in the practice which responds to the theory, and, at present, the practice gives no such response' (p. 197). But where Adorno and Horkheimer had been driven towards an almost unmitigated cultural pessimism, Marcuse still clung to the hope that others might prove better qualified to serve as the midwife of history. In the book's closing pages, he looked to 'the substratum of the outcasts and outsiders', located 'underneath the conservative popular base', for the chance that 'the historical extremes may meet again: the most advanced consciousness of humanity, and its most exploited force' (pp. 199–200). His actual hopes were invested in people 'of other races and other colours, the unemployed and the unemployable' (p. 200), but with a little poetic licence student radicals were soon also able to imagine themselves thus.

Marcuse's strictly aesthetic notions recapitulate much that is in Adorno: both in *Eros and Civilisation* and in *The Aesthetic Dimension* he argued that art must retain its negativity and autonomy, at a distance from everyday practices, precisely so as to preserve its politically subversive potential. In Adorno, Horkheimer and Marcuse, as in the Leavises, high art is privileged as the site of authenticity, mass culture anathematised and sociologically 'explained' as the site of manipulation. Only in the so-called 'second generation' of Frankfurt School critical theorists, represented paradigmatically by Jürgen Habermas, Adorno's successor to the Chair of Sociology and Philosophy at Frankfurt, do we finally encounter a growing awareness of the institutional bases of all culture.

HABERMAS: FROM CRITICAL THEORY TO THE SOCIOLOGY OF CULTURE

The biographical connections between Habermas and Adorno are as direct as those between Williams and Leavis: Habermas was Adorno's assistant from 1956 to 1959 and, aside from a 10-year hiatus at the Max Planck Institute in Starnberg, he taught at Frankfurt from 1964 until his retirement in 1996, when he was in turn succeeded by Honneth. Habermas subscribes to a radical-democratic critique of contemporary capitalism, inspired in part by Weber, in part by Marx. More specifically, he has explicitly affirmed his indebtedness to 'Lukács, Korsch, Gramsci and the Frankfurt School' (Habermas, 1979, p. 83); that is, to the expressly humanist elements within western Marxism. This is a debt he was willing to reaffirm even after the collapse of Eastern European Communism, even in discussion with a Polish intellectual (Habermas & Michnik, 1994, pp. 9–10). Insofar as Habermas refers to the base/superstructure model, he regards it, as did Williams, as a historical rather than an ontological proposition: 'the mark of a seal that must be broken' (Habermas, 1990, p. 16). This, then, is a distinctly Weberian 'Marxism'. Indeed, both Weber's rationalisation thesis and his elaboration of the different types of rational action are central to Habermas. The latter's defence of Enlightenment reason can thus be read as resuming the earlier preoccupations of Weber as much as those of Marx.

The public sphere

For Habermas, the Enlightenment had been sustained by quite distinctive institutional forms. Their novelty had inspired his first major work, *The Structural Transformation of the Public Sphere*, which attempted to explain the socio-historical emergence, during the seventeenth and eighteenth centuries, of a middle-class public opinion, relatively independent of the absolute monarchy. This 'bourgeois public sphere' was 'the sphere of private people come together as a public', a public made up of formally free and equal, rational individuals. These bourgeois would-be citizens, Habermas wrote, 'soon claimed the public sphere . . . against the public authorities themselves . . . The medium of political confrontation was peculiar and without historical precedent: people's use of their reason' (Habermas, 1989, p. 27). The key institutions included the *salons* in France, the learned and literary societies in Germany and the coffee houses in England. Habermas traced the historical evolution of the institutions of public opinion through to their apparent decline in the modern social-welfare state, where state and society penetrate each other, thus producing an apparent 'refeudalization' (p. 231) of society. The collapse of the liberal public sphere has made room for staged and manipulative publicity of the kind registered by Adorno and Horkheimer, he observed, but the state still clings to the mandate of a critical public sphere (p. 232).

The problem for Habermas therefore became not the wholesale refusal enacted by the first generation of critical theorists, but rather how to create new forms of critical public opinion within the institutional contexts already established by an increasingly 'organised' capitalism. In *Legitimation Crisis*, Habermas distinguished between society viewed as 'system' and as 'life-world'. The first referred to the sphere of the economy and the state, of money and power, which functions through the logic of instrumental reason; the second to the world of everyday experience, social discourse and cultural values, science, politics and art. Habermas believed that in the life-world a realm of 'undistorted communication' between free and equal citizens could establish values able to counteract the dominative tendencies of the system. But the life-world is increasingly subject to 'colonisation' by the system, which threatens radically to reduce the possibilities for collective, communicative action. This led him to a concern with how late capitalist societies are legitimated and with the crisis tendencies inherent within them. He argued that economic crises were increasingly 'resolved' through politicisation and that this process itself foregrounded problems of legitimacy and hence the political effects of culture.

In this context, art became for Habermas merely one institutional order among others. Following Weber, he viewed cultural modernity as characterised by 'the separation of the substantive reason expressed in religion and metaphysics into three autonomous spheres . . . science, morality and art' (Habermas, 1985, p. 9). Capitalist societies have never been able to provide adequate motivation for their individual actors, he argued, without resort to more traditional forms of religious belief, but these have become decreasingly effective over time (Habermas, 1975, pp. 77–8). Where religion had been largely system-supportive, art and aesthetics are less obviously suited to this function. Increasingly autonomous from both economics and politics, 'bourgeois' art collects together the human needs that cannot be met by either, which thus become 'explosive ingredients built into the bourgeois ideology' (p. 78). Avant-garde art in particular 'strengthens the divergence between the values offered by the socio-cultural system and those demanded by the political and economic systems' (p. 86). With the benefit of hindsight, it is difficult to avoid the suspicion that Habermas was overimpressed by the immediate impact of the counter-culture of the 1960s. Returning to the problem in 1980, and rehearsing some of the themes outlined in Bürger's *Theory of the Avant-Garde* (Bürger, 1984), he would come to the rather different conclusion that the historical avant-garde's attempt to force a reconciliation between art and life, by destroying the autonomy of art, had been doomed to failure. 'A reified everyday praxis can be cured', he wrote, 'only by creating unconstrained interaction of the cognitive with the moral-practical and the aesthetic-expressive elements. Reification cannot be overcome by forcing just one of those highly stylized cultural spheres to open up and become more accessible' (Habermas, 1985, pp. 11–12). As with Bürger, Habermas' final judgement on the avant-garde is much less sanguine than is Adorno's.

Communicative rationality

Habermas emphasised the essential ambiguity of modernity: the historical need for emancipation from the rigid social structures of pre-rational tradition on the one hand, the 'colonisation of the lifeworld' by instrumental reason on the other. For Habermas, reason is immanent within sociality, and especially within language: through the structure of language, he wrote, 'autonomy and responsibility are posited for us. Our first sentence expresses unequivocally the intention of universal and unconstrained consensus' (Habermas, 1971, p. 314). This notion of unimpeded communication provided him with criteria by which to critique existing social reality and elaborate the utopian possibilities for real social change. The end result was the magisterial two-volume theory of communicative action (Habermas, 1984, 1987a). Habermas' early work had sought to secure the emancipatory potential in Enlightenment reason from Adornian cultural pessimism. Increasingly, however, the irrationalist threat appeared to emanate from French post-structuralism and post-modernism as much as from his own one-time mentors (Habermas, 1987). Though sympathetic to the postmodern 'new social movements' (Habermas, 1981), he would remain deeply suspicious of postmodern theoretical relativism. Hence the dismissive comment on Foucault and Derrida: 'On the basis of modernist attitudes they justify an irreconcilable antimodernism' (Habermas, 1985, p. 14).

He also became increasingly concerned with how to reconcile the utopian ideal of free, rational communicative interaction with the degraded reality of contemporary modern society. This might explain his growing interest in the law, the interface between the normative claims of the life-world and the imperatives of state and market systems. This returned him to the problem of legitimation: laws cannot be self-legitimating because of their inherent rationality, as Weber had supposed (Habermas, 1988, p. 219); their validity must flow from their moral and political dimensions, their ability to guarantee and reflect the will of people, as this is generated in intersubjective communicative action. In other words: 'There can be no autonomous law without the realization of democracy' (p. 279). Habermas' later writings have become increasingly political in tenor, dealing by turn with immediately German problems, such as those posed by reunification, and with more generally European problems, such as the relationship between the European Union and globalising capitalism (Habermas, 1994; Habermas, 1998). He has continued to argue that 'there are alternatives' to the privatisation of the social threatened by the peculiar combination of corporate globalisation and ideological individualism. Confronted by the individualism of the so-called 'Berlin generation', he is insistent on the need for 'a language capable of skewering the phenomena of the hour as mercilessly as Adorno did in the early days of the Federal Republic' (Habermas, 1998a, p. 11). In *The Postnational Constellation*, Habermas has even called for the reconstitution of the welfare state at a supranational level, precisely as a counterweight to the globalisation of the economic system (Habermas, 2001).

Habermas has thus continued the work of critique initiated by the first generation of critical theorists, even if this has become increasingly a matter of commentary and polemic rather than social theory in the grand fashion. In the latter respect, Adorno's mantle appears to have passed to Honneth, whose work promises to add a distinctly subjectivist dimension to post-Adornian critical theory by substituting 'recognition' for undistorted communication as its guiding normative principle (Honneth, 1996). There are obvious parallels between second-generation critical theory and cultural materialism, which have on occasion been remarked upon (Eagleton, 1990, pp. 404, 409). But there are also crucial differences, which are partly disciplinary and partly national-cultural in origin. For cultural materialism the concretely experiential has remained stubbornly relevant, not so much as the antithesis but as the complement to abstract reason. As Eagleton observes: 'Williams's subtle sense of the complex mediations between such necessarily universal formations as social class, and the lived particularities of place, region, Nature, the body, contrasts tellingly with Habermas's universalist rationalism' (p. 409). It is difficult to avoid the conclusion that for Habermas the disciplinary habits of sociology tend to pose a recurrent threat to the claims of particularity. Whether or not Honneth's interests in recognition will provide an adequate solution to this problem remains to be seen. The characteristically abstract quality of German critical theory serves to remind us, however, that cultural studies emerged from a distinctively British intellectual environment barely touched by sociology. This might not be quite the burden it has sometimes seemed.

ZIZEK: CRITICAL THEORY GOES LACANIAN

Insofar as critical theory can be defined in terms of its combination of post-Marxist social critique and post-Freudian psychoanalysis, then Slavoj Zizek, Senior Researcher at the Institute of Social Studies in Ljubljana, Slovenia, has at least as much claim to the title as Habermas or Honneth. Zizek's work has combined a version of Marxism derived in the first instance from the philosopher Louis Althusser with a version of psychoanalysis strongly influenced by Jacques Lacan. Both Althusser and Lacan were loosely (post-) structuralist thinkers (we will consider their work in greater detail in the next chapter). But if Zizek's theoretical sources were indeed (post-) structuralist, his object has remained social critique of a peculiarly controversial kind. Zizek is an immensely prolific writer, whose work has ranged across a wide variety of cultural phenomena, moving with apparent ease between philosophy and politics, literature and film, in an often startling blend of Hegel and Hitchcock, Lacan and Lukács (Zizek, 1992; Zizek, 2001). Quite apart from its applications to clinical practice, Zizek has brought Lacanian psychoanalysis to bear quite centrally on philosophy and politics, especially as these are understood from the perspective of ideology critique.

In two early works, *The Sublime Object of Ideology* and *Looking Awry*, Zizek had established, by turn, a Lacanian reconstruction of the theory of ideology from Marx to Althusser (Zizek, 1989) and a critical account of the politics of Lacan's return to Freud

(Zizek, 1991). The clearest account of his own conception of ideology, however, is in the introduction to a collection of essays he would edit entitled *Mapping Ideology*. Here he distinguished three senses of the term 'ideology': as a doctrine or set of beliefs; as materialised in institutions and practices; and as 'the elusive network of implicit, quasi-"spontaneous" presuppositions and attitudes that form an irreducible moment of the reproduction of "non-ideological" (economic, legal, political, sexual ...) practices' (Zizek, 1994, p. 15). The latter is clearly what interests him the most. It acquired a distinctly psychoanalytic twist, moreover, through Zizek's resort to a Lacanian model of psycho-social reality as comprising three dimensions, respectively the Imaginary, the Symbolic and the Real. The Imaginary refers to the Freudian pre-Oedipal stage of infant development; the Symbolic to the world of language, social communication and culture; the Real to all that is inaccessible both to the Imaginary and to the Symbolic, but that nevertheless impinges on subjectivity and its functioning.

The Real is more or less synonymous with the unconscious and with the individual's real desires: 'the irreducible kernel of *jouissance* that resists all symbolization' (Zizek, 1999, p. 14). Zizek was especially fascinated by Lacan's move away from an earlier structuralist sense of the unconscious as 'structured like a language', preoccupied with the boundary between the Imaginary and the Symbolic, and towards a later exploration of the radical implications both of the Real itself and of the boundary between it and the Symbolic. Following Lacan, Zizek claimed that symbolisation, or representation, will always fall short of reality, which can never be wholly revealed 'in itself'. The aspects of reality that resist symbolisation take the form of a spectre, he argued, an unsettling (ideological) closure. For Zizek, this is the 'pre-ideological kernel' of ideology: '*What the spectre conceals is not reality but its "primordially repressed", the irrepresentable X on whose "repression" reality itself is founded*' (Zizek, 1994, p. 21). Zizek cites as an example Lévi-Strauss' explanation for the fundamentally different spatial conceptions of the ground plan of a village held by its two main subgroups. These conflicting conceptions were evidence not simply of a difference of perspective, Lévi-Strauss had concluded, but of an irresolvable social antagonism, with which neither group had been able to come to terms. This 'splitting' of perception, Zizek observed, 'implies the hidden reference to a constant—not the objective, "actual" arrangement of buildings but a traumatic kernel, a fundamental antagonism the inhabitants were not able to symbolize . . . [or] come to terms with: an imbalance in social relations that prevented the community from stabilizing itself into a harmonious whole'. This traumatic kernel is the Lacanian Real masked by the social structure: 'the structure of social reality materializes an attempt to cope with the real of antagonism' (p. 26).

Marx's critique of political economy yielded a similar insight, according to Zizek, when it referred to the 'fetishistic', or idolatrous, quality of commodities, which shadows the 'official spirituality' of western capitalist industrialisation. If 'the "official" ideology of our society is Christian spirituality', wrote Zizek, 'its actual foundation [its Real] is none the less the idolatry of the Golden Calf, money' (p. 20). The most basic function of ideology, then, is to conceal these deeper social antagonisms, which are not so much aberrations of the social world as the key to its constitution. Zizek is thus a Marxist without the messianism. He agrees with Marx that class conflict and other similar social antagonisms provide the motor force of social reality. But for Zizek these are unamenable to any final resolution, whether through an ideal communist state, a triumphant liberal-capitalist 'end of history' or a New Age return to pastoral harmony. His notion of ideology, as that which papers over the 'senseless contingency of reality', defines real life itself as necessarily always ideological. For Zizek, then, the ultimate source of social antagonism lies within the subject itself as a 'constitutive lack' rather than in the symbolic field of power relations into which the subject is inserted.

Ideology as fantasy

The aim of ideology critique is thus to expose or deconstruct the field of social or ideological fantasy. Zizek argues that the factual impossibility of social harmony tends to be be 'displaced' onto the Other, who is imagined as preventing entry into plenitude, whether this Other be the black, the Jew or the Communist. Paradoxically, such displacement is actually a hatred of oneself and of one's own deep-seated desires, which, if allowed to come to the conscious surface of subjectivity, would imperil the stability secured by ideological fantasy. Hence, the key task of contemporary ideology critique: 'to designate the elements within an existing social order which—in the guise of "fiction", that is, of "Utopian" narratives of possible but failed alternative histories—point towards the system's antagonistic character, and thus "estrange" us to the self-evidence of its established identity' (p. 7).

If the central focus falls on individual subjectivity, this has profound social and political implications. The 'dispersed, plural, constructed subject' celebrated by much postmodernist theory is, for Zizek, simply the *'form of subjectivity that corresponds to late capitalism'*. Capital itself, he writes, 'is the ultimate power of "deterritorialization", which undermines every fixed identity'; late capitalism is the power that weakens the 'traditional fixity of ideological positions (patriarchy, fixed sexual roles, etc.)', so as to remove all possible barriers to the 'unbridled commodification of everyday life' (Zizek, 1993, p. 216).

For Zizek, ideology involves both misrecognition and illusion, but what people misrecognise is not so much their social reality as the illusions that structure it. 'They know very well how things really are', he writes: 'but still they are doing it as if they did not know. The illusion is therefore double: the illusion which is structuring our real, effective relationship to reality. And this overlooked, unconscious illusion may be called the *ideological fantasy*' (Zizek, 1989, pp. 32–3).

In an essay aptly entitled 'It's the *Political* Economy, Stupid!', he argues that a crucial contemporary illusion is the refusal of many in the new social movements to acknowledge the significance of capitalist relations of production. Though conceding the value and necessity of their politics, he insists that their goals will be thwarted unless they can contribute towards 'some kind of radical limitation of Capital's freedom, the subordination of the process of production to social control—the radical *repoliticization of the economy*' (Zizek, 1999a, p. 353).

Zizek's applications of Lacanian psychoanalysis to culture and politics have yielded strikingly original interpretations, none more so than in his film criticism. But like Adorno and Marcuse, he tends both to exaggerate the social system's capacity for dominative integration and to underestimate the possibilities for resistance and change. In *The Ticklish Subject*, for example, he analyses two British films, *Brassed Off* and *The Full Monty*, as 'stories about the traumatic disintegration of old-style working-class male identity' (p. 351). In the first film, Zizek's interest is in the brass band's decision to continue playing despite the loss of their jobs; in the second, in the striptease that marks its conclusion. These represent 'two modes of coming to terms with the catastrophic loss', he writes, 'heroically renouncing the last vestiges of false narcissistic dignity and accomplishing the act for which one is grotesquely inadequate'. The sad thing, he continues, is that this is precisely our situation today: 'none of the critics of capitalism, none of those who describe so convincingly the deadly vortex into which the so-called process of globalization is drawing us, has any well-defined notion of how we can get rid of capitalism' (p. 352). For all the exuberance with which Zizek prosecutes his practical criticism, his work tends thus to repeat that most fundamental of Frankfurt School tropes, its enduring cultural pessimism.

BOURDIEU: FROM THE SOCIOLOGY OF CULTURE TO CRITICAL THEORY

Pierre Bourdieu (1930–2002), Professor of Sociology at the Collège de France, might appear an unlikely candidate for inclusion under the rubric of critical theory. An erstwhile structuralist, whose work sometimes seemed to run parallel to that of Foucault, an erstwhile anthropologist and former student of Lévi-Strauss, he was in many respects a quintessentially 'French' theorist. But he distanced himself from the 'objectivism' of structural anthropology, while remaining stubbornly resistant to post-structuralist deconstruction (Bourdieu, 1977; Bourdieu, 1984, p. 495). Moreover, his work engaged very directly with both Marxist and Weberian traditions in social theory. One commentator has even observed that it 'is best understood as the attempt to push class analysis beyond Marx and Weber' (Eder, 1993, p. 63). Certainly, if critical theory is defined in terms of its aspiration to change the world, then Bourdieu was as critical a theorist as any. During the late 1990s, he emerged as by far the most prominent academic intellectual to join in active solidarity with the new 'anti-globalisation' movements. His *La Misère du monde*, first published in hardback in 1993, and in paperback in 1998, became a bestseller in France and a major source of political inspiration to the movement, both in the original and in its English translation as *The Weight of the World*. He was directly involved in militant 'anti-globalisation' activism, speaking at mass meetings of striking railway workers in 1995 and unemployed workers in 1998 (Bourdieu, 1998, pp. 24n, 88n); he launched the 1996 petition for an 'Estates General of the Social Movement' and its May Day 2000 successor, the appeal for a pan-European Estates General; he co-founded the radical 'Raisons d'agir' group and its associated publishing house; he publicly called 'for a left Left' (Bourdieu, 1998a); and he was a regular contributor to the radical French monthly, *Le Monde diplomatique*. We might add that, like Marx, Bourdieu attached a distinctive subtitle to what is still his best-known work: *Distinction: A Social Critique of the Judgement of Taste* (Bourdieu, 1984).

Bourdieu's reputation as a sociological thinker revolves around the 'theory of practice', in which he attempted to theorise human sociality as the outcome of the strategic action of individuals operating within a constraining, but not determining, context of values. Famously, the term Bourdieu coined to describe this was 'the habitus' (Bourdieu, 1977), by which he meant 'an acquired system of generative schemes objectively adjusted to the particular conditions in which it is constituted' (p. 95). It is simultaneously structured and structuring, materially produced and very often generation-specific (pp. 72, 78). Elsewhere, he describes it as 'a kind of transforming machine that leads us to "reproduce" the social conditions of our own production, but in a relatively unpredictable way' (Bourdieu, 1993, p. 87). Like Marx and Weber, Bourdieu considers contemporary capitalist societies to be class societies. But for Bourdieu, their dominant and dominated classes are distinguishable from each other not simply as a matter of economics, but also as a matter of habitus: 'social class, understood as a system of objective determinations', he insisted, 'must be brought into relation . . . with the class habitus, the system of dispositions (partially) common to all products of the same structures' (Bourdieu, 1977, p. 85).

Cultural capital

Bourdieu's most widely cited study, however, and certainly the most influential in cultural studies, has been *Distinction*, a work that takes as the object of its critique precisely the same kind of high modernism as that privileged in Frankfurt School aesthetics. Where Adorno and Horkheimer had insisted on a radical discontinuity between capitalist mass culture and avant-garde modernism, Bourdieu would focus on the latter's own deep complicity with the social structures of power and domination. The book was based on an extremely detailed sociological survey, conducted in 1963 and in 1967/68, by interview and by ethnographic observation, of the cultural preferences of over 1200 people in Paris, Lille and a small French provincial town (Bourdieu, 1984, p. 503). Analysing his sample data, Bourdieu identified three main zones of taste: 'legitimate' taste, which was most widespread in the educated sections of the dominant class; 'middle-brow' taste, more widespread among the middle classes; and 'popular' taste, prevalent in the working classes (p. 17). He characterised legitimate taste primarily in terms of what he called the 'aesthetic disposition' to assert the '*absolute primacy of form over function*' (pp. 28, 30). Artistic and social 'distinction' are thus inextricably interrelated, he argued: 'The pure gaze implies a break with the ordinary attitude towards the world which, as such, is a social break' (p. 31). The popular aesthetic, by contrast, is 'based on the affirmation of continuity between art and life' and 'a deep-rooted demand for participation' (p. 32). The characteristic detachment of this 'pure gaze', Bourdieu argued, is part of a more general disposition towards the 'gratuitous' and the 'disinterested', in which the 'affirmation of power over a dominated necessity' implies a claim to 'legitimate superiority over those who . . . remain dominated by ordinary interests and urgencies' (pp. 55–6).

Bourdieu's general sociology had posited that, without exception, all human practices can be treated as 'economic practices directed towards the maximizing of material or symbolic profit' (Bourdieu, 1977, p. 183). Hence his inclination to view the intelligentsia as self-interested traders in cultural capital. For Bourdieu, it followed that professional intellectuals were best considered as a subordinate fraction of the same social class as the bourgeoisie. Defining the dominant class as that possessed of a high overall volume of capital, whatever its source—whether economic, social or cultural—he located the intellectuals in the dominant class by virtue of their access to the latter. The dominant class thus includes a dominant fraction, the bourgeoisie proper, which disproportionately controls 'economic capital', and a dominated fraction, the intelligentsia, which disproportionately controls 'cultural capital'. The most apparently disinterested of cultural practices are therefore, for Bourdieu, essentially material in character. Even when analysing the more 'purely artistic' forms of literary activity, the 'anti-economic economy' of the field of 'restricted' as opposed to 'large-scale' cultural production, he noted how '*symbolic, long-term profits* . . . are ultimately reconvertible into economic profits' (Bourdieu, 1993a, p. 54) and how avant-garde cultural practice remained dependent on the 'possession of substantial economic and social capital' (p. 67).

The artistic and academic fields

In *The Rules of Art*, Bourdieu resumed many of the themes first broached in *Distinction*, especially the role of cultural discernment as a marker of class position. Here he explained how Flaubert, Baudelaire and Manet had been crucial to the institution of an 'autonomous artistic field' of salons, publishing houses, producers, commentators, critics, distributors, and so on; and to the establishment of a notion of 'art for art's sake', which measured authenticity as 'disinterestedness'. For Bourdieu, the latter notion marked the genesis of the modern artist or writer as 'a fulltime professional, dedicated to one's work in a total and exclusive manner, indifferent to the exigencies of politics and to the injunctions of morality' (Bourdieu, 1996, pp. 76–7). This new artistic field had created a zone of autonomy, free from both the market and politics, in its 'heroic' phase, during the latter part of the nineteenth century. But in the twentieth century, Bourdieu argued, modernist art had developed not as a critique of the 'iron cage' of instrumental rationality, but as a function of the power games of the dominant classes, its capacities for critical distance progressively eroded through cooption by both the market and the state education system.

Bourdieu detected analogously 'interested' processes at work in the academic intelligentsia. The academic profession is a competitive struggle for legitimacy and cultural distinction, he explained, which functions to reproduce the wider structures of social class inequality: whether applied to the world, to students, or to academics themselves, academic taxonomies are 'a machine for transforming social classifications into academic classifications' (Bourdieu, 1988, p. 207). Later he would stress the central significance of the elite graduate schools, the so-called 'grandes écoles', to the power of the French social and economic elite, showing how their credentialism operated as a kind of 'state magic' for a supposedly rationalised society (Bourdieu, 1996a, p. 374). Tracing the growing incidence of academic credentials among the chief executives of the top 100 French companies, he concluded that the apparent substitution of academic for property titles actually performed a crucial legitimating function: company heads 'no longer appear . . . the heirs to a fortune they did not create', he wrote, 'but rather the most exemplary of self-made men, appointed by their . . . "merits" to wield power . . . in the name of "competence" and "intelligence"' (p. 334).

Where the Frankfurt School had worked with a model of theory as explicitly critical, Bourdieu tended to affect a quasi-positivistic objectivism, so that the moment of critique was often concealed behind a mask of scientific 'objectivity'. In *The Weight of the World*, he used a combination of ethnographic interviews and sociological commentary to mount a stunning indictment of contemporary utilitarianism—in the shape of 'economic liberalism'—as creating the preconditions for 'an unprecedented development of all kinds of ordinary suffering' (Bourdieu et al., 1999). But even here, in his most explicitly engaged work, he still insisted that sociological 'science' could itself uncover 'the possibilities for action' that politics will need to explore (p. 629). Where the Frankfurt School had conceived of intellectuals as significantly productive of critical sensibility, Bourdieu tended to detect only material self-interest. This kind of 'reflexive' critique is necessary, he argued, to break with the 'habits of thought, cognitive interests and cultural beliefs bequeathed by several centuries of literary, artistic or philosophical worship' (Bourdieu 2000, p. 7). But such cynicism can easily lead to a radical overestimation of the reproductive powers of the social status quo.

Bourdieu struggled to find ways of thinking the role of the intellectual that could allow for his own developing aspiration to activism. Hence his interest in what he termed the 'corporatism of the universal', the idea that intellectuals have a kind of collective self-interest in the defence of the culture sphere, which can somehow translate into something close to a traditional humanist politics (Bourdieu, 1989; Bourdieu, 1996). The problem should be obvious, however: the approach belied his own scepticism about the intelligentsia's pretensions to distinction, while simultaneously understating the general moral significance of his own political interventions. As a British socialist writer observed: 'Bourdieu's political stance . . . is . . . less a reflection [of] than an antidote to aspects of his theoretical vision' (Wolfreys, 2000, p. 99). Whatever the limits and possibilities of Frankfurt School critical theory, this could hardly ever be said of either Adorno or Habermas.

4

Semiology: from structuralism to post-structuralism

Critical theory shared with culturalism at least two—essentially humanist—theoretical presuppositions: the analytical postulate of a fundamental contradiction between cultural value and the developmental logics of utilitarian capitalist civilisation; and the prescriptive imperative to locate some social institution, or social grouping, powerful enough to sustain the former against the latter.

Culturalism's hopes were variously invested in the state, the church, the literary intelligentsia and the labour movement; critical theory's in the Lukácsian proletariat and Marcuse's outcasts, but more importantly in the critical intelligentsia, its art and philosophy or, as in Bourdieu, its sociology. Semiology, the science of the study of signs, accepted neither analytical postulate nor prescriptive imperative. In its earlier structuralist phases, it replaced the former with a dichotomy between appearance and essence, in which essence was revealed in structure; the latter with a scientistic epistemology that denied both the need for prescriptive practice and the possibility of meaningful group action. Each of these positions was subject to revision in its later post-structuralist phases, but neither, as we shall see, in directions that moved toward humanism.

DURKHEIM AND SAUSSURE

We have referred to semiology as 'structuralist', and so it was, at least in its earlier phases. But there are many different versions of structuralism, both in general and as applied to literature and culture. For our purposes, however, structuralism is best defined as an approach to the study of human culture centred on the search for constraining patterns, or structures, which claimed that individual phenomena have meaning by virtue of their relation to other phenomena as elements within a systematic structure. More specifically, semiology—or semiotics, as it is sometimes known—also claimed that the methods of structural linguistics could be applied to all aspects of human culture (Robey, 1973, pp. 1–2). Structuralism was until comparatively recently an overwhelmingly Francophone affair: a perfectly plausible case can be mounted for Auguste Comte (1778–1857) as a central precursor to the structuralist tradition; much less controversially, the title belongs to the French anthropologist (and sociologist) Emile Durkheim (1858–1917), and, more importantly, to Ferdinand de Saussure (1857–1913), the French-speaking Swiss linguist. Saussure's work on language and Durkheim's on 'primitive' religion directly anticipated the subsequent histories of the two academic disciplines most directly implicated in structuralism: semiology itself and 'structural' anthropology.

Durkheim and the collective consciousness

Durkheim made no strong claim for the special significance of linguistics, though, interestingly, he did nominate language as an important instance of the archetypal 'social fact' (Durkheim, 1964, p. 3). But his general social theory was quite significantly proto-structuralist. His last major work, *The Elementary Forms of the Religious Life*, first published in 1915, is as much concerned with knowledge itself as with religion. Here he explicitly rejected both the empiricist view, that what we know is given by experience, and the rationalist, that the categories of knowledge are somehow immanent within the human mind. Rather, he argued, these categories are constituted by and through systems of thought that are themselves socially variable: 'A concept is not my concept; I hold it in common with other men' (Durkheim, 1976, p. 433). The 'collective consciousness is . . . a synthésis *sui generis* of particular consciousness ...', he wrote, '[and] this synthesis has the effect of disengaging a whole world of sentiments, ideas and images which, once born, obey laws all of their own' (pp. 423–4). The collective consciousness is thus absolutely central to social order: it is only through it that society is able to control, indeed construct, the individual human personalities that inhabit it.

This understanding of systems of thought as ultimately determining is quasi-structuralist, though the language in which it was expressed, that of consciousness, is not. In his more specific treatment of religious belief, Durkheim introduced a further structuralist trope, that of the binary opposition. The 'real characteristic of religious phenomena', he argued, 'is that they always suppose a bipartite division of the whole universe . . . into two classes which embrace all that exists, but which radically exclude each other' (p. 40). These two classes were the sacred and the profane. What mattered, for Durkheim, was not the specific content of either, but rather the relation between the two. Sacred things were thus *'things set apart and forbidden'* (p. 47), whatever they might be, and defined only in relation to the profane, to things not set apart and not forbidden.

Saussure on language

Saussure's *Course in General Linguistics* was first published in 1916, only a year after *The Elementary Forms*. Its central thesis was that every language is in itself an entirely discrete system, the units of which can be identified only in terms of their relationships to each other, and not by reference to any other linguistic or extra-linguistic system. Saussure distinguished between *langue*, the social and systemic rules of language, and *parole*, the individual and particular instance of speech, or utterance. Only the former, he insisted, can properly be the object of scientific study, for it alone is social rather than individual, essential rather than accidental. 'Language is not a function of the speaker', argued Saussure: 'it is a product that is passively assimilated by the individual . . . Speaking . . . is an individual act. It is wilful and intellectual' (Saussure, 1974, p. 14). This distinction between institution and event would be of central importance to almost all subsequent structuralisms, for it was the institution—the structure—that became the defining preoccupation for structuralist analysis.

Just as Durkheim had insisted on the essential arbitrariness of the specific content of sacredness and of profanity, so too Saussure insisted that '*the linguistic sign is arbitrary*' (p. 67). For Saussure, language is a system of signs; and a sign is the union of signifier—or symbol—and signified—the idea or concept, as distinct from the thing that is symbolised. Thus: 'The linguistic sign unites, not a thing and a name, but a concept and a sound-image' (p. 66). This suppression of the referent, or 'thing', freed the signifier both from the referent itself and from the signified. Language is thus entirely a matter of social convention, in which the signifier and the signified, and the relations between them, are all radically arbitrary. Each element in the language is definable only in terms of its relation to other elements in the system of signs. And, just as Durkheim had defined the sacred and the profane in terms of their difference from each other, so too Saussure insisted that 'in language there are only differences *without positive terms* . . . language has neither ideas nor sounds that existed before the linguistic system, but only conceptual and phonic differences that have issued from the system' (p. 120).

Saussure also posited a sharp distinction between synchronic analysis, of the structure of a given language at a given point in time, and diachronic analysis, of how the language changes over time. Given that every language operated at any given time as an independent system, it followed that historical analysis was synchronically irrelevant: 'Since changes never affect the system as a whole . . . they can be studied only outside the system' (p. 87). In this respect, as in many others, Saussure was the archetypical proto-structuralist thinker: where Durkheim had continued to adhere to a residual evolutionism (Durkheim, 1976, p. 3), Saussure initiated an in principle methodological antipathy to historicist modes of explanation that was to prove characteristic of almost all subsequent structuralisms and post-structuralisms.

Saussure's single most daring theoretical move, however, was to foreshadow the eventual creation of semiology, a general science of signification, itself: 'Language is a system of signs that express ideas, and is therefore comparable to a system of writing, the alphabet of deaf mutes, symbolic rites, polite formulas, military signals, etc. . . . *A science that studies the life of signs within society is conceivable* . . . I shall call it *semiology*' (Saussure, 1974, p. 16). A general science of signs, using methods similar to those of Saussure's own structural linguistics, would thus prove applicable to all meaningful human actions or productions, since insofar as human behaviour is meaningful, it is indeed signifying. Thus construed, semiology aspired to direct our attention towards the basis of human social life in convention, and towards the systems of rules, relations and structures that order it. For Saussure, as for Durkheim, and for later structuralisms, what is at issue is not the relation between culture and some other extra-cultural structure of social power, but the social power of discourse, the power of the system of signs itself.

Structuralism: a general model

Structuralism has been at its most theoretically influential in the disciplines of anthropology and semiology. Durkheim had tended to think of his field as 'sociology', a French word coined originally by Comte. But his own most important work, and much of the later intellectual effort of the French Durkheimian school, was directed towards what is customarily regarded as 'anthropology' in the Anglophone world. The obvious instances included Durkheim's nephew, Marcel Mauss (1872–1950), and Lucien Lévy-Bruhl (1857–1939). The key figure, however, was Claude Lévi-Strauss, Professor of Social Anthropology at the Collège de France, whose anthropological researches were indebted not only to Durkheim but also to Saussure. During the late 1950s and the early 1960s, this continuing tradition of post-Durkheimian anthropology coincided with a positively Saussurean revival of semiology, initiated in the first place by

Roland Barthes (1915–80), and with the translation into French of a series of texts from the Russian Formalist school of literary criticism, which together generated, finally, the theoretical moment of French (and Italian) high structuralism. This was, above all, the moment of Barthes, Lévi-Strauss, Michel Foucault (1926–84) and, in Italy, Umberto Eco, but tangentially also that of Louis Althusser (1918–90).

Before we proceed to a more detailed exposition of the work of particular structuralists, let us attempt a brief sketch of what we mean by structuralism in general. It seems to us best characterised by five major characteristics: its positivism; its anti-historicism; its adherence to a (possible) politics of demystification; its theoreticism; and its anti-humanism. As to the first, it should be obvious that from Durkheim and Saussure on, the structuralist tradition has exhibited both a habitual aspiration to scientificity and, normally, a correspondingly positive valorisation of science—described either pejoratively as scientistic or, more neutrally, as positivist. This understanding of itself as a science sharply distinguished structuralism from both culturalism and critical theory. So too does anti-historicism. Both critical theory and culturalism translate their antipathy to utilitarian capitalist civilisation into a historicist insistence that this type of civilisation is only one among many; they are then able to invoke either the past or an ideal future against the present. By contrast, structuralism typically inhabited a never-ending theoretical present. The only important exception to this observation was Durkheim, whose residual evolutionism we have already noted.

A stress on structures as deeper levels of reality submerged beneath, but nonetheless shaping, the realm of the empirically obvious can very easily allow for a politics of demystification in which the structuralist analyst is understood as penetrating through to some secretly hidden truth. As long as this hidden reality is seen as somehow confounding the truth claims of the more obvious realities, such a stance can remain compatible with an adversarial intellectual politics. Even then all that eventuates is a peculiarly enfeebled, and essentially academic, version of intellectual radicalism, in which the world is not so much changed, as contemplated differently. And again, while structuralism is certainly compatible with such radicalism, it does not require it. Hence the rather peculiar way in which the major French structuralist thinkers proved able to shift their political opinions, generally from Left to Right, without much corresponding amendment of their respective theoretical positions. For structuralism, as neither for culturalism nor critical theory, the nexus between politics and theory appeared essentially contingent.

This combination of positivism and what we might well term 'synchronism' with a commitment to the demystification of experiential reality propelled the entire structuralist enterprise in a radically theoreticist direction. A science of stasis, marked from birth by an inveterate anti-empiricism, it became almost unavoidably preoccupied with highly abstract theoretical, or formal, models. Hence the near ubiquity of the binary opposition as a characteristically structuralist trope. Theoretical anti-humanism arose from much the same source: if neither change nor process nor even the particular empirical instance are matters of real concern, then the intentions or actions of human subjects, whether individual or collective, can easily be disposed of as irrelevant to the structural properties of systems. In this way, structuralism notoriously 'decentred' the subject.

RUSSIAN FORMALISM: FROM SHKLOVSKY TO BAKHTIN

Before finally proceeding to French structuralism, we should briefly recall the theoretical legacy of the Russian Formalists, who were themselves directly influenced by Saussurean linguistics. The Petrograd Society for the Study of Poetic Language, founded by Victor Shklovsky (1893–1984) in 1916, and the Moscow Linguistic Club, founded a year earlier by Roman Jakobson (1896–1982), had both hoped to establish the study of literature on properly scientific and systematic foundations. Suppressed by the Soviet government in 1930, the exiled Jakobson continued his work through the Prague Linguistic Circle; it was eventually transmitted to France by Tzvetan Todorov, the Franco-Bulgarian literary theorist, who published a selection of Formalist writings in French translation in 1965 (Todorov, 1965).

Shklovsky and Jakobson

The Formalists aspired to understand literature as a system, just as Saussure had done with language. Literary science, Jakobson argued, should study not the supposedly empirical facts of literature, but rather 'literariness'—whatever it is that endows literature with its own distinctively systemic properties. Literariness, the Formalists concluded, was that process by which literary texts 'defamiliarise', or make strange, both previous literature and also the world itself (Shklovsky, 1965, p. 12). The artistic text is thus defined neither by its fictionality nor its inventedness, but by its 'deformation' of everyday language, which Jakobson exaggeratedly described as 'organized violence committed on ordinary speech' (Jakobson cited in Erlich, 1955, p. 219). The central focus for the Formalists thus became those formal literary 'devices' by means of which such defamiliarisation is achieved. It should be obvious, however, that what defamiliarises can itself become familiar, and thereby cease to be literary, in Formalist terms at least. Literariness is not, then, essentially a property of the text, nor even of the particular devices that the text might deploy, but of the literary system itself, of what later structuralists would term the relations of intertextuality between texts. The literary text is thus to the system of texts as *parole* is to *langue*, a singular element within a system of arbitrary conventions, the meaning of which is explicable neither referentially nor historically, but only synchronically. In yet another, more explicitly Saussurean, version of literariness, Jakobson proposed a six-factor model of the speech event in which the poetic function of language was defined as attached to the linguistic message itself, as distinct from the addresser, addressee, context, contact and code, to each of which is attached a different linguistic function (Jakobson, 1960, pp. 356–7). In short, language fulfils a poetic, or literary, function to the extent that it becomes self-conscious of itself as language. Both variants of literariness, it should be noted, provide an implicit theoretical legitimation for literary modernism, as no doubt they were intended to.

Bakhtin and Volosinov

Mikhail Bakhtin (1895–1975) and the other members of the so-called 'Leningrad Circle', such as Valentin Volosinov, were much less committed than Shklovsky and Jakobson to a strictly Saussurean model, though their work certainly had its origins in debate with Formalism. As against Saussure's concern with '*the relationship of sign to sign within a closed system*' (Volosinov, 1973, p. 58), Volosinov argued that criticism should seek to explain how concrete utterances are produced in particular socio-cultural contexts. This led him to an understanding of ideology as a culturally specific representation of the world through language: 'Wherever a sign is present, ideology is present too', he wrote: '*Everything ideological possesses semiotic value*' (p. 10). If signification is socially produced in this way, then it follows that '*word is a two-sided act*. It is determined equally by *whose* word it is and *for whom* it is meant . . . I give myself verbal shape from another's point of view, ultimately from the point of view of the community to which I belong' (p. 86). This, in turn, suggests that speaker and addressee share patterned speech situations, which condition what can be communicated, but are in turn conditioned by such dialogue. As a result, speech situations are both more open-ended and more subject to inflection according to class, profession, generation, region and so on than in a conventionally Saussurean account. This open-ended multiplicity is what Bakhtin variously denoted by the terms 'heteroglossia', 'dialogism' and 'polyphony'.

Bakhtin found evidence of such polyphony in the novels of Dostoevsky, where the characters are 'not voiceless slaves' subject to a monological and unitary consciousness, but rather '*free* people, capable of standing *alongside* their creator, capable of not agreeing with him and even of rebelling against him' (Bakhtin, 1984, p. 6). Later, he would find similarly dialogic tendencies in Cervantes, Defoe, Sterne and Fielding, in Menippean satire, confessions, drama and poetry, and, above all, in Rabelais (Bakhtin, 1981; Bakhtin, 1965). According to Bakhtin, Rabelais' *Gargantua and Pantagruel* had used 'the popular-festive system of images' to attack 'the fundamental dogmas and sacraments, the holy of holies of medieval ideology' (p. 268). In Rabelais, as in medieval reality, the 'carnivalesque crowd', he wrote, 'is the people as a whole, . . . organized *in their own way*, . . . outside of and contrary to all existing forms of the coercive socioeconomic and political organization, which is suspended for the time of the festivity . . . The people become aware of their sensual, material bodily unity and community' (p. 255). The carnival is also a world of language mixing, of the parodic speech forms of folk humour, of debunking and 'decrowning' the official Latin of the priest caste, of the free play of words in a context of collapsed hierarchies: 'The hard, official dividing lines between objects, phenomena, and values begin to fade. There is an awakening of the ancient ambivalence of all words and expression . . . revived in a free and gay form' (p. 420).

Bakhtin remains an enduring influence on contemporary cultural theory, if only as a brake on more conventionally Formalist conceptions of structure as asocial, ahistorical and immanent. The concepts of dialogism and heteroglossia suggest a levelling of ideological viewpoints, which in reality, as distinct from fiction, occurs only very rarely outside the carnival. And even the concept of the carnivalesque seems problematic once extracted from the social context of the medieval marketplace. As Stallybrass and White have observed, its displacement from the marketplace to the bourgeois home, through the novel form, hardly disrupts the dominant norms (Stallybrass & White, 1986). Hirschkop has asked how might the carnivalesque be 'translated into the very different kinds of popular culture one finds in modern capitalist societies?' (Hirschkop, 1989, p. 3). The answer is that in most cases it can't. Indeed, the subversive potential of the carnivalesque might only still exist in the so-called Third World, where capitalist modernity has not yet fully dissolved pre-modern ways of life. Perhaps the true value of the notion lies neither with the novel nor with any other contemporary literary form, but with its capacity to remind us of our common bodily ties in 'an age gravely threatened with common biological extinction' (Eagleton, 1989a, p. 188).

HIGH STRUCTURALISM

Lévi-Strauss

Both Barthes and Lévi-Strauss came into contact with Saussurean linguistics partly by way of the legacy of Russian Formalism and the Prague School. Lévi-Strauss' *The Elementary Structures of Kinship*, first published in 1949, dealt with a typically 'anthropological' subject—marriage and descent—but in a typically semiological fashion, through the attempt to construct a 'grammar' of kinship (Lévi-Strauss, 1969). The incest taboo, he would conclude, 'is in origin neither purely cultural nor purely natural' (Lévi-Strauss, 1985, p. 24). He believed it could be explained only in conjunction with kinship structures and, to this end, turned to an analogous symbolic system, 'phonology', as theorised by Jakobson. Both kinship and phonology are systematic; in both, individual terms or entities are determined by their difference from others in the system; both function as unconscious structures; both are governed by general laws (Lévi-Strauss, 1963, p. 33). For Lévi-Strauss, the principle of 'reciprocity', of gift and counter-gift based on the exchange of goods and women, provided the common element uniting all manifestations of kinship structure, and was thus also the source of the incest prohibition.

In the four volumes of *Mythologiques*, published between 1964 and 1971, he sought to explain how the passage from nature to culture was symbolised in the indigenous cultures of North and South America. All the Indian peoples, he concluded, 'seem to have conceived of their myths for one purpose only: to come to terms with history and, on the level of system, to re-establish a state of equilibrium capable of acting as a shock-absorber for the disturbances caused by real-life events' (Lévi-Strauss, 1981, p. 607). Meaning did not inhere in the myths themselves; the myths were media or 'grids' through which to make sense of a world that can never be known in itself. The Osage Indians of

North America, for instance, venerated the eagle, not for itself, but for the classificatory possibilities it provided: rather than an eagle in general, it is a bald eagle, a golden eagle or a spotted eagle; it is white, spotted or red; it is young, adult or old. These differences then provide an analogous or parallel structure to that of Osage society. For Lévi-Strauss, totemism was therefore a code whose primary function is to express social difference by analogy with the natural world: there is no mysterious identification between an individual or group and a totemic animal or plant; the latter is significant only because of its position in a series, its difference from others of the same or other species. In this view, Freud's Oedipus complex is merely one culturally specific myth in a great chain of myths that deal with incest prohibition.

In the second volume of *Structural Anthropology*, Lévi-Strauss writes that 'no civilization can define itself if it does not have at its disposal some other civilizations for comparison' (Lévi-Strauss, 1976, p. 272). Here he identified three stages in the history of western humanism that allowed the West to acquire such a perspective on its own culture: Renaissance humanism, which looked back to antiquity to define itself in comparison with the past; 'bourgeois' humanism, when Europe became aware of the Orient and came to define itself as superior; and 'democratic' humanism, which subscribes to an ethic of tolerance and respect for different cultures (pp. 271–4). His own work was intended as a contribution to this contemporary democratic trend. Hence his suspicion of categories such as 'progress', and the lack thereof, or the idea of some civilisations being 'inside' history, others 'outside' or closer to nature. Most societies, he claimed, have experienced progress and technological development. The difference is in the fact that western culture 'has proved to be more cumulative than others' (p. 350).

The word 'savage' in the title of Lévi-Strauss's *The Savage Mind* is thus ironic. It was central to his argument, in fact, that supposedly 'savage' thought was not at all savage, in the sense of being either alien or primitive. Rather, he stressed that both totemic religion and primitive 'science' actually 'work' perfectly well in their own systemic terms. 'This science of the concrete', he wrote, 'was necessarily restricted by its essence to results other than those destined to be achieved by the exact natural sciences but it was no less scientific and its results no less genuine. They were secured ten thousand years earlier and still remain at the basis of our own civilization' (Lévi-Strauss, 1966, p. 16). Consider the famous parallel between primitive science and the role of the modern French *bricoleur*: both build up structured sets from the 'debris of events'; and in practice both 'reach brilliant unforeseen results' (pp. 16–22). This conception releases us from notions of cultural superiority and unilinear narratives of progress from 'backwardness' to 'enlightened' modernity. If any superiority is attached to either, for Lévi-Strauss it would have been to the 'primitive'. The West 'started by cutting man off from nature and establishing him in an absolute reign', he observed: 'This 'radical separation of humanity and animality . . . initiated a vicious circle' that eventually governed even the relations between supposedly 'civilised' men and supposedly 'primitive'. For Lévi-Strauss, it was thus a humanism 'corrupted at birth by taking self-interest as its principle and its notion' (Lévi-Strauss, 1976, p. 41).

Roland Barthes

Barthes was perhaps the single most important, representative figure of French high structuralism, an immensely prolific writer, literary critic, sociologist and semiologist, structuralist and, later, post-structuralist, whose bizarre death—he was run over by a laundry truck—was as untimely as it was improbable. His most famous work, *Mythologies*, was first published in 1957. Strongly influenced by Saussure, it sought to analyse semiologically a whole range of contemporary myths, from wrestling to advertising, from striptease to Romans in the cinema. Here Barthes aspired to 'read' washing powder advertisements, for example, as languages, that is, as signifying systems with their own distinctive grammars. The book included a long essay, entitled 'Myth Today', which attempted to sketch out the theoretical corollaries of the often very entertaining, almost journalistic and invariably insightful, particular analyses that occupied the bulk of the text.

In 'Myth Today', Barthes defined 'myth' as a second-order semiological system, in which the signs of language, that is, both signifiers and signifieds, function as the signifiers of myth, signifying other mythical signifieds (Barthes, 1973, pp. 114–5). By 'myth', he meant something very close to a Weberian legitimation. In bourgeois society, he argued, myth is 'depoliticized speech', which 'has the task of giving an historical intention a natural justification, and making contingency appear eternal' (p. 142). By so naturalising the historically contingent, myth proves fundamentally supportive of the social status quo. Hence Barthes' famous observation that: 'Statistically, myth is on the right' (p. 148). At this point in his intellectual career Barthes was still clearly on the left (cf. Jameson, 1998a, p. 172). Indeed, the essay provides an excellent example of the way structuralism as demystification can be linked to an adversarial intellectual stance. In *Mythologies*, as in the later *Elements of Semiology* and *The Fashion System*, first published in 1964 and 1967 respectively (Barthes 1968; Barthes 1983), Barthes' semiology strayed furthest from the realm of the literary, and into fashion, food, furniture and cars. His central theoretical preoccupation, however, remained writing.

At his most structuralist, and at his most influential, during the late 1960s and early 1970s, Barthes was concerned to develop a set of highly formal analyses of the structures of narrative; to develop and redefine the Formalist conception of literariness; and to describe and celebrate 'the death of the author'. His narratology is striking both for its manifest scientism and for its clear indebtedness to themes originally initiated by Shklovsky and Jakobson. His treatment of literariness is similarly inspired. Writing and language are not instrumental, Barthes maintained, but function in their own right and for themselves: the verb 'to write' is thus an apparently intransitive verb; the writer doesn't write something, but rather just writes (Barthes, 1970, pp. 141–2). Despite the originality of the formulation, there is an obvious parallel between this stress on the near-intransitivity of writing and Jakobson's on the self-consciousness of the poetic function. And, as with Jakobson, so with Barthes, this understanding of literariness is necessarily aligned to an endorsement of modernist aesthetics. Hence Barthes' enthusiasm for the attempt by 'modern literature . . . to substitute the instance of discourse for the instance of reality (or of the referent), which has been, and still is, a mythical "alibi" dominating the idea of literature' (p. 144). For Barthes, as for Jakobson, an apparently descriptive aesthetic rapidly acquired prescriptive capacity.

Barthes' much quoted essay on the death of the author insisted that literary texts be understood in terms of intertextuality rather than supposed authorial intentions. The essay itself was intended as a polemic against the more traditionally humanist view of the writer as author (literally, the source) of literary meaning. Formally, Barthes recognised the reader as the point where intertextual meaning can finally become focused: the reader, he wrote, is the '*someone* who holds together in a single field all the traces by which the written text is constituted'. But this reader was still 'without history, biography, psychology' (Barthes, 1977, p. 148). That is, Barthes was concerned not so much with the empirically concrete reader as with the structural role of the reader, to borrow a phrase from Eco (Eco, 1981). Barthes' structuralism was thus concerned not with the intrinsic properties of the text, but with the conventions that render it intelligible to the reader. This intelligibility is, however, a function of the discourse itself, rather than of any individual reader's capacities and interests. The entire argument, which became extremely influential both in France and elsewhere, was informed by a rigorous theoretical anti-humanism, in no way belied by its rhetorical conclusion that 'the birth of the reader must be at the cost of the death of the Author' (Barthes, 1977, p. 148).

Umberto Eco

Umberto Eco, Professor of Semiotics at the University of Bologna, occupied a roughly analogous position within Italian semiotics to that of Barthes in French semiology. Perhaps Italy's most renowned contemporary intellectual, Eco has enjoyed an unusual status as both a celebrated cultural critic and a world-famous author. But the enthusiastic reception of his first novel, *The Name of the Rose* (Eco, 1994), merely enhanced the reputation of a career that had ranged from medieval aesthetics to postmodern fiction. Eco's general theory of semiotics has framed his more detailed readings of music, architecture, the modernist novel, comic strips, film, advertising and popular fiction. Originally part of the so-called Italian 'neo-avant-garde', he played a key role, during the 1960s, in introducing Italian intellectual circles to, by turn, structuralism, Russian Formalism, semiotics, German Critical Theory and American New Criticism. Structuralism and semiotics in particular attracted Eco's interest, providing him with a framework for theorising narrative structure that would subsequently inform his own novels, themselves now widely considered exemplary instances of postmodern fiction.

His first major publication, *The Open Work*, was a treatise on modernist aesthetics and, in particular, on James Joyce. Here Eco posited the distinction between traditional 'closed' works of art and modernist 'open' works, marked by the plurality of readings and the net 'increase in information' they offer (Eco, 1989, p. 43). Joyce's *Finnegan's Wake* is the exemplary model of an open text for its 'chaotic character, the polyvalence, the multi-interpretability of this polylingual *chaosmos*' (p. 41). While this concentration on immanent structure might seem to disregard the text's social context, Eco recovers this dimension by treating truly 'important' works of art as 'epistemological metaphors', representations of 'a widespread theoretical consciousness (not of a particular theory so much as of an acquired cultural viewpoint)' (p. 87). What is social in art is thus its form: 'Art knows the world through its formal structures . . . its true content . . . Literature is an organization of words that signify different aspects of the world, but the literary work is itself an aspect of the world in the way its words are organized' (p. 144).

This investment in form as the true marker of 'quality' in literature, best exemplified in high modernism, had prompted Eco's initially hostile response to popular or mass culture. But in a number of influential essays on various aspects of the media, Eco attempted to free his own cultural criticism from its essentially elitist stance vis-à-vis popular culture. The critical intellectual should aim to expose the inner ideological workings of social control, as these are embedded in mass cultural messages and products, he concluded, rather than simply to reject them *en bloc*. Eco's *La struttura assente*, first published in 1968 (and its subsequent revision and re-issue in English as *A Theory of Semiotics* (Eco, 1976)), inaugurated a lasting engagement with 'semiology', or 'semiotics', as Eco preferred to call it. Despite the difference in terminology, there is no doubting Eco's indebtedness here to Barthes' *Mythologies*. But equally, the shift from 'structuralism' to 'semiotics' also reflected something of the political tenor of the late 1960s. As de Lauretis observes: 'structuralism came to denote a reactionary and narrow view of critical activity . . . in Italy structuralism was transformed into semiotics by a conscious political shift' (de Lauretis, 1978, p. 5).

The Role of the Reader signalled a further shift in focus, away from cultural production and towards reception. Here Eco treats the author as 'nothing else but a textual strategy establishing semantic correlations and activating the Model Reader' (Eco, 1981, p. 11). As with Barthes, however, the focus falls on the structural role of the reader, as constructed by the text, rather than on an ethnography of empirical readerships. Here, too, Eco reformulated the distinction between open and closed works, so as to apply the latter to popular fiction. A closed text was now one that aimed 'at arousing a precise response on the part of more or less precise empirical readers' (p. 8): Superman comic strips, Ian Fleming's James Bond novels or Eugène Sue's *Les Mystères de Paris*, for example. Eco insisted that because such texts presupposed a sociologically 'average' reader, they were in fact 'immoderately open' to any possible 'aberrant' decoding by non-average readers. Open texts, again represented by Joyce, were by contrast those that 'work at their peak revolutions per minute only when each interpretation is reechoed by the others, and vice versa'. Here 'the pragmatic process of interpretation is not an empirical accident independent of the text *qua* text, but is a structural element of its generative process' (p. 9). Here there are more or less competent readings, since an open text outlines a closed project of its model reader as a component of its own structure.

In his reading of the Bond novels, Eco outlined their formulaic structure and what he termed 'the elements for the building of a machine that functions basically on a set of precise units governed by rigorous combinational rules' (p. 146). In a classically structuralist analysis, he identified five levels of narrative structure, each ruled by value oppositions such as 'Free World-Soviet Union', 'Duty-Sacrifice', 'Love-Death', and 'Loyalty-Disloyalty'. These binary oppositions are combined with only minor variations in a plot structure that recurs from novel to novel, in which Bond foils yet another plot by an evil madman, in the process winning the sexual favours of the beautiful woman he frees from the villain's clutches. Eco wittily summarised the eight basic steps in this repetitive schema as 'Bond moves and mates in eight moves' (p. 156). Unlike the typical leftist criticism of the period, which saw in Fleming's novels only reactionary ideology, Eco had discovered 'a narrative apparatus . . . remarkably close in tone and structure to the classic fairy tales of Western culture' (Bondanella, 1997, p. 64). But he clearly underestimated the sophistication of popular texts and popular readers. As Bennett and Woollacott would later observe, he construed popular reading as 'socially and culturally unorganized' only because he lacked familiarity 'with the determinations which mould and configure' it (Bennett & Woollacott, 1987, p. 79).

Foucault's archaeology

Where Barthes and Eco had happily declared themselves as structuralists, Foucault repeatedly denied any such theoretical affinities and predilections (Foucault, 1980, p. 114). In the most specifically Saussurean of senses, we might very well endorse such protestations. But in a more general sense, Foucault's earlier work was indeed structuralist. His first truly influential books, *Madness and Civilisation* and *The Birth of the Clinic*, were published in French in 1961 and 1963 (Foucault, 1965; Foucault, 1973). In both, Foucault was concerned to establish the systematic, and in its own terms perfectly valid, nature of the dominant understandings of madness and illness in the seventeenth and early eighteenth centuries, and to contrast these with the new, equally systematic, and equally internally valid, conceptions that emerged, very rapidly, in the late eighteenth century. For Foucault, the later conceptions were merely different, not better.

What matters is not the epistemological problem of truth, but rather the sociological problem of the fit between new ways of knowing and new institutional practices. This earlier institutional emphasis was temporarily superseded by a more deliberate focus on discourse as such, both in *The Order of Things*, first published in 1966 as *Les Mots et les Choses*, and in *The Archaeology of Knowledge*, first published in 1969 (Foucault, 1973a; Foucault, 1972). Here Foucault defined the objects of his inquiry as 'discursive formations' or *epistemes*—in short, ways of knowing: systematic conceptual frameworks that define their own truth criteria, according to which particular knowledge problems are to be resolved, and that are embedded in and imply particular institutional arrangements. The central focus fell, unsurprisingly, on a contrast between the classical *episteme*, which governed knowledge in the seventeenth and in the early eighteenth century, and the modern *episteme*, which developed from the late eighteenth century and was only now coming to be challenged by a putatively postmodern, in fact structuralist, *episteme*.

The structuralism of this entire project should be readily apparent. Despite Foucault's profession as historian, his work remained radically anti-historicist, unable either to judge between *epistemes* or to explain the shift from one to another (hence the characteristically structuralist sense of change as discontinuity). Moreover, Foucault pursued a typically structuralist strategy of demystification towards, for example, modern medicine and modern psychiatry. And his approach was clearly theoretically anti-humanist. Thus the strength of the new sciences of psychoanalysis and structural anthropology consisted in their ability 'to do without the concept of man . . . they dissolve man' (Foucault, 1973a, p. 379). One very interesting essay of Foucault's quite specifically took up Barthes' theme of the death of the author and sought to explain authorship by its various institutional uses (Foucault, 1977). Finally, we should add that Foucault's earlier writings were also deeply positivist in inspiration. Given his obvious animus towards modern science, his persistent attempt to demystify and relativise 'scientific knowledge', this might well appear the strangest of observations. And yet this vast archaeology—a history of previous *epistemes*, no less—was unthinkable except as knowledge of an object produced by a subject external to it, which was precisely the positivist, and structuralist, position.

Althusser's Marxism

We have referred to Althusser, Foucault's onetime teacher, as also having been tangentially involved in the moment of high structuralism. At the time, this would have seemed a strange judgement, since Althusser was a member of the French Communist Party and quite probably France's best-known Marxist intellectual. But it is clear in retrospect that his distinctive contribution had been to reread Marx's 'historical materialism' as a structuralism. For Althusser, Marxism was a science, sharply distinguished from, and counterposed to, ideology, both by its own defining 'knowledge function' and by the 'epistemological break' by which it had been founded (Althusser, 1977). This science was characterised by a new mode of explanation, in which 'structural causality' was substituted for mechanical and expressive. Culture was thus neither superstructural effect nor an expression of the truth of the social whole, but rather a relatively autonomous structure, with its own specific effectivity, situated within a wider structure of structures. Each level of this structure was subject to '*determination of the elements of a structure . . . by the effectivity of that structure . . .* (and) *determination of a subordinate structure by a dominant structure*' (Althusser & Balibar, 1970, p. 186). Clearly, the transparent structuralism of the model was more than a matter of mere semantics.

In a much-quoted essay on 'Ideology and Ideological State Apparatuses', Althusser argued that ideology was necessarily embedded in institutions, or 'ideological state apparatuses', as he termed them; that its central social function was the reproduction of structured social inequality, or the 'relations of production'; that it functioned by constituting biological individuals as social 'subjects'; and that it thereby represented the imaginary relation of individuals to their real conditions of existence (Althusser, 1971). This was very obviously a reworking of Gramsci's theory of hegemony, but one that repressed the notion of agency in favour of structural determination. And since art, though not itself ideology, according to Althusser, alluded to ideology (p. 122), it became possible to read culture 'ideologically'. Althusser had also developed a theory of symptomatic reading, which sought to reconstruct the 'problematic' of the text (Althusser & Balibar, 1970), the structure of determinate absences and presences that occasion it. For Althusser the object of this symptomatic reading had been Marx's 'scientific' discoveries. But for Althusserian cultural criticism, as represented most importantly by Pierre Macherey in France (Macherey, 1978) and the young Terry Eagleton in England (Eagleton, 1976), such readings could be directed both at art and at popular culture, with a view to exposing ideology itself as their real object. Althusserianism exercised a considerable fascination for radical critics, both socialist and feminist, during the 1970s, but fell very rapidly out of favour after 1980, when Althusser killed his wife, Hélène, in what appeared to have been a fit of madness.

From structuralism to post-structuralism

But quite apart from the personal tragedy of the Althussers, structuralism seemed already to have run its course. Where structuralism had displayed a recurrent aspiration to scientificity, post-structuralism would betray this aspiration through its equally recurrent insistence that meaning can never be pinned down, not even by semiology itself. At the end of *The Archaeology of Knowledge*, Foucault confesses, uncomfortably, that his discourse was 'avoiding the ground on which it could find support' (Foucault, 1972, p. 205). The embarrassment was distinctive; the problem was not. For Durkheim and Lévi-Strauss, Saussure and Barthes, as for Foucault, the central repressed problem had always been how to guarantee the scientificity of a knowledge that was itself, according to the logics of their own argument, either social or intra-discursive. No solution to this problem seemed possible from within structuralism itself. Hence the move by both Barthes and Foucault, during the 1970s, towards different versions of post-structuralism. Hence, too, the meteoric rise to intellectual pre-eminence, during the same period, of Jacques Derrida.

For Barthes himself, the key moment of transition probably occurred with *S/Z*, his study of Balzac's short story, *Sarrasine*. In what appeared initially as conventionally structuralist narratology, he divided the text into 561 'lexias', or units of reading, and analysed them, exhaustively, in terms of five main codes. He also distinguished between 'readerly' and 'writerly' texts—those which position the reader as passive consumer, and those which demand that the reader actively participate as co-author of the text, respectively (Barthes, 1974, p. 4). But if *Sarrasine* was a writerly text, as Barthes argued, then it followed that it could have no single meaning: 'to decide on a hierarchy of codes . . . is *impertinent* . . . it overwhelms the articulation of the writing by a single voice' (p. 77). The five codes were thus self-confessedly arbitrary, and the story itself possessed of no determinate meaning, but rather both plural and diffuse. This distinction between readerly and writerly texts was soon reformulated as that between *plaisir* and *jouissance*, or 'pleasure' and 'bliss', in a move that called attention to the corporeal erotics of reading. Barthes was still too much of a structuralist to contemplate a return to the reading subject, but the reading body, 'my body of bliss' (Barthes, 1975, p. 62) had become a very different matter. The text of *jouissance* was thus necessarily incomplete, just as the body is more erotic 'where the garment gapes' than when completely naked (p. 9). This was Barthes at play in a double sense, then, both as eroticism and also as indeterminacy, that is, as the play of meanings that would fascinate Derridean deconstruction.

POST-STRUCTURALISM: DECONSTRUCTION AND GENEALOGY

Post-structuralism is itself a portmanteau concept, so polysemic as to be of only questionable theoretical value. In general, however, it has been used to denote four relatively distinct theoretical movements: Derridean 'deconstruction'; Foucault's 'genealogical' writings on the theme of the knowledge/power relation; the various reworkings of psychoanalysis as semiotics inspired by the work of Jacques Lacan (1901–81); and the anti-Freudian 'rhizomatics' of Gilles Deleuze (1925–95) and Félix Guattari (1930–92).

Derrida and deconstruction

Derrida is perhaps the post-structuralist thinker *par excellence*, a more profound thinker than Barthes with no properly structuralist past, a philosopher rather than a critic, to use a distinction of which neither approved. Insofar as the developing discourse of post-structuralism was concerned, the key theoretical option during the late 1970s and 1980s was that between Derrida and Foucault. Derrida's three major works, *Writing and Difference*, *Speech and Phenomena* and *Of Grammatology*, all first published in 1967, thus marked the founding moment of French post-structuralism. His much-quoted essay, 'Structure, Sign, and Play in the Discourse of the Human Sciences' (Derrida, 1970), had been written for an international symposium that was planned to introduce French structuralism into American intellectual life, held at Johns Hopkins University in 1966. Ironically, it would achieve quite the opposite: a radical calling into question of all that structuralism had argued. Subsequently included in *Writing and Difference*, this essay clearly anticipated many of the characteristic themes and preoccupations of what would later become post-structuralism. It turned the logic of structuralism against itself, insisting that the 'structurality of structure' had been repressed in structuralism, in ways that limit precisely 'the *play* of the structure' itself (Derrida, 1978, p. 278). Taking as his text Saussure's distinction between signifier and signified and Lévi-Strauss' between nature and culture, Derrida showed how both undermine their own presuppositions, so that 'what appears most fascinating . . . is the stated abandonment of all reference to a *center*, to a *subject*, to a privileged *reference*, to an origin' (p. 286). The alternative to structuralism is thus not a return to humanism, but an affirmation of play itself and so a new interpretation of interpretation: 'the affirmation of a world of signs without fault, without truth, and without origin' (p. 292). This is what Derrida would come to designate as 'deconstruction'.

Derrida rejected what he termed the 'logocentric' notion of

language as 'voice', that is, as the expression of intentional human meaning, and of writing as technology and technique. 'The system of writing . . . is not exterior to the system of language', he argued. Quite the contrary, the system of language associated with western phonetic-alphabetic writing is precisely what has made possible the production of 'logocentric metaphysics' (Derrida, 1976, p. 43). Just as for Saussure *langue* was more permanent and durable than *parole*, so for Derrida writing outlives and outlasts its supposed authors. But Derrida takes the argument a stage further: where Saussure had privileged sign over referent, Derrida privileges signifier over signified; so much so, in fact, that writing consists, he says, not of signs, but of signifiers alone. Thus for Derrida, the 'meaning of meaning' is an indefinite referral of signifier to signifier 'which gives signified meaning no respite . . . so that it always signifies again' (Derrida, 1978, p. 25). Linguistic meaning thereby entails an 'infinite equivocality'. Though subject to later psychoanalytic reformulation as 'phallogocentrism', the critique of logocentrism has remained fundamental to Derrida's thought. The entire western philosophical tradition, from Plato on, is judged 'metaphysical' insofar as it imagines 'presence' prior to discourse.

If 'metaphysics' is the problem, then 'difference' is the solution. Derrida takes from Saussure the notion that language is founded on difference, but coined the neologism, *différance*, to stress the double meaning of the French verb, *différer*—to differ and to defer or delay (Derrida, 1982, pp. 7–8). Thus difference is also the deferral, for the moment at least, of other, alternative meanings. 'What is written as *différance*', he explained, 'will be the playing movement that "produces" . . . these differences, these effects of difference' in language (p. 11). Différance is thus 'neither a word nor a concept', but rather a device by which to think strategically 'what is most irreducible about our "era"' (p. 7). That characteristically Derridean device, the pun, is deployed precisely so as to enable a remorseless worrying away at the other possible meanings of words. Deconstruction itself is best understood as pushing textual meaning to its limits, in order to discover the differences within a text, the ways it fails to say what it means to say. A distant but by no means entirely hostile observer has described it as 'a form that posits some prior text of which it claims to be a commentary, appropriating portions—and in particular terminological subsections—from that text provisionally to say something which the text does not exactly say as such in its own voice or language' (Jameson, 1995, p. 78).

Demystification as relativisation

This might appear little more than a peculiarly obtuse form of literary criticism—and so it was interpreted by the Yale School of American 'Derrideans' (cf. Bloom et al., 1979). But for Derrida himself, deconstruction has been as much a philosophy and a politics as a type of literary criticism. So when he famously insisted that there '*is nothing outside of the text*', he would add that 'in what one calls . . . real life . . . there has never been anything but writing' (Derrida, 1976, pp. 158–9). Real life is thus itself a text and can, therefore, be deconstructed. Indeed, he has explicitly argued that deconstruction should interfere 'with solid structures, "material" institutions, and not only with discourses or signifying representations' (Derrida, 1987, p. 19). Derrida's insistence on the indeterminate openness of meaning is clearly intended as subversive of all authoritarianisms, whether epistemological, ethical or political, and of the fear of change that often inspires such authoritarianism. Hence his concluding invocation at Johns Hopkins of 'the as yet unnamable which is proclaiming itself and which can do so . . . only under the species of the nonspecies, in the formless, mute, infant, and terrifying form of monstrosity' (Derrida, 1978, p. 293). A Derridean politics is thus, above all, a politics of demystification through relativisation.

For all the mobility of Derrida's thought, it betrays no obvious line of movement, such as in Barthes' from structuralism to post-structuralism, or Foucault's from 'archaeology' to 'genealogy'. Indeed, Derrida's work resists such classification. He has written widely on subjects as diverse as the social organisation of higher education, the nuclear arms race, art and aesthetics, literary criticism, Marxism, archiving and email, friendship, psychoanalysis, forgiveness and reconciliation, but always as the philosopher, always the deconstructionist (Derrida, 1983;

Derrida, 1984; Derrida, 1987; Derrida, 1992; Derrida, 1994; Derrida, 1996; Derrida, 1997; Derrida, 1998; Derrida, 1999). The argument develops not by way of theoretical refinement, but by a succession of shifts in textual focus, so elaborated as to become themselves theoretical refinements. In *Specters of Marx*, for example, the focus is on Marx and the 'anti-Marxist conjuration' of Fukayama and others during the early to mid-1990s. Taking as its occasion the first noun of *The Communist Manifesto*—'A spectre'—and Marx's own love of Shakespeare, whose most famous ghost had haunted Hamlet's Elsinore, Derrida explores the logics of 'spectrality', showing how Marx 'scares himself' with ghosts, spectres and *Geist*, but also how anti-Marxism seeks to exorcise Marx, pronouncing him dead so as to make him so (Derrida, 1994). In *Archive Fever*, the focus is on the concept of the archive, the name of which derives from the Greek word for town hall, and how it is at once both public and private, the site of origin and perpetuity, preservation and discovery (Derrida, 1996). In *Resistances of Psychoanalysis*, the focus moves to psychoanalysis and its own resistances to itself, its lack of susceptibility to its own methods, in Freud, Lacan and Foucault (Derrida, 1998).

The deeper affinities between Foucault and Derrida, despite their apparent mutual animosity, reside around this persistent scepticism vis-à-vis discourse, a scepticism that seeks to identify the possibilities within discourse, which discourse itself seeks to repress. Both thereby adopted an adversarial stance towards dominant discourse, a stance that is the hallmark of a peculiarly post-structuralist politics of demystification. But there can be no positive content to any such politics. Thus even in his most expressly political work, Derrida characterises his would-be 'new international' only as a negativity—not as what it will be, but as what it will not: 'without status, without title, and without name, . . . without contract, . . . without coordination, without party, without country, without national community . . . without co-citizenship, without common belonging to a class' (Derrida, 1994, p. 85). The central achievement and aspiration in Derrida is the discovery not so much of hidden truths as of marginalised inconsistencies.

Foucault on knowledge and power

In Foucault's writings from the mid-1970s, we find a similar repudiation of the older structuralist aspirations to scientificity. Here, however, post-structuralism had moved in a very different, even opposed, direction: certainly, Foucault himself remained dismissive of Derrida's 'little pedagogy' (Foucault, 1972a, p. 602). Foucault relativised discourse not by any radical reconstruction of the notion of signification itself, but by the attempt to substitute relations of power for relations of meaning. 'I believe one's point of reference should not be to the great model of language . . . and signs', argued Foucault, 'but to that of war and battle. The history that bears and determines us has the form of a war rather than that of a language' (Foucault, 1980, p. 114). The term coined to describe this later approach was 'geneaology', as distinct from 'archaeology'. The text that announced the shift was *Discipline and Punish*, a study of the birth of the modern prison (Foucault, 1979). For Foucault himself, there was little novelty in a focus on the interconnectedness of discursive and institutional practices as such. The real theoretical innovation here consisted, first, in a new sense of this connectedness as necessarily *internal* to discourse; and, second, in a growing awareness of the human body itself as the central object of control in such institutions as the prison, but also as the source of possible resistance to that control.

For Foucault, power in modern society had become essentially ubiquitous. Thus he spoke of its 'capillary form of existence . . . the point where power reaches into the very grain of individuals, touches their bodies and inserts itself into their actions and attitudes, their discourses, learning processes and everyday lives' (Foucault, 1980, p. 39). Famously, Foucault takes Bentham's plan for a 'Panopticon'—a central tower from which a supervisor would be able to monitor simultaneously the behaviour of a large number of supervised prisoners, patients, madmen, workers or whatever—as 'the architectural figure' of this radical extension of the mechanisms of control, regulation and self-control in modern societies (Foucault, 1979, p. 200). The argument has been misrepresented as itself Benthamite and Foucault as himself some kind of latter-day utilitarian (Bennett, 1998, pp. 82–4). But the almost archetypically anarchist quality of Foucault's practical politics is evident, for example, in his prison reform agitation. Moreover, the implicit hostility to Enlightenment rationality of the earlier archaeological writings becomes increasingly explicit and at times reminiscent of Adorno and Horkheimer in the later genealogy. It is true that, for Foucault, the ubiquity of power renders it open and indeterminate: 'it induces pleasure, forms knowledge, produces discourse. It needs to be considered as a productive network which runs through the whole social body' (Foucault, 1980, p. 119). There is, then, no single structure of power, but rather a play of powers. This provided a rationale for anarchism, rather than for what Bennett means by 'reform'. It aimed not so much at an 'objective' account of discourse as at a strategic, or tactical, but nonetheless militant, intervention into that play.

Foucault on sexuality

Perhaps the most telling example of this approach was the first volume of the *History of Sexuality*, where Foucault upturned the then widely accepted 'repression hypothesis' concerning Victorian sexuality and argued, to the contrary, that new 'techniques of power exercised over sex' and a new 'will to knowledge . . . constituting . . . a science of sexuality' had in effect created the modern sexual subject, precisely through a 'putting into discourse of sex' (Foucault, 1978, pp. 12–13). His conclusion, directed against Freud and Lawrence, is both striking and original. Distinguishing between the 'idea' of 'sex' and the social organisation of 'sexuality', he argued that what had been perceived as the chronicle of 'a difficult struggle' to remove censorship should rather be seen as the 'centuries-long rise of a complex deployment for compelling sex to speak, for fastening our attention and concern upon sex, for getting us to believe in the sovereignty of its law when in fact we were moved by the power mechanisms of sexuality' (p. 158). The much-anticipated later volumes of the history, *The Use of Pleasure* and *The Care of the Self*, were far more scholarly in character, indeed prodigiously so. They also seemed less radical in theoretical import—in part, no doubt, because of their determined focus on classical Greek and Roman antiquity, rather than on direct comparison between it and modernity, and in part because the genealogy promised in the first volume was abandoned in favour of a concentration on the 'games of truth' through which men think their nature as selves (Foucault, 1987, pp. 6–7). This renewed concern with discourse, as distinct from practice, might well be read as a retreat from genealogy into something closer to the early archaeology.

In these two volumes, Foucault succeeded in demonstrating the radical difference of classical conceptions of self and sexuality, not only in such relatively obvious matters as 'homosexuality' and 'the love of boys', but also in the more fundamental question of the nature of ethical conduct itself. For the Greeks, he concluded, sexual ethics were not so much a means of internalising 'general interdictions' as of developing 'an aesthetics of existence, the purposeful art of freedom perceived as a power game' (pp. 252–3). The radically encultured character of human sexuality clearly followed as a necessary corollary of the entire analysis. By implication, at least, this called into question the supposed naturalness of dominant contemporary sexual codes, most obviously their heterosexism. Foucault's implied sympathy for the Greek ethic of self-regulated sexuality had an obvious relevance to a subculture defined quite specifically in terms of its sexuality. Written under the shadow of his own developing sickness from AIDS, there was also a terrible poignancy to Foucault's concern for the 'care of the self'. Little wonder, then, that he should have become a gay martyr (cf. Halperin, 1995). The problem remains, however, that for most of us, whether gay or straight, both subjectivity and right conduct are about a great deal more than sex. Moreover, as Foucault had himself made clear, Greek sexual ethics rested on a 'harsh system of inequalities and constraints' for 'women and slaves' (Foucault, 1987, p. 253). This ethic of self-mastery was made possible, then, only by the exclusion of most of the population and of a whole range of human conduct—work, for example—from ethical consideration. It is difficult to avoid the observation that we owe these inclusions, in part, to that same Enlightenment Foucault had so cordially detested.

POST-STRUCTURALISM: LACAN, DELEUZE AND GUATTARI

Jacques Lacan

We referred to Lacan in the previous chapter's discussion of Zizek. Like Barthes and Foucault, Lacan too had a structuralist past: influenced, in turn, by Lévi-Strauss, Saussure and Jakobson, he had used structural linguistics to recover what he saw as the essential kernel of Freudian psychoanalysis. Hence his insistence that '*the unconscious is structured like a language*' (Lacan, 1977, p. 20). Unlike Freud, Lacan came to see the unconscious not as a key to understanding and thus curing the aberrations of the conscious ego, but as an end in itself, the centre of our being. Expelled from the International Psychoanalytic Association as a result, he founded the École Freudienne in Paris, in 1964, and from there presented the two series of lectures, subsequently published as *Écrits* and *The Four Fundamental Concepts of Psycho-Analysis*, which formed the basis of his thinking. Lacan reversed the Freudian conception of the subject's trajectory: instead of a pre-Oedipal subject self-present to its own unity and only later 'split' by socialisation, he saw the subject as wholly constructed through the child's contact with the external world of people and language. There is therefore no core of self or subjectivity prior to the child's insertion into the social. Moreover, Lacan saw language itself as providing the key to understanding how human subjectivity is constructed. Interestingly, he claimed that this was already implied in Freud's *The Interpretation of Dreams* (Lacan, 1977a, p. 159).

As we noted in chapter 3, Lacan developed a tripartite model of the pyscho-social world, comprising the Imaginary, the Real and the Symbolic. During the infant stage, the child inhabits a pre-linguistic, pre-Oedipal 'Imaginary' characterised by speechless identity between child, mother and world. During the 'mirror stage', between the ages of six and eighteen months, primordial symbolisation in the *fort-da* games of presence and absence develops a sense of subjectivity in the infant and hence also awareness of its being and of existence in general. The subject is formed, therefore, by the insertion of the child's awakening consciousness into the symbolic system of language that, as it were, 'speaks' it: 'It is the world of words that creates the world of things' (p. 65). But entry into the 'Symbolic' and the acquisition of subjectivity are achieved only at the price of a loss of this imaginary identity with the mother. The symbolic order is thus masculine: it is, in short, the Law of the Father. Though a child might have no empirical father present, it is nonetheless socialised into pre-existent symbolic social structures under the agency of paternity. The Law of the Father is symbolised by the 'phallus', which is not the actual penis, but rather the 'transcendental signifier', as Lacan terms it, that grounds the social order.

Lacan's third term, the Real, stands in opposition both to the Symbolic (language, the social, culture, other people) and to the Imaginary (the subject's sense of its relationship to the Symbolic). The Real is not 'reality', however; it is all that lies outside and inside the subject, but which is never directly accessible. For Lacan, the original lack is not the lost unity with the mother, but the lack of self. Driven to fill this originary lack, which can never be wholly sutured over, the individual is traversed by insatiable desires, which are displaced from object to object in search of recognition and acceptance. Here, Lacan distinguished between the 'big Other' the 'little other'. The former is all that the subject desires to know and bond with in its plenitude and full presence, but which forever remains at a remove. In consequence, the subject 'transfers' this desire to substitute versions represented by the 'little other'. In his later theorisations, Lacan would redefine the big Other as the Real.

Lacan was particularly interested in Lévi-Strauss' emphasis on the function of the signifier, as distinct from the signified, an idea that led him to the notion of 'an incessant sliding of the signified under the signifier' (p. 154). In short, meaning can never be definitively fixed on a signifier, but is constantly displaced from signifier to signifier, much as Derrida imagined, in a chain of perpetual signification. Lacan saw Freud's concepts of 'displacement' and 'condensation' as corresponding to metonymy and metaphor, the primary figures of language in Jakobson. Metaphor points to the substitution for one signifier of another and is thus the 'very mechanism by which the symptom, in the analytic sense, is determined' (p. 166). This is the 'transference-function' of the signifier: to represent what the unconscious will not allow to be presented in its raw truth—desire. Metonymy, by contrast, refers to the continual displacement of desire along the chain of signifiers as the ego drives the subject's endless search for unity.

Lacanian psychoanalysis has been employed widely in post-structuralist literary and cultural criticism, perhaps most influentially so in work on the 'gaze'. Lacan derived this notion from Freud's account of 'scopophilia', or the pleasure of looking, in *On Metapsychology*. The child's displacement of its auto-erotic drive onto others during the Oedipal phase involves a scopophilic drive, in which the gaze directed towards the other produces pleasure. Freud viewed the process as at the root of narcissism, voyeurism and masochism. In Lacan, however, scopophilia was extended into the very formation of subjectivity itself, through the notion that we seek confirmation of self in the gaze of others. It is this illusory confirmation that 'sutures' the impossibility of uniting with the big Other. Lacan's conception of subjectivity is reminiscent of Bakhtin's theory of the self as formed in dialogue with others. But Lacan's version of the psyche is essentially negative, leaving little hope for any eventual resolution of personal or civilisational discontents. As Roudinescou describes it: 'psychoanalysis can never be an agent in the adaptation of man to society . . . it is doomed to live in the world and to see disorder in the world as a disorder of consciousness' (Roudinescou, 1997, p. 216). Some of the more persuasive uses of the theory of the gaze have been made by feminists inquiring into the 'male gaze'. The obvious problem remains that Lacan's notion of 'desire as lack' seems quite unable to explain conflictual desires, arising from the specific contexts of real individuals, especially non-normative sexuality. Even Elizabeth Grosz, a theorist who found in Lacan an important source of inspiration (Grosz, 1990), came to question the value of a theory unable to 'account for, to explain, or to acknowledge the existence of an active and explicitly female desire, and, more particularly, the active and sexual female desire for other women that defines lesbianism' (Grosz, 1994, p. 275).

Deleuze and Guattari

Lacan's negativity stands in marked contrast to the radically positive possibilities for a politics of difference and desire enthusiastically elaborated in the two volumes of Deleuze and Guattari's *Capitalism and Schizophrenia*, both written during the 1970s: *Anti-Oedipus* and *A Thousand Plateaus*. They also collaborated on *Kafka: Toward a Minor Literature* and on their last work, *What is Philosophy?*, first published in 1975 and 1991 respectively. Their work of the 1970s combined Deleuze's Nietzschean philosophy of difference with Guattari's psychoanalytic approach to micro-politics after the style of Foucault. Theirs was a radical libertarianism, which read Marxism and psychoanalysis as aiming to liberate the subject from structures of control, social or psychic, only in order to re-inscribe it into the equally controlling structures of the authoritarian state and psychological normalcy. Their theoretical vocabulary and concerns clearly shared the more generally post-structuralist hostility towards 'totalising' thought: 'We no longer believe in a primordial totality that once existed', they declared, 'or in a final totality that awaits us at some future date' (Deleuze & Guattari, 1983, p. 42).

Rejecting the Freudian unconscious as 'classical theatre' and the Lacanian subject as 'an idealist . . . conception' (p. 25), Deleuze and Guattari imagined the unconscious as a positive and productive 'desiring-machine', seeking ever new creative connections in a constant state of becoming. The aim of *Anti-Oedipus* was thus to promote the creation of 'schizo-subjects', 'nomadic desiring-machines', who would be able to 'unscramble the codes' of a jaded modernity. The schizophrenic thus became the model for a psychic condition able to resist the restrictive and manipulative control of capitalist mechanisms: 'What we are really trying to say is that capitalism, through its process of production, produces an awesome schizophrenic accumulation of energy or charge, against which it brings all its vast powers of repression to bear, but which nonetheless continues to act as capitalism's limit' (p. 34). Deleuze and Guattari also attempted to explain the rise of fascism: not in terms of repression, nor as a crisis of capitalist accumulation, but rather as a logical outcome of the deformed channelling of desire into the paranoid, fascistic ego-structures capitalism typically induces. But as Foucault noted in his introduction, they were not so much interested in Nazi Germany or Mussolini's Italy as in the 'fascism in us all, in our heads and in our everyday behaviour, the fascism that causes us to love power, to desire the very thing that dominates and exploits us' (Foucault, 1983, p. xiii). This fascism of the mind, Deleuze and Guattari believed, is unamenable to explanation in terms of ideology.

In *A Thousand Plateaus* Deleuze and Guattari adopted the term 'rhizome' to denote the 'de-territorialisation' of desire. Here their subversive 'schizo-subjects' become 'nomads', waging guerrilla warfare against 'state machines' and their structures of control. *A Thousand Plateaus* attempted to think through the implications of 'rhizomatic' thinking for both the personal and the social. Moreover, its structure performed the theory and practice it expounded: a horizontal, non-hierarchical form of writing, it invited the reader to begin anywhere in its 36 chapters ('plateaus'), since it proposed no overarching narrative or system. The book was written in direct opposition to what they saw as the dominant western mode of thought, which is 'arborescent'—organised like a tree structure, based on vertical, hierarchised and systematic principles linked to foundational roots. Rhizomatic writing, by contrast, whether in Kafka or Nietszche or in their own work, is that which opens out into multiple expressions of liberated desire and against the false constraints of society's bureaucratised institutions of repression.

There is a wonderfully anarchistic exuberance to these writings of the 1970s, with their mockery of psychoanalysis, Marxism and structuralism. But for all this enthusiasm, it is often very difficult to take their argument seriously. Why should we believe that thought is rhizomatic? As Best and Kellner ask perplexedly: 'how do Deleuze and Guattari know this? Why is this claim correct, as opposed to . . . the structuralist claim that the mind naturally organizes reality according to binary divisions . . .?' (Best & Kellner, 1991, p. 106). The answer seems to be that we are supposed to take it on trust. If the social and natural worlds are as rhizomatic as Deleuze and Guattari claim, then how do we explain the near-ubiquity of 'arborescent' structures, except as a result of coercion and/or ideology? And why is the 'fascism in our heads' better explained by deformed desire than by the notions of ideology and rationalisation used in critical theory? Again, the answer seems to be that we should take it on trust. As it turned out, this was a trust that Deleuze and Guattari would breach in their own last collaboration, an oddly aestheticist celebration of the western philosophical canon, rewritten as 'geophilosophy' rather than historicism, and pitted against both science and art (Deleuze & Guattari, 1994). The 'young conservatism' Habermas claimed to detect in Foucault and Derrida (Habermas, 1985, p. 14), is as apparent here, in the not-so-young Deleuze and Guattari, as anywhere in post-structuralism. For it finally becomes clear that the 'universal capitalism' Deleuze and Guattari abhor is actually modernity itself.

The transition from structuralism to post-structuralism entailed a retreat both from 'macropolitics' of the kind once familiar to both Left and Right, and from the historical 'grand narratives' that tended to accompany them. Indeed, the attempt to undermine the epistemological and political status of historical knowledge is characteristic of the entire semiological enterprise: structuralism was profoundly anti-historicist; post-structuralism further radicalised this anti-historicism by deconstructing the notion of structure itself. In its place we find a rejection of the truth both of science and of theory, in favour of the infinitely plural pleasures of a textuality possessed of no determinate relation either to the signified or to the referent, and a stress on the radical contemporaneity and radical indeterminacy, in short the radical textuality, of our current constructions of the past. Neither position is entirely without insight. But in comparison with either critical theory or theoretical culturalisms, whether of the Left or the Right, post-structuralism often seems both pedagogically and politically inconsequential.

Its retreat into an indefinite pluralism, which was neither historical nor properly speaking critical (since criticism presupposes some real object external to itself), easily entailed a kind of textual frivolity as intellectually self-indulgent as Leavis or Adorno had been intellectually censorious. Bourdieu once observed of Derrida that: 'Because he never withdraws from the philosophical game, whose conventions he respects, even in the ritual transgressions at which only traditionalists could be shocked, he can only philosophically tell the truth about the philosophical text and its philosophical reading, which (apart from the silence of orthodoxy) is the best way of not telling it' (Bourdieu, 1984, p. 495). At its best, as in Foucault or in Derrida at his least playful, post-structuralism can be much more than this; at its worst, as in the silly word games about even sillier television programmes that sometimes seem to fill cultural studies journals, it can be very much worse.

5

The cultural politics of difference

Différance, we have seen, is one of the key notions in post-structuralist cultural theory. But it was also, according to Derrida, what was most irreducible about our 'era'. Taking this remark as a cue, we turn now to the kind of cultural theory inspired, at least in part, by the politics of difference associated with the 'new social movements', as the French sociologist Alain Touraine dubbed them (Touraine, 1981, pp. 9–10). From feminist movies to gay newspapers, there is no doubting the practical achievements of these new movements in effecting an unprecedented 'decentring' of white, straight, male, cultural authority. When cultural theory embraced this new 'postmodern' pluralism, it opened up the theoretical space within which some, at least, of the culturally marginalised could assert their own cultural specificities. The results have become familiar, not only in cultural studies, but also across many of the older humanities: radical feminism, queer theory, postcolonial theory, black studies and so on. This 'difference theory', as we termed it in chapter 1, has been characterised by an attempt to theorise the nexus between the operations of différance in language and culture and those of socio-historical difference, especially in respect of gender and sexuality, nationality, race and ethnicity. The key concepts in this theoretical formation are difference itself, and its apparent antonym, identity. In this chapter we will track these and related concepts as they have been figured and refigured in cultural theory.

SEX, GENDER AND SEXUALITY

Historically, the first of the new movements to generate its own distinctive cultural theory was 'second-wave' feminism. Women's resistance to patriarchal oppression is very probably as old as patriarchy itself, and certainly long predated the various types of cultural theory and cultural politics that concern us here. A recognisably feminist political vision can be traced back at least to the French revolutionary period: witness Mary Wollstonecraft's *A Vindication of the Rights of Women* or Olympe de Gouges's *Déclaration des droits de la femme et de la citoyenne* (Wollstonecraft, 1975; MacLean, 1990). But contemporary feminism remains essentially a product of the 1960s. Like the New Left, this second-wave feminism had aspired to a level of theoretical articulacy and sophistication unimagined by previous radical movements. Like the New Left, this second-wave feminism also came increasingly to define cultural theory itself as a matter of both particular interest and peculiar political relevance. This was so, in part, because many feminist intellectuals happened to be already employed in teaching in the humanities, especially in literary studies, in part because they perceived women's oppression as having cultural, rather than biological, roots, and in part because they saw women's cultural production as central to 'consciousness raising', and hence to social change.

All intellectual movements have their pre-histories, however, and second-wave feminism acknowledged both Virginia Woolf (1882–1941) and Simone de Beauvoir (1908–86) as major sources of intellectual inspiration. Woolf had initiated an enduringly feminist concern with the material constraints on women's cultural production, while also registering the possibility of a peculiarly female type of sentence, 'of a more elastic fibre . . . capable of stretching to the extreme, of suspending the frailest particles, of enveloping the vaguest shapes' (Woolf, 1979, p. 191). In her criticism and fiction she had forged a more or less deliberate connection between women's consciousness and literary modernism, which fascinated later feminist intellectuals (cf. Gilbert & Gubar, 1988). For de Beauvoir, the central philosophical conundrum had been that of how woman, 'a free and autonomous being like all human creatures . . . finds herself living in a world where men compel her to assume the status of the Other' (de Beauvoir, 1972, p. 29). Her understanding of femininity as a masculine project to construct women as objects, with which women themselves were nonetheless complicit (p. 21), anticipated much subsequent feminist debate over the objectification of women, as well as over the distinction between biological 'sex' and culturally constructed 'gender'. That Woolf and de Beauvoir were both novelists seems more than coincidental, given the peculiar salience of writing about writing in second-wave feminist discourse.

Culture, ideology and gender

Despite the occasionally 'separatist' ambitions of feminist politics, feminist cultural theory was far from self-contained. As Ruthven rightly noted, feminist cultural criticism drew on a number of 'discursive categories' originally 'marxist, structuralist, and post-structuralist or deconstructionist' in character (Ruthven, 1984, p. 26). Ruthven might have been 'the Crocodile Dundee of male feminism', as Elaine Showalter described him (Showalter, 1989, p. 366), but she had made much the same point herself: 'English feminist criticism, essentially Marxist, stresses oppression; French feminist criticism, essentially psychoanalytic, stresses repression; American feminist criticism, essentially textual, stresses expression. All, however, have become gynocentric' (Showalter, 1985, p. 249). She misrecognised post-structuralism as psychoanalysis (it was both more and less), but quite rightly drew attention to a 'textual' focus in American feminist criticism, which actually bespoke the often unacknowledged influence of older culturalist notions of tradition and disinterestedness. Showalter herself is Professor of English at Princeton University and a longstanding opponent of dependence on French or Marxist 'masters', but there was clearly a parallel indebtedness to culturalist 'practical criticism' at work in her own writing.

When Showalter referred to all three feminisms as having 'become gynocentric', she called attention to how second-wave feminism had evolved from an initial critique of 'androcentrism', or male-centredness, into a later celebration of 'gynocentrism', or female-centredness. This probably wasn't as uniform a trajectory as she suggested, but it was very common, nonetheless, especially in the English-speaking world. Kate Millett's *Sexual Politics*, the most important pioneering work of Anglophone feminist cultural theory, had been concerned precisely to develop a critique of sexist culture. The book had culminated in a sustained critique of the work of three male novelists, 'counterrevolutionary sexual politicians' (Millett, 1977, p. 233), as she termed them: D.H. Lawrence, Henry Miller and Norman Mailer. So, for example, she described how in *Lady Chatterley's Lover* Lawrence 'uses the words "sexual" and "phallic" interchangeably, so that the celebration of sexual passion for which the book is so renowned is largely a celebration of the penis of Oliver Mellors . . . This is . . . the transformation of masculine ascendancy into a mystical religion' (p. 238). Millett's work initiated a whole range of studies into how androcentric cultures constructed persistently negative images of women—these extended well beyond her own focus on masculine high culture, to include both elite and popular forms, produced by and for both men and women. This interest in negative gender stereotyping also laid the groundwork for an account of male pornography as representing women in acutely misogynist form (Dworkin, 1974), which became increasingly relevant to practical feminist politics.

The early critique of sexism moved quite quickly, however, towards the recovery and celebration of women's culture. The term Showalter coined for this latter development was 'gynocritics', a translation of the French *la gynocritique*, to mean the discovery of 'woman as the producer of textual meaning' (Showalter, 1985, p. 260). One important line of argument here was the attempt to discover a female tradition, sometimes even a female Great Tradition. Showalter's *A Literature of Their Own*, for example, and Ellen Moers' *Literary Women* both explored such notions (Showalter, 1978; Moers, 1978). But where many American feminists had found culture, a female literary tradition and female realism, many British feminists, working with concepts drawn from Marxism, discovered ideology and the impress within ideology of the mode of material production. As the Marxist-feminist Literature Collective had announced at Essex University in 1977: 'Literary texts are . . . ideological in the sense that they cannot give us a knowledge of the social formation; but they do give us . . . an imaginary representation of real relations' (Marxist-feminist Literature Collective, 1978, p. 185). This is almost exactly the Althusserian formulation of the theory of ideology. It should come as little surprise, then, that the Collective's preferred reading strategy, deriving from Macherey, was to 'analyse the incoherences and contradictions in . . . texts' (p. 186) and relate these to historical developments in the social formation. Michèle Barrett, then a member of the Collective, now Professor of Literary and Cultural Theory at Queen Mary College, University of London, later developed a detailed account of what she identified as the four key mechanisms by which textual representations reproduced gender ideology: stereotyping; compensation, via the discourse about the supposed moral value of femininity; collusion, that is, manipulation of consent; and recuperation—the negation of challenges to the dominant gender ideology (Barrett, 1988, pp. 108–12).

Feminist post-structuralism

Thus far, we have considered both properly culturalist formulations and those versions of Marxist feminism which, though redefining culture as ideology, still adopted a fundamentally 'cultural' model of difference. In French feminism, by contrast, we find persuasive instances of biological, linguistic and psychoanalytic models. This is not to suggest that there were no Anglophone instances of any of these (cf. Spender, 1980; Daly, 1978; Mitchell, 1974), only that they were much less representative of Anglophone feminist discourse during the 1970s and 1980s than of French. In the work of Hélène Cixous and Luce Irigaray, for example, female difference was at once both a cause for celebration and also irretrievably biological in origin. In Cixous, a quasi-Derridean antipathy to the dualisms of logocentric thought was combined with de Beauvoir's strong sense of woman as subordinate term to produce a kind of feminist deconstruction.

Thus, for Cixous, logocentrism was inextricably connected to phallocentrism: 'the logocentric plan had always, inadmissibly, been to create a foundation for (to found and fund) phallocentrism' (Cixous & Clément, 1986, p. 65).

As with Derrida, it was différance in writing, the difference of *écriture féminine*, as Cixous termed it, that would subvert such dualisms. While she was prepared to concede that not all men repress their femininity, even that some women 'more or less strongly, inscribe their masculinity' (p. 81), she nonetheless pursued the notion that women's writing somehow articulated the female body. Like the later Barthes, she connected writing to *jouissance*: 'the difference . . . becomes most clearly perceived on the level of *jouissance*, inasmuch as a woman's instinctual economy cannot be identified by a man or referred to the masculine economy' (p. 82). In her 1975 essay, 'The Laugh of the Medusa', Cixous had argued for an explicitly physiological connection between *écriture féminine* and the female body as a site of decentred eroticism: 'A woman's body, with its thousand and one thresholds of ardor . . . will make the old single-grooved mother tongue reverberate with more than one language', she wrote: 'More so than men . . . women are body. More body, hence more writing' (Cixous, 1981, pp. 256–7).

Irigaray also stressed the *jouissance* of the female body, and its connectedness to the type of deconstructive pluralism so highly prized in post-structuralist thought. 'Her sexuality . . . is *plural*', she observed: 'Is this the way texts write themselves/are written now? . . . *woman has sex organs more or less everywhere*. She finds pleasure almost everywhere . . . the geography of her pleasure is far more diversified, more multiple in its differences, more complex, more subtle, than is commonly imagined—in an imaginary rather too narrowly focused on sameness' (Irigaray, 1985, p. 28). This was a matter not only of writing, but also of speech. For Irigaray, the female body gave rise to a distinctive women's language, *parler femme*, in which '"she" sets off in all directions . . . in what she says . . . woman is constantly touching herself' (p. 29). Showalter's insistence that 'there can be no expression of the body which is unmediated by linguistic, social, and literary structures' (Showalter, 1985, p. 252) was, of course, true, but it was much less pertinent to the kind of argument advanced by Cixous and Irigaray than it appeared. What was at issue was not biological determinism, as Showalter supposed, but rather the nature of writing and of female sexuality, and of their possible connections, given the undoubtedly mediated ways in which the body finds cultural expression. A more serious objection was that directed by Juliet Mitchell at Julia Kristeva, but which could easily also be turned towards Cixous and Irigaray: that insofar as femininity is indeed like this, then it is so only by virtue of the effects of patriarchal oppression. This 'is just what the patriarchal universe defines as the feminine', Mitchell wrote, 'all those things that have been assigned to women—the heterogeneous, the notion that women's sexuality is much more one of a whole body, not so genital, not so phallic. It is not that the carnival cannot be disruptive of the law; but it disrupts only within the terms of that law' (Mitchell, 1984, p. 291).

Interestingly, Mitchell and Kristeva shared a common interest in Lacan. The key Kristevan text was almost certainly *Revolution in Poetic Language,* first published in 1974, the central analytical framework of which is clearly Lacanian. Kristeva renamed Lacan's 'Imaginary' the 'semiotic' and insisted that it persists into adulthood as an alternative mode of signification. She borrowed from Plato the term *chora,* meaning womb or enclosed space, to refer to the pre-Oedipal pulsions with which the semiotic is linked. 'Our discourse—all discourse—moves with and against the *chora*', she wrote, 'in the sense that it simultaneously depends upon and refuses it . . . The *chora* . . . is not a sign . . . it is not yet a signifier either . . . it is, however, generated in order to attain to this signifying position . . . the *chora* precedes and underlies figuration . . . and is analogous only to vocal or kinetic rhythm' (Kristeva, 1984, p. 26). Once the symbolic order is entered, she argued, the semiotic is repressed, but not thereby superseded. Rather, it continues to constitute the heterogeneous and disruptive aspects of language. Where the symbolic is masculine, the semiotic is akin to, though not identical with, the feminine—it is repressed and marginal. The semiotic is thus culturally subversive, insofar as it deconstructs the binary oppositions that are fundamental to the structures of symbolic language.

As the 1980s proceeded, post-structuralist claims became increasingly pressing upon Anglophone feminisms. When Showalter herself came to produce an updated account of the evolution of recent feminist theory, she would recognise the gynocritical moment as having been succeeded, though not supplanted, by feminist post-structuralism, or 'gynesic' criticism, as she termed it (Showalter, 1989, p. 359). In the United States, new styles of feminist deconstruction had indeed acquired a very considerable importance, especially in the field of literary studies: obvious instances included the work of Gayatri Chakravorty Spivak, for example, and of Barbara Johnson (Spivak, 1987; Johnson, 1987). The enthusiasm for French post-structuralism among Australian feminists went so far as to prompt Barrett's description of the synthesis between Lacanian psychoanalysis and Barthesian semiology as the 'New Australian Feminism' (Barrett, 1988, p. xxix). British feminists had also come to celebrate the apparently happy marriage between post-structuralist theory and feminist practice (Weedon, 1987). Barrett herself would soon subject her earlier post-Althusserianism to a rigorously post-structuralist critique, finally opting for a Foucauldian 'politics of truth', as opposed to what both she and Foucault termed Marxism's 'economics of untruth' (Barrett, 1991, pp. vii, 155). The politico-intellectual effects of the developing union between feminism and post-structuralism were essentially twofold: first, there was a shift in general feminist preoccupations from political economy and sociology to literary and cultural studies, what Barrett termed 'an extensive "turn to culture" in feminism' (Barrett, 1999, p. 21); second, there was a shift within feminist cultural studies, away from a characteristically structuralist interest in how the patriarchal text positions women, and towards a new interest in how women readers produce their own resistant, or at least negotiated, pleasures from such texts.

The sheer scale of this Anglophone feminist enthusiasm for French post-structuralism very nearly marginalised alternative approaches within feminism. Such psycho-semiotic feminisms were especially persuasive, moreover, to scholars working in philosophy or in the more cosmopolitan areas of literary and cultural studies. Indeed, the Australian philosopher, Elizabeth

Grosz, now Professor of Women's Studies at Rutgers University in New Jersey, had defined 1980s feminist theory, as distinct from the feminism of the 1960s, in terms of a set of quite specifically 'French' and post-structuralist thematics: as aspiring to autonomy (difference) rather than equality; as engaged theoretically not with 'Marx, Reich, Marcuse', but 'Freud, Lacan, Nietzsche, Derrida, Deleuze, Althusser, Foucault' (Gross, 1986, pp. 190–3); and as contesting singular or universal concepts of truth so as to 'encourage a proliferation of voices . . . a plurality of perspectives and interests' (p. 204). Such feminisms were often uncompromisingly 'intellectual' in character. Hence the not uncommon activist doubt that an intellectual practice centred on the deconstruction of male-dominated academic knowledges, rather than on the empirical reality of women's life in patriarchy, might prove both elitist and unfeminist. Grosz herself confronted the objection head on: 'feminist struggles are . . . occurring in many different practices, including the practice of the production of meanings, discourses and knowledges . . . This struggle for the right to write, read and know differently is not merely a minor or secondary task within feminist politics' (Grosz, 1989, p. 234).

Queer theory: Butler and Grosz

One important line of development from feminist post-structuralism has been the kind of 'queer theory' developed by writers such as Grosz herself, Eve Kosofsky Sedgwick, Teresa de Lauretis and Judith Butler, Professor of Rhetoric at the University of California at Berkeley. 'Queer' here has the semantic force both of 'homosexual', as in the old homophobic jibe, and of 'deconstructive', as in unsettling and strange. Queer theory has been concerned above all with the identity claims of non-normative sexualities. It proceeded from a more generally post-structuralist sense of the contingency of identity towards a radical deconstruction of the categories of 'gender' and 'sexuality' themselves. For Butler, gender was not merely cultural, but something close to a cultural fiction, almost entirely socially constructed, albeit in part out of materials provided by bodies: 'Gender is the repeated stylization of the body', she insisted, 'a set of repeated acts within a highly regulatory frame that congeal over time to produce the appearance of substance, of a natural sort of being' (Butler, 1990, p. 33). It is thus a discursive practice rather than a form of essential identity. There 'is no gender identity behind the expressions of gender', she argued, because 'identity is performatively constituted by the very "expressions" that are said to be its results' (p. 25). Neither male nor female nor gay nor lesbian nor straight identities have any essence, therefore; they are merely different variants of performativity, some subversive, some not, but all in some sense 'regulated'. The debt to Foucault should be apparent.

This was much more radical than the older culturalist distinction between sex and gender, if only because Butler saw 'sex' itself as gendered, that is, as something we perform. Sex, she wrote, 'was always already gender . . . Gender ought not to be conceived . . . as the cultural inscription of meaning on a pregiven sex', but 'must also designate the very apparatus of production whereby the sexes themselves are established' (p. 7). This can easily be trivialised as meaning that we simply choose to put on and take off our gender and sexuality like changing clothes. Indeed, Butler had cited 'drag' as an example of performativity: '*In imitating gender, drag implicitly reveals the imitative structure of gender itself—as well as its contingency*' (pp. 137–8). But she subsequently clarified the notion of performativity so as to highlight its non-voluntarist character: 'Performativity cannot be understood outside of . . . a regularized and constrained repetition of norms. And this repetition is not performed *by* a subject; this repetition is what enables a subject' (Butler, 1993, p. 95). The political implications for gay or feminist politics ran parallel to Foucault's deconstruction of the 'sexual revolution' in Freud and Lawrence: being gay or female was neither an essence to be liberated nor even a cultural ethnicity, but rather an amalgam of the 'identity effects' of certain institutionally located signifying practices, and thus itself a site of contestation between the oppressively normalising and the liberatory destabilising.

Grosz further radicalised the position by challenging the idea that gender, rather than sex, is at the heart of performativity. Gender '*must* be understood as a kind of overlay on a pre-established foundation of sex', she argued, 'a cultural variation of a more or less fixed and universal substratum' (Grosz, 1994, p. 139). Butler's mistake, for Grosz, lay in the failure to acknowledge 'the instabilities of sex itself, of bodies themselves . . . [of what] the body is . . . capable of doing, . . . what anybody is capable of doing is well beyond the tolerance of any given culture' (p. 140). 'Human subjects never simply *have* a body', she wrote: 'rather, the body is always necessarily the object and subject of attitudes and judgments' (p. 81). For Grosz, bodies are neither purely biological nor purely cultural; they act as a mediating term, a zone of exchange, between the private and the public, the psychological and the social. The object of feminist critique cannot, then, be to liberate the 'natural' female body from socially dominant misrepresentations, since all bodies are unavoidably socially and culturally marked in some way. The issue is, rather, which particular cultural stereotypes 'are used and with what effects' (p. 143). It should be apparent that these radical critiques of gender, sexual identity and the body are as applicable to the category 'homosexual' as to 'lesbian'. Thus David Halperin writes that: '"Homosexual", like "woman", is not a name that refers to a "natural kind" of thing . . . It's a discursive, and homophobic, construction that has come to be misrecognised as an object under the epistemological regime known as realism' (Halperin, 1995, p. 45). Presumably, Grosz' argument concerning the sexed body is as applicable to the gay male body as to the female.

Butler has claimed that 'deconstruction of identity is not the deconstruction of politics' (Butler, 1990, p. 148). Elsewhere, she has even argued that a viable radical politics requires 'affiliation with poststructuralism', since only this 'way of reading' will allow us to insist that 'difference remain constitutive of any struggle' (Butler, 1999, p. 44). There is, however, a strong sense in which the relativising logic of feminist deconstruction threatens to undermine the ground from which a specifically feminist or queer critique of patriarchal culture could be mounted. What is so important, after all, about a critique of institutional oppression, if what are oppressed are merely fictional identities? As Lynne Segal, Professor of Psychology at Birkbeck College, University of London, has recently observed: 'deconstructive feminism ... avoids the perils of generalizations about female subjectivity. But it courts the danger that its own interest in endlessly proliferating particularities of difference ... endorses a relativity and indeterminacy which works to undermine political projects' (Segal, 1999, p. 32). Hence Showalter's earlier insistence that: 'Feminist criticism can't afford ... to give up the idea of female subjectivity, even if we accept it as a constructed or metaphysical one' (Showalter, 1989, p. 369). Barrett makes much the same point, albeit with a less assured sense of her own political certainties: 'If we replace the given self with a constructed, fragmented self, this poses ... the obvious political question of who is the I that acts and on what basis, ... who is the I that is so certain of its fragmented and discursively constructed nature' (Barrett, 1999, p. 25).

NATIONALISM, MULTICULTURALISM AND POSTCOLONIALISM

Nationalism

As with gender and sexuality, so too with the debates over the cultural politics of nationalism, multiculturalism and postcolonialism—an originally culturalist discourse has taken on an increasingly post-structuralist character. Nations are often understood as political, geographical or even biological phenomena, but there is an obvious sense in which they are primarily cultural. Nationalism is clearly not the politico-cultural effect of an already existing nationality, but its cause. As the social philosopher Ernest Gellner observed: 'Nationalism is not the awakening of nations to self consciousness: it invents nations where they do not exist' (Gellner, 1964, p. 169). Nations are not so much matters of natural 'fact', then, as forms of collective imagining. That there is some deep connection between the developing social role of the modern intelligentsia and the creation of such imaginings has become something of a theoretical commonplace. If it is no longer possible to hold German idealist philosophy entirely responsible for the subsequent history of nationalism, this is largely because attention shifted, in Gellner's own work and in that of Tom Nairn, for example (Gellner, 1997; Nairn, 1977; Nairn, 1997a), away from formal, philosophical systems of thought and towards the needs and aspirations of intelligentsias, understood as particular, historically specific social groupings.

Benedict Anderson's *Imagined Communities* considerably advanced this line of argument through its focus on the specific nexus connecting intellectuals to the printing industries. A nation, he wrote, 'is an imagined political community . . . imagined as both inherently limited and sovereign' (Anderson, 1991, p. 15). Nations are imagined in a very particular way, moreover: as passing through a homogeneous empty time in which simultaneity is indicated only by temporal coincidence in terms of clock and calendar. This is a distinctly modern type of imagination, he observed, the technical preconditions for which are provided by the novel and the newspaper. Print-capitalism has thus been central to the rise of nationalism: the capitalist publishing industry, driven by a restless search for markets, assembled the multiplicity of pre-modern vernaculars into a much smaller number of print-communities, each of which prefigured a modern nation. Anderson himself identified four main waves of nationalism: first, early American nationalism, in which language *per se* was irrelevant, but in which printer-journalists, producing self-consciously 'provincial' as opposed to 'metropolitan' newspapers, powerfully shaped the development of national consciousness; second, European popular nationalisms centred on middle-class reading coalitions, which mobilised the popular masses in opposition to the polyvernacular dynastic state; third, the official nationalism of those polyvernacular dynasties that sought, through 'Russification' or 'Anglicisation', to impose a nationalism from above; and last, those anti-imperialist nationalisms in which an intelligentsia educated within the confines of the colonial educational system came to imagine and later constitute the colony itself as a nation.

Insofar as the former Soviet Union and the continuing United Kingdom could each be construed as successors to the nineteenth-century polyvernacular dynastic state, then Lithuanian and Welsh nationalisms can be understood as contemporary variants of nineteenth-century European popular nationalism. The more obviously communitarian and solidaristic aspects of such nationalism sit fairly comfortably with equivalently communitarian and solidaristic elements in culturalist theory. Whatever its emancipatory intent, however, radical nationalism seems open to two fundamental objections: first, that in a world becoming increasingly internationalised and culturally cosmopolitan it articulates a by now demonstrably 'retrospective', rather than 'prospective', structure of feeling; and second, that it threatens to repress cultural identities other than its own. There might thus be a necessary and unavoidable conflict of interest between a nationalist imagination centred on the category of nation and a feminist imagination centred on gender; between nationalism and the kinds of socialist imagination centred on class; between nationalism and the 'multicultural' imaginings of non-national or sub-national ethnic groups. Though the Welsh or the Quebecois, for example, might well still choose between nationalism and multiculturalism, only the latter remains available to the Afro-Caribbean and Bengali communities in Britain or to the Greek and Italian communities in Canada or Australia. For these last, multiculturalism seems likely to remain structurally incompatible with any but the most tentative of cultural nationalisms.

Solidarity, community and culture are, of course, vital and important: they render social life meaningful, creative and sometimes even genuinely co-operative. But the imagined community of the nation-state remains a very special case, as it seems unimaginable except as superordinate to and sovereign over all other imaginable communities: the nation-state is not simply a community, but also a state, and states are by definition sovereign. How, then, to square this circle? Arguing in defence of Irish nationalism, Eagleton borrowed from Williams an analogy between class and nation (Williams, 1964, p. 322), which pointed to the need to go, not so much around nationality, as 'all the way through it and out the other side'. 'To wish class or nation away, to seek to live sheer irreducible difference *now*', Eagleton continued, 'is to play straight into the hands of the oppressor' (Eagleton, 1990, p. 23). In Ireland, the whole process of nation-state building is so obviously already under way, and yet so obviously stalled, that nationality is perhaps an almost unavoidable politico-cultural referent. But in fully sovereign 'postcolonial' states such as Australia or Canada, the practical import of cultural nationalism appears both less radical and less unavoidable. The invariable consequence of 'going through' nationality tends to be not its supersession, but its installation into a position of monopolistic cultural privilege, typically the central site and source of a more or less conservative cultural hegemony. It is against such cultural hegemony that multiculturalism has tended to assert the rights of minorities.

Multiculturalism

The term 'multiculturalism' is often understood in the most banal of senses, as the availability of different 'ethnic' foods, music, art and literature in the one society. The effects are much less banal, however, if cultural diversity is extended into the legal system, labour laws, educational institutions and government policy towards health and housing. John Rex, Professor of Sociology at the University of Warwick, defined the 'multicultural alternative' in terms of a belief that it should be possible, without undue threat to the overall unity of a society, to recognise that resident minorities have rights: 'to their own language in family and community contexts, . . . to practise their own religion, . . . to organise domestic and family relations in their own way, and . . . to maintain communal customs' (Rex, 1996, p. 91). Torres distinguishes between multiculturalism 'as a social movement' and 'multicultural education' as a 'reform movement'. The former is the more far-reaching: 'a philosophical, theoretical, and political orientation that goes beyond school reform and tackles issues of race, gender, and class relations in society at large' (Torres, 1998, pp. 175–6).

Multiculturalism was one of the central matters at issue in the American 'culture wars' of the 1990s. In its earliest formulations, both as theory and as policy, it had been conceived as almost the archetypal instance of a 'left-culturalist' squared circle, that is, as a plurality of unitary cultures. The obvious objection is that this is a contradiction in terms. Certainly, its conservative opponents understood it thus and also, therefore, as necessarily divisive, insofar as it focused on the needs and complaints of specific social groups defined by ethnicity or race. A threat to national stability and traditional values, according to Arthur Schlesinger, multiculturalism could even lead to the 'disuniting of America' (Schlesinger, 1991). At the other extreme, radical critics tended to see multiculturalism as a strategy of containment, accepting the need to recognise and foster the cultural diversity of a society, but within the pre-established and overarching institutions and values that traditionally harboured discriminatory and exploitative policies. According to this argument, society and culture are irreparably marked by divisions of class, gender and race that are repressed by unitary conceptions of culture, even if these are ethnically multicultural. To cite an American example again: 'Such pluralism tolerates the existence of salsa, it enjoys Mexican restaurants, but it bans Spanish as a medium of instruction in American schools. Above all it refuses to acknowledge the class basis of discrimination and the systematic economic exploitation of minorities that underlie postmodern culture' (JanMohamad & Lloyd, 1990, p. 8).

Multicultural theory has increasingly tended to invoke ethnic 'difference' as in itself a discursively and politically subversive category. Writing from a country where multiculturalism conventionally denoted 'ethnicity' rather than 'race', Australian feminist Sneja Gunew, now Professor of English at the University of British Columbia, argued that it would 'deconstruct' the dominant unitary national narratives, become 'a strategy which interrogates hegemonic unities' and thereby establish the 'basis for constructing "signifying breakthroughs", the preconditions for a revolutionary, non-repetitive, history' (Gunew, 1985, p. 188). Later, she would borrow from Michael Fischer the notion of a poetics of ethnicity, which could seek 'mutual illuminations in reading those juxtaposed dialogic texts or utterances that swerve away from . . . binary structures', and thereby substitute 'irony . . . for authenticity' (Gunew, 1994, p. 49; cf. Fischer, 1986). Writing from a country where multiculturalism often denoted 'race', Stuart Hall's work of the 1990s increasingly gave pride of theoretical place to the relatedly 'diasporic' issues of multiculturalism and 'hybridity', postcolonialism and globalisation. Interestingly, this was also the point at which he emerged as a commanding figure in cultural studies, not only in Britain, but also internationally (cf. Gilroy et al., 2000). There is no denying either the necessity for or the importance of this work of 'decentring', in which liberalism was exposed as 'the culture that won' rather than the 'culture . . . beyond culture', Britishness as subject to a 'major internal crisis of national identity' (Hall, 2000, pp. 228–9). But Hall's approach to these matters remains theoretically problematic, especially insofar as it tended to read difference in increasingly post-structuralist terms.

Postcolonial cultural theory

Postcolonial cultural theory derived from much the same empirical datum as multiculturalism, that of the collapse of European imperialism, and of the British Empire in particular. What multiculturalism meant to the former metropoles, postcolonialism meant to the former colonies. Postcolonial theory was initially very much the creation of 'Third World' intellectuals working in literary studies within 'First World' universities. The key figures were Edward Said and Gayatri Spivak, the first Palestinian, the second Indian, both now Professors of Comparative Literature at Columbia University. But one could easily add to the list: Homi Bhabha is Indian and Professor of English at the University of Chicago; Dipesh Chakrabarty is Indian and Professor of South Asian Languages, again at Chicago (cf. Bhabha, 1990; Bhabha, 1994; Chakrabarty, 2000). The resulting combination of Third Worldist cultural politics and post-structuralist theory has become an important, perhaps even characteristic, feature of the contemporary First World radical academy. As with multiculturalism, the argument commenced not so much with a celebration of subordinate identity as with a critique of the rhetoric of cultural dominance, which sought to 'decentre' the dominant—white, metropolitan, European—culture. The central 'postcolonialist' argument is thus that postcolonial culture has entailed a revolt of the margin against the metropolis, the periphery against the centre, in which experience itself becomes 'uncentred, pluralistic and nefarious' (Ashcroft et al., 1989, p. 12).

Hence its supposedly 'inevitable tendency towards subversion' (p. 33).

Said and Bhabha

The origins of postcolonial theory can be traced to Said's *Orientalism*, an impressively scholarly account not of 'the Orient' itself, but of how British and French scholarship had constructed the Orient as 'Other'. For Said, Orientalism was a 'discourse' in the Foucauldian sense of the term: 'an enormously systematic discipline by which European culture was able to manage—and even produce—the Orient . . . during the post-Enlightenment period' (Said, 1995, p. 3). The 'Orient', he wrote, became an object 'suitable for study in the academy, for display in the museum . . . for theoretical illustration in anthropological, biological, linguistic, racial and historical theses about mankind and the universe, for instances of economic and sociological theories about development, revolution, cultural personality, national or religious character' (pp. 7–8). This wasn't simply a matter of academic ideas reflecting other political interests, as a Marxist might argue. Rather: 'Orientalism is—and does not simply represent—a considerable dimension of modern political–intellectual culture' (p. 12). Moreover, it functioned by way of a system of binary oppositions in which the West, its possessions, attributes and ethnicities were valorised positively against the inferior status of colonised peoples. The 'major component in European culture', Said concluded, 'is precisely . . . the idea of European identity as a superior one in comparison with all the non-European peoples and cultures' (p. 7). Western accounts of the Orient were thus at least as much an effect of the West's own dreams, fantasies and assumptions about the Other as of any referential 'reality' within the 'Orient' itself.

Drawing on Said's understanding of this fantastic quality in western constructions of the East, Bhabha drew attention to the fundamentally ambivalent operations of colonial stereotyping. If the overarching logic of colonial discourse was to 'construe the colonized as a population of degenerate types on the basis of racial origin' (Bhabha, 1994, p. 70), it nonetheless also set up a fundamental split in the construction of otherness, which itself led to a peculiar ambivalence. Colonial discourse, wrote Bhabha, 'produces the colonized as a social reality which is at once an "other" and yet entirely knowable and visible' (pp. 70–1). The result is a characteristic 'hybridity', or 'in-betweenness', greater than or at least different from the sum of its colonising and colonised parts. Insofar as the colonising power attempted to 'reform' the subjectivity of its colonised subjects, what Bhabha calls colonial 'mimicry' became central to the form of this hybridity: an 'ironic compromise' between domination and difference, which produced an Other that is almost, but not quite the same. Mimicry is thus the sign of a 'double articulation', according to Bhabha: 'a complex strategy of reform, regulation and discipline, which "appropriates" the Other as it visualizes power'; but also 'the sign of the inappropriate . . . a difference or recalcitrance which coheres the dominant strategic function of colonial power, intensifies surveillance, and poses an immanent threat to . . . "normalized" knowledges and disciplinary powers' (p. 86). The result of this inevitably flawed 'colonial mimesis' is thus a 'strategic failure' in which, to cite the Indian case, 'to be Anglicized is *emphatically* not to be English' (pp. 86–7). The colonial encounter tends towards its own deconstruction, therefore, as it turns 'from *mimicry*—a difference that is almost nothing but not quite—to *menace*—a difference that is almost total but not quite' (p. 91).

Gayatri Spivak

At the level of practical politics, such critiques of European misrepresentation might seem to suggest the need for a counter-assertion of an authentically postcolonial identity. This move is precluded by the logic of post-structuralism, however, for if Europeanness and non-Europeanness are each constituted within and through discourse, then there can be no extradiscursively 'real' postcolonial identity to which a counter-cultural politics might appeal for validation. For Said himself, this was much less of a problem than for later theorists. His work has never been simply (or even complexly) post-structuralist: there is a great deal of healthy eclecticism in his writing and many other influences at play, most obviously Gramsci and Williams (Said, 1995). For Spivak, however, the issue became much more pressing, if only because she is not only the translator into English of Derrida's *Of Grammatology*, but also a famously 'obscure' deconstructionist critic in her own right (Derrida, 1976; Spivak, 1999; Eagleton, 1999). Hence her tortuous discussion of the (im)possibility of 'subaltern' speech and its equally tortuous rewriting in *A Critique of Postcolonial Reason*. In both versions, Spivak argued for the theoretical superiority of Derridean deconstruction over Foucauldian genealogy and Deleuzian rhizomatics. But in the earlier essay she had been much more explicit: 'Derrida . . . is less dangerous . . . than the first-world intellectual masquerading as the absent nonrepresenter who lets the oppressed speak for themselves . . . he articulates the *European* Subject's tendency to constitute the Other as marginal to ethnocentrism and locates *that* as the problem of all logocentric . . . endeavors' (Spivak, 1988, pp. 292–3; cf. Spivak, 1999, pp. 279–81). Hence the conclusion that the 'subaltern cannot speak', which is neither explicitly reaffirmed nor withdrawn in the rewritten version (Spivak, 1988, p. 308; Spivak, 1999, p. 308–11).

One way out of the dilemma is suggested by Spivak's notion of 'strategic essentialism': '*strategically* adhering to the essentialist notion of consciousness, that would fall prey to an anti-humanist critique, within a historiographic practice that draws many of its strengths from that very critique' (Spivak, 1987, pp. 206–7). Which means, in short, that whatever deconstruction's theoretical purchase when directed at European, white, male, bourgeois humanism, postcolonial theorists must nonetheless proceed *as if* humanism were still valid, *as if* the subject had still not been decentred, *as if* deconstruction had failed, if ever they are adequately to represent insurgent, or subaltern, consciousness. As Spivak continued: 'the Subaltern Studies group . . . must remain committed to the subaltern as the subject of history. As they choose this strategy, they reveal the limits of the critique of humanism as produced in the West' (p. 209). This resort to a kind of 'strategic' humanism is neither as shocking nor as original as Spivak believed. It is reminiscent, at one level, of Derrida's decision to exempt Marxism from deconstructive critique in his deliberate refusal to join the 'anti-Marxist concert' of the post-1968 period in France (Fraser, 1984, p. 133). But the *necessity* for this resort to strategic essentialism—in Spivak, in Derrida, even in Showalter (Showalter, 1989, p. 369)—surely casts doubt on the wider anti-humanist enterprise. For what use is a theory that requires, for its effective application, that we pretend not to believe in it?

Postcolonialism, post-structuralism and radical humanism

Said canvassed a very different solution in his *Culture and Imperialism*, a book that takes as its theme the 'general relationship between culture and empire' (Said, 1993, p. xi). His conclusions warrant repetition at some length:

> there seems no reason except fear and prejudice to keep insisting on . . . separation and distinctiveness, as if that was all human life was about. Survival in fact is about the connections between things . . . It is more rewarding—and more difficult—to think concretely and sympathetically, contrapuntally, about others than only about "us". But this also means not trying to rule over others, not trying to classify them or put them in hierarchies, above all, not constantly reiterating how "our" culture or country is number one (or *not* number one, for that matter) (p. 408).

This wasn't so much strategic essentialism as essentialism itself, a clear affirmation, in short, of the continuing political and intellectual relevance of a radicalised humanism. Yet it is a humanism as capable as any post-structuralism of undermining the Eurocentric certainties of the older liberal humanisms. Said's reading of Jane Austen's *Mansfield Park*, for example, as 'part of the structure of an expanding imperialist venture', was both powerfully demystifying and indisputably 'anti-imperialist'. But it also deliberately avoided the 'rhetoric of blame', in favour of what Said himself described as the 'intellectual and interpretive vocation to make connections . . . to see complementarity and interdependence' (pp. 114–15).

Aijaz Ahmad, an Indian academic working in India, has

argued against the entire postcolonial argument on the grounds that it substitutes textualism for activism and nation for class (Ahmad, 1992, pp. 92–3). Moreover, in Ahmad's view, much of the intellectual legitimacy attaching to postcolonial theory actually derived from its deep complicity with the structures of social privilege enjoyed by 'First World' and 'Third World' intellectuals and by 'Third World' ruling classes. 'The East', he wryly observed, 'seems to have become, yet again, a *career*—even for the "Oriental" this time, and within the Occident too' (p. 94). Any commentary on these debates from a 'First World' source is open, by a roughly similar logic, to the accusation of its own complicity in the profits of imperialism. But let us here hazard the observation that such textualist politics as post-structuralism enjoins do generally function much as Ahmad argues: to defer activism and to bestow the spurious illusion of political radicalism on what is in fact an almost entirely conventional academic activity. Doubtless, the possibilities for activism are peculiarly circumscribed for a Palestinian exile in New York. Doubtless, professors of literature are professionally obliged to have a preoccupation with problems of textuality, and doubtless Said and Spivak are as entitled to their profession as Ahmad is to his. Doubtless, Said's more popular writings (Said, 1986; Said, 1979) also attest to a more activist political intention than Ahmad appeared to allow. But whatever these particular qualifications, the more general logic of post-structuralism does indeed seem to lead in the direction to which Ahmad points. As Eagleton has observed: 'Post-structuralism is among other things a kind of theoretical hangover from the failed uprising of '68 . . . blending the euphoric libertarianism of that moment with the stoical melancholia of its aftermath' (Eagleton, 1992, p. 6).

Postcolonialism in settler societies

That this is so becomes particularly apparent in the more recent appropriations of postcolonial theory by 'First World' intellectuals. These are increasingly premised on the dubious assumption that the settler societies of the Americas and Australasia can be meaningfully assimilated to the formerly colonised societies of

Africa and Asia as in some sense analogously postcolonial. Moreover, the category of 'postcolonial' has often been expanded to include not simply the post-independence period, but all writing 'affected by the imperial process from the moment of colonization to the present day' (Ashcroft et al., 1989, p. 2). The paradoxical effect of this argument is to obliterate rather than celebrate difference: both between pre-independence and post independence periods and, more importantly, between colonisers and the colonised. The colonies of white settlement are not postcolonial in any sense other than that posited by a strict periodisation between pre-independence and post-independence. In every other respect they are instances of a continuing colonisation, in which the descendents of the original colonists remain dominant over the colonised indigenous peoples.

Accounts of how European colonial discourse had constructed the non-European as 'Other' cannot plausibly be applied either to Australia or to Canada, still less to the United States. To the contrary, the colonies of European settlement were typically imagined precisely as overseas extensions of Europe itself, as 'Self' rather than 'Other'. Postcolonial literature—defined both as exclusive of non-English language writing and as inclusive of settler writing—has thus increasingly come to represent little more than a fashionable refurbishment of what used to be called 'Commonwealth literature'. And, as Salman Rushdie rightly insisted: '"Commonwealth literature" should not exist. If it did not, we could appreciate writers for what they are, whether in English or not; we could discuss literature in terms of its real groupings, which may well be national, which may well be linguistic, but which may also be international, and based on imaginative affinities' (Rushdie, 1991, p. 70).

To be fair, the New Zealand postcolonial theorist Simon During, Professor of English at, by turn, the University of Melbourne and Johns Hopkins University, had conceded the distinction between the postcolonialism of the post-colonised and that of the post-coloniser (During, 1990, pp. 128–9). But no such distinction was registered in Ashcroft, Griffiths and Tiffin, for whom the logic of their own argument compelled the inclusion of the United States within the category 'postcolonial' (Ashcroft et al., 1989, p. 2). The implication, that American culture is somehow subversively peripheral to a European centre, seems almost wilfully perverse, given that many of the dominant cultural forms of our time—science fiction, jazz, rock, the Hollywood movie, some important television subgenres—are characteristically American in origin. It can be sustained only at the price of a systematic indifference to such 'popular' cultural forms and a corollary insistence on the special value of 'Literature'. For it is only in the very peculiar and increasingly socially marginal instance of high literary studies that such notions of American marginality retain an even residual credibility. Elsewhere, American centrality is surely almost self-evidently obvious. There is, then, a certain irony in the way postcolonial theory proclaims its own antipathy to the Anglocentrism of traditional English studies, while simultaneously rejoicing in notions of Literature clearly reminiscent of Leavisite culturalism.

We have referred to postcolonialism as performing a similar function in the former colonies to that of multiculturalism within the former metropoles. But the former colonies—and especially the settler colonies—are also themselves imaginable as multicultural. And here the practical politico-cultural dilemma arises: how exactly does one reconcile a postcolonial identity, the external difference of which is predicated upon its own internal unity, to a multicultural diversity that will threaten all national cultural unities, including even the postcolonial? In During's opinion, 'today, in writing in a First World colony . . . one ought to be nationalistic' and 'nationalism in postcolonial nations has virtues . . . it lacks elsewhere' (During, 1990a, pp. 139, 151). This is especially so, he continued, in those settler societies where 'nationalism is not used *against* large minority racial/tribal groups' (p. 139). By contrast, Gunew insisted that multiculturalism must seek to 'confound those who believe that the land speaks . . . literary nationalism' (Gunew, 1990, p. 116).

Ironically, Gunew was writing against exactly the kind of 'virtuous' postcolonial nationalism During had sought to celebrate. No doubt nationalism 'has different effects and meanings in a peripheral nation than in a world power' (During, 1990a, p. 139). But these differences might matter much less for those whose own difference is lived in the peripheral nation—women, subordinate social classes, ethnic minorities, indigenous peoples—than for the postcolonial national intelligentsia itself. Postcolonial theory is thus repeatedly hoisted by its own post-structuralist petard. Ahmad's critique of Said and Rushdie clearly implied as much. And Said himself conceded something of the same when he wrote that: 'The national bourgeoisies . . . tended to replace the colonial force with a new class-based and ultimately exploitative one, which replicated the old colonial structures in new terms' (Said, 1993, p. 269).

RACE AND ETHNICITY IN BLACK AND LATINO CULTURAL STUDIES

Race-based cultural politics are normally forged from the common experience of racism. From indigenous movements for the recovery of land and the protection of cultural heritage through to the struggles of immigrant populations to overcome racial and ethnic stigmatisation, the politics of race are played out daily in almost every part of the world. But it is in relation to the African diaspora that it has proven the most bitter and fractious. As Stephen Howe puts it: 'the central object of the obsession has always been distinctions between black and white' (Howe, 1998, p. 21). It is precisely these issues and these obsessions that are problematised in the work of black cultural theorists such as Hall and Paul Gilroy in Britain, and Cornel West, Henry Louis Gates, Jr, and bell hooks in the United States.

Hall and Gilroy

British cultural studies had first begun to explore the multiculturalism of its own society through a critique of the way white racism constituted blackness as 'Other'. Hall and a number of his colleagues from the Birmingham Centre co-authored a highly acclaimed 'cultural studies' account of 'mugging', showing how media constructions of black criminality conferred popular legitimacy on state authoritarianism (Hall et al., 1978). This turn towards race—and ethnicity, gender and sexuality—was a necessary corrective, Hall would later claim, to an economic reductionism that gave all social antagonisms the master signifier of 'class'. Black politics, he explained, 'give priority to political issues which are not the same as [those that concern] the white working class' (Mullan, 1996, p. 273). We have observed how Hall's recent work has focused on the politics of representation, especially the stereotyping of the 'racialised Other' (Hall, 1997). Looking back on the development of black cultural studies, he has identified two key moments: the first, when 'black' came to stand for the 'common experience of racism and marginalization and . . . provide the organizing category of a new politics of resistance' (Hall, 1996, p. 441); the second, when 'black' was itself recognised as a 'politically and culturally constructed category', referring to an 'immense diversity and differentiation of . . . historical and cultural experience' (Hall, 1996, pp. 441, 443). For Hall, as for Gilroy, such diversity would be approached through the idea of 'a *diaspora* experience . . . of unsettling, recombination, hybridization' (p. 445).

Gilroy has worked on both sides of the Atlantic, as Professor of Sociology at Goldsmiths College, University of London, and at Yale University. His first major work, *There Ain't No Black in the Union Jack,* analysed the intersection of race, nation and class in post-industrial Britain, calling particular attention to what he perceived to be the blind spot of 'race' in British cultural studies. Intended as a 'corrective' to the more 'ethnocentric dimensions' of cultural studies, it argued that the new discipline 'tends towards a morbid celebration of England and Englishness from which blacks are systematically excluded', and that this was true 'even when cultural studies have identified themselves with socialist and feminist political aspirations' (Gilroy, 1992, p. 12). For Gilroy, such Left nationalism was a consequence of an imagined 'imperative' to 'construct national interests and roads to socialism' from out of a political language already necessarily 'saturated with racial connotations' (pp. 12–13). Even the founding fathers of cultural studies, Williams and Thompson, were singled out for special mention in the indictment. To Williams' stress on social identity as a product of 'long experience',

Gilroy would retort: 'how long is enough to become a genuine Brit?' (p. 49). At one point, Gilroy famously accused Williams of an 'apparent endorsement of the presuppositions of the new racism' (p. 50).

In *The Black Atlantic*, Gilroy proceeded to analyse the way black intellectuals and writers have negotiated the tensions of being simultaneously European and black. The result, he argued, had been the 'stereophonic, bilingual, or bifocal cultural forms' and 'structures of feeling' of 'the black Atlantic world' (Gilroy, 1993, p. 3). Here, the stress falls overwhelmingly on the inevitable hybridity, modernity and sense of constant becoming of diaspora cultures. He found this embodied quintessentially in black vernacular art forms, especially in the various mutations of jazz, of Hendrix, of soul and reggae, of the novels of Wright, Ellison, Morrison, Walker and Baldwin. A culture such as this can only be adequately appreciated and nurtured, he would conclude, by a response to racism that 'doesn't reify the concept of race . . . that doesn't try to fix ethnicity absolutely but sees it instead as an infinite process of identity construction' (p. 223).

More recently, Gilroy has deliberately sought to counterpose the notion of the diasporic to what he sees as the 'race-thinking' or 'raciology' (Gilroy, 2000, p. 12) that is present not only in dominant white cultures, but also in some varieties of militant black rap and hip-hop culture, in Afrocentrism and in the racialisation of commodified black cultural expression. His own interests and hopes lay with the utopian possibilities of what he termed 'planetary humanism' and 'strategic universalism', rather than with ethnic cultural absolutisms based on race. The adjectival qualification—planetary, as against European—invokes earlier black thinkers, such as Frantz Fanon and Aimé Césaire, rather than the Enlightenment, but functions nonetheless as a kind of calling to account in which humanism is required to live up to its own unrealised promise. This resort to the 'planetary' is meant to sidestep the post-structuralist critique of liberal humanism, but it is difficult to see why 'planetary' should turn out to be any less abstract, universalising or essentialist a notion than 'human'. Gilroy is on much firmer ground in his concern that the 'biopolitics' of contemporary black culture might actually shore up the boundaries of racial particularity. As he writes in the introductory chapter: 'if ultranationalism, fraternalism, and militarism can take hold, unidentified, among the descendants of slaves, they can enter anywhere. Past victimization affords no protection against the allure of automatic, prepolitical uniformity' (p. 8).

It is easy to sympathise with Gilroy's unease at the re-racialisation of commodity culture in the name of black 'freedom'. But the 'planetary', conceived as a radical universalisation of the diasporic, surely isn't the solution, if only because the problem lies with the commodity form itself and with its capacity for alienation. Which returns us to Gilroy's earlier critique of British cultural studies. His accusation of racism had been directed at the pages in *Towards 2000*, where Williams contrasted the 'alienated superficialities' of 'formal legal definitions' of citizenship with the more substantial reality of 'deeply grounded and active social identities' (Williams, 1983, p. 195). Gilroy read Williams as in effect replicating the racist distinction between 'authentic and inauthentic types of national belonging' (Gilroy, 1992, p. 49). This has been a widely influential reading, much repeated in later cultural studies debates (cf. Hall, 1993, pp. 360–3; Hall & Chen, 1996, p. 394; Hall, 2000a; Bennett, 1998, p. 26). It is, however, a misreading. The pages at issue were those where Williams developed his own critique of the legalism of mainstream liberal anti-racism. At no point had he denied that 'blacks can share a significant "social identity" with their white neighbours', as Gilroy suggests (Gilroy, 1992, p. 50). Rather, Williams merely insisted that the appeal to legality was in itself an inadequately counter-hegemonic response to racism (cf. Jones, 2000). Indeed, he quite specifically argued that the 'real grounds of hope' lay in 'working and living together, with some real place and common interests to identify with' (Williams, 1983, p. 196).

Rooted settlement or diasporic hybridity?

Insofar as there was something substantial at issue here, as distinct from mere misreading or misunderstanding, it hinged on Williams' critique of 'alienated superficialities', rather than on his supposed racism. He had argued that liberal and radical intellectuals, especially the 'nationally and internationally mobile', were often so in thrall to 'market and exchange relations' as to prefer legal solutions to problems of relationship, which would be best resolved only from the lived experience of the 'rooted settlements' in which most people, black and white, derive their 'communal identities' (pp. 195–6). This, surely, is the heart of the difference between Williams, Gilroy and Hall: their opposed valuations of 'rooted settlement' as against 'diasporic hybridity'. Hence their quite different evaluations of 'socialism' as against 'liberalism': Hall's hybrid subjects, who '*produce themselves anew and differently*' (Hall, 1993, p. 362), are able to do so, in practice, only by way of 'market and exchange relations'. For Gilroy and Hall, rooted settlement and diasporic hybridity are coded racially as, respectively, white and black. But there is no reason to believe either that Williams intended it thus or that they need be imagined thus.

In Australia, for example, immigrants are disproportionately white, black people typically not immigrants at all, but rather the native first peoples, many of whom live in settlements far more 'rooted' than anything Williams imagined. Multiculturalism's aspiration to relativise all positions and claims tends to trivialise the status of exactly these peoples, whose historical trajectories have typically been much more painful than those of more recently arrived minority groups. Such indigenous cultures suffer from a double misrecognition. As the original inhabitants of the land, they have reason to resent the subordination of their customs, law and social organisation to an externally imposed dominant culture. As the inheritors of a particular tribal history and cultural context, they have reason to resist their absorption into a pan-indigenous identity fabricated largely by the dominant national ethnicities. Whatever the pleasures of the diaspora, social justice sooner or later requires recognition of the human value of these most deeply settled of cultures. Such recognition seems unlikely to be forthcoming from dominant cultures determined to transcend even their own limited histories of rooted settlement. Commodity culture invites us to produce ourselves anew and differently, on a daily basis, whenever it insists that we consume.

And this is what Hall's later work comes perilously close to celebrating: the alienated superficialities of the market. In this respect, it represents a more general tendency for cultural studies to transform itself into what one Brazilian writer dubs 'commodity studies' or 'image studies' (Cevasco, 2000, p. 438). Gilroy sees the problem, of course, but his solution, planetary humanism, is in danger of raising alienated superficiality to an even higher level of abstraction.

West and Gates

Black cultural nationalism and cultural politics have had a much longer history in the United States than in Britain, dating arguably from the pre-Civil War years, certainly from the Harlem Renaissance of the 1920s. But black cultural studies and the cultural theory that accompanied them date only from the 1970s. The most prominent of contemporary black cultural theorists is almost certainly Cornel West, Professor of African-American Studies and Philosophy of Religion at Harvard University. For West, an adequate understanding of 'race' relations in America had to begin 'not with the problems of black people but with the flaws of American society—flaws rooted in historic inequalities and longstanding cultural stereotypes' (West, 1993, p. 15). Though disagreeing with Afrocentrism, he recognised the frustration it expressed: 'Afrocentrism', he wrote, 'is a gallant yet misguided attempt to define an African identity in a white society perceived to be hostile' (p. 4). This same sense of frustration also underpins the growing 'nihilism' among black populations, he argued, a nihilism that 'feeds on poverty' and on the 'shattered cultural institutions' that previously sustained black communities (pp. 15–16). Such fragmentation has been driven by 'corporate market institutions', the persistence of white supremacism and an exaggerated ethic of individualism. A keen observer of black popular culture, West noted the irony that 'just as young black men are murdered, maimed, and imprisoned in record numbers, their styles have become disproportionately influential in shaping popular culture'. He cites hip-hop as an example, commenting that insofar as it expresses the despair of the black underclass, its popularity among western urban youth amounts to the 'commodification of black rage' (p. 88).

In an essay first published in 1990 in the journal *October*, West heralded the arrival of a 'new kind of cultural worker . . . associated with a new politics of difference'. The new politics would be distinguished by its rejection of 'the monolithic and the homogenous in the name of diversity, multiplicity and heterogeneity'; by its repudiation of the abstract, general and universal in favour of the concrete, specific and particular; and by its aim 'to historicize, contextualize and pluralize' (West, 1999a, p. 119). Here West quite explicitly identified the movement towards difference in the fields of race, gender and sexuality, and the 'shattering of male, WASP cultural homogeneity' (p. 127), as running parallel with and being fuelled by decolonisation and revolutionary nationalism in the 'Third World'. But these struggles had been at least as much a matter of equality as of difference. Hence Klor de Alva's criticism that in self-identifying as racially 'black' or ethnically 'African-American', West and other black intellectuals had actually perpetuated a racialised discourse based on skin colour. For Klor de Alva, himself a Chicano and an anthropologist, this merely played into the hands of racism, trapping 'blacks' and 'other so-called people of color, in a social basement with no exit ladder'. West's response was to argue that a sense of group identity based on skin colour is necessary for 'protection, association and recognition' (p. 501). Identifying as black had been both positive and affirmative, he continued, arguing that it was 'important not to conflate overcoming racial barriers with dismantling racial language'. The latter, West concluded, 'ignores or minimizes the history of racism' (p. 509).

Like West, Henry Louis Gates, Jr, also worked at Harvard, where he is Chair of the Afro-American Studies Department. One of the leading voices in black literary and cultural studies in the United States, his work is a mixture of cultural criticism, literary theory and autobiographical disclosure. As with West, much of Gates' work has been a recovery of 'black' cultural tradition and the collective African-American past from under and inside the dominant white version of American history. In *Figures in Black* and *The Signifying Monkey*, Gates investigated the black vernacular tradition, aiming to uncover both the key tropes in 'the use of black figurative language' and the processes by which 'the white written text speaks with a black voice, [which] is the initial mode of inscription of the metaphor of the double-voiced' (Gates, 1988, pp. 84, 131). Gates found in the work of Ismael Reed a literary language that posited a 'structure of feeling' that simultaneously critiqued both 'the metaphysical presuppositions inherent in Western ideas and forms of writing' and 'the received and conventional structures of feeling' inherited from the Afro-American tradition itself (p. 250).

bell hooks

In the United States, as in Britain, black cultural criticism has been an overwhelmingly male affair. The obvious exception has been bell hooks, whose *Ain't I A Woman?* was written against both black male sexism and white feminist racism, as well as addressing more general questions concerning black women's involvement in the women's movement (hooks, 1981). Her work has inspired a developing chorus of voices willing to challenge not only racism, but also male hegemony, 'classism' and black 'essentialism' within the 'coloured' communities themselves (cf. Anzaldúa, 1990; Moraga & Anzaldúa, 1981; Carbey, 1987).

In *Outlaw Culture*, hooks critiqued both the commodification of feminism in Madonna's media-constructed image as 'unrepressed female creativity and power' (hooks, 1994, p. 11) and its glamorisation by white professional feminists such as Naomi Wolf, Camille Paglia and Catherine MacKinnon. She also insisted that radical academics need to use a language comprehensible to the ordinary people for whom, and presumably to whom, they speak. Hence her own use of terms like 'dick' and 'pussy': 'Talking sex in meta-language and theoretical prose', she argues, will never capture the imagination of the masses of people 'working daily to understand how their lives have been affected by shifting gender roles and expectations and how sexism fucks us all up' (p. 79).

If hooks' invocation of blackness against feminism and

feminism against blackness might seem almost quintessentially 'postmodern', this is not how it appeared to her. To the contrary, she argued that for all its talk of 'difference' and 'otherness', postmodernism displays a studied *in*difference to manifestations of blackness, other than those 'associated solely with concrete gut level experience'. For hooks, this merely perpetuated racism by assuming that 'no meaningful connection' could be made between 'black experience and critical thinking about aesthetics or culture' (hooks, 1990, p. 1). And this is so, she claims, because postmodernism is predominantly the creation of 'white male intellectuals and/or academic elites', with little relevance for black writers in general, let alone black women. She notes wryly that as perceptive a critic as the Australian feminist Meaghan Morris could provide a bibliography of important contributions to the discourse on postmodernism by women, not one of which refers to work by black women (p. 3).

Latino studies

As with black cultural studies, the growth of Hispanic/Latino studies has reflected the growing influence of 'minority' groups on the political and cultural mainstream in the United States. 'Hispanic' is the term used by the Government Census Bureau, but 'Latino' appears to have superseded it in popular usage. The Spanish language and a distinctive Latin American-derived popular music are perhaps the key elements in a cultural imaginary shared across the Americas. The largest minority in the United States, Latinos actually exhibit the full range of skin pigmentation from 'white' to 'black'. They have nevertheless been dubbed the 'brown race', a label perpetuated even by some Latino activists. Darder and Torres have shown how, from the 1960s on, 'race' came to supplant 'ethnicity' when Latinos borrowed an 'internal colony model' from radical black scholars to theorise their own oppression. The idea of a brown race thus provided a 'discursively powerful category of struggle and resistance' through which 'to build in-group identity and cross-group solidarity with African Americans' (Darder & Torres, 1998, p. 9). But as Klor de Alva observed in debate with West, racial identity politics will be self-defeating insofar as 'white' continues to stand for citizenship, 'black' or 'brown' (and 'yellow') for minority 'subservient' status (West, 1999, p. 501). Moreover, such race talk might well perpetuate racist discourse within Latino communities themselves. Following Hall, Darder and Torres opt for a 'critical notion of ethnicity', able to 'position' already 'racialized populations' in relation to their 'particular histories' (Darder & Torres, 1998, p. 10).

This history has been one of 'conquest and colonization, . . . proletarianization and disempowerment' (p. 17). The resulting struggles, over bilingualism in education, assimilation, urban space, media representation, welfare and the status of illegal aliens, provided much of the raw material for Latino studies. The initial impetus towards an independent Latino politics came from the Californian and Texan farm strikes of the mid-1960s, which triggered a more general mobilisation of Mexican Americans and the beginnings of a distinctly nationalist vision. Mexican-American activists appropriated the pejorative terms, Chicano and Chicana, transforming them into a sign of positive political identity. The movement evolved into a full-blown cultural nationalism, complete with artistic and theatrical works exalting peasant and indigenous cultural values, an assertion of racial pride (*¡Viva la raza!*) and a resuscitated mythology of Aztlán, the legendary home of the Aztecs. As with most other cultural nationalisms, it largely ignored class, gender and sexual differences within the Mexican-American community. Hence the backlash from Chicana feminists who, in the early 1980s, had begun to challenge the *machismo* of Chicano nationalism.

The rather different situation of Puerto Ricans has been perceptively analysed by Juan Flores in his *From Bomba to Hip-Hop*. He argued that the question of cultural identity is crucial for diasporic nations, especially so for Puerto Ricans, given that half the population of the island now lives in the United States. The continuous migration flows have kept alive cultural memory and a sense of national belonging, but have also created tensions between the islanders and the diaspora, as well as conflicts of loyalty that are played out within the class and racial hierarchies of the dominant society. Combining sociological insight with

Latin music history and a participant–observer's eye for complexity and tension, Flores draws a cultural map of Puerto Rico, a 'national imaginary', sensitive to the nuances of these struggles over identity and representation, both on the island and in the United States itself.

Stubbornly unfashionable, Flores insists on the colonial character of relationships between the United States and Puerto Rico, and on the continuing relevance of popular culture and its links to 'supposedly outmoded forms of vernacular, community, and "folk" culture' (Flores, 2000, p. 14). Community-based cultural practices are the lifeblood of ethnic minorities like the New York Puerto Ricans, in their rearguard action against submersion in an amorphous pan-Latino identity that will obscure the specificities of their class position and national origin, both of which are unresolved problems for most Hispanics. Puerto Ricans are second only to Mexican-Americans in terms of both numbers and the duration of their settlement in the United States, yet they are still the Hispanic group 'most characteristically cast as the bottom rung, the "exception" to the Hispanic rule' (p. 8). Despite all the rhetoric of 'commonwealth status' or 'free association', the most obvious explanation for this peculiarity of the Puerto Rican experience is that their identity derives not from an independent nation-state, but from 'a colony by all indicators of international relations' (p. 9). This relationship is mirrored on the mainland by the structured social inequalities that construct the 'racialized, stigmatized, inner-city Puerto Rican' as the 'spic', whose 'only cultural cousin has been the similarly placed "pachuco" and the "greaser" from the cities of the Southwest' (pp. 8–9).

One important object of Latino cultural critique has been their stereotyping in Hollywood film, television and popular culture generally. Writing in 1993, Guillermo Gómez-Peña objected to the way American multiculturalism conceptualised Latinos as 'objects of desire' within a 'meta-landscape of Mac Fajitas, La Bamba craze, MTV border rock, Pepsi ads in Spanish, and Chicano art without thorns'. '[O]ur art is . . . "colorful", "passionate", "mysterious", "exuberant", "baroque"', he continued, 'all euphemistic terms for irrationalism and primitivism' (Gómez-Peña, 1993, p. 51). Latino cultural studies has coined the term 'tropicalism', as equivalent to what Said had meant by 'Orientalism', in its own attempt to come to terms with the new post-nationalist, globalised political and cultural space. By tropicalism they mean 'the system of ideological fictions . . . with which the dominant (Anglo and European) cultures trope Latin American and U.S. Latino/a identities and cultures' (Aparicio & Chávez-Silverman, 1997, p. 1). There is much to be said for this intervention at the specifically cultural level of analysis. What worries more traditional Latino radicals, however, is the possibility that an equivalently 'postmodern' turn in political theory might conceptualise 'the ideas of capitalism, labor, and class struggle out of existence' (Darder & Torres, 1998, p. 5). There is no necessary incompatibility between cultural studies and political economy, either in general or in the specific instance of Latino studies. How the issue will be resolved in practice remains to be seen.

This tension between the cultural and the material is precisely what the break from literary into cultural studies was intended to circumvent. There is an awful poignancy, then, to Segal's insistence that feminist cultural studies now requires 'repoliticization', that the rifts between economic and cultural analysis need to be overcome once again (Segal, 1999, pp. 223–4). But so they do, because this is where we have come to. As Nancy Fraser laments: 'the politics of recognition is becoming increasingly dissociated from the politics of redistribution' (Fraser, 1997, pp. 180–1). The promise of difference theory, that culture be understood as radically in excess of both 'nation' and 'class', has been as politically exciting as any in recent intellectual history. Insofar as the combination of identity politics and difference theory has worked in and against the peculiarly 'postmodern' realities of late-capitalist culture, it has sometimes attained a more fully contemporary relevance than any other kind of theory. But insofar as it has become one of a number of theoreticist manoeuvres by which sections of an erstwhile progressive radical intelligentsia have sought to theorise, and dramatise, their own emergent depoliticisation, then it is also increasingly complicit with the dominant politico-cultural logics of a society that is still deeply utilitarian and capitalist in character.

6

Postmodernism and cultural theory

In this chapter we turn to what Meaghan Morris, Professor of Cultural Studies at Lingnan University in Hong Kong, once described as contemporary cultural theory's 'own version of cinema's blockbuster: the state-of-the-globe, state-of-the-arts, Big Speculation' (Morris, 1988, p. 242); that is, to postmodernism. The types of cultural theory we have discussed thus far—culturalism and cultural materialism, critical theory, structuralist and post-structuralist semiology, difference theory—all pursued their own kinds of strategy towards the analysis of cultural artefacts *in general*. Postmodernism is not a cultural theory of this kind, however; indeed it is not, properly speaking, a theory at all. Rather, the term refers, in the first instance, primarily to a whole set of artistic movements, in literature, painting and architecture for example, dating mainly from the second half of the twentieth century, which self-consciously defined themselves in opposition to earlier, equally self-consciously modernist movements. It is only in a secondary sense that the term also refers to a set of efforts from within cultural theory to define the specific nature of these movements in relation to other equally specific aspects of contemporary society and culture. The former is postmodernism; the latter is what Morris termed the 'postmodern debate'. These self-consciously postmodernist movements were, for the main part, a product of the 1960s, 1970s and 1980s, rather than of the past ten years. But what Scott Lash says of architecture is almost certainly true of the other arts: 'As a movement, postmodernism . . . is a thing of the past. As a presence at the end of the 1990s . . . it is ubiquitous' (Lash, 1999, p. 56).

POSTMODERNISM, POSTMODERNITY AND 'POST-WAR' LATE CAPITALISM

Like all blockbusters, postmodernism's success derived in part from its capacity to appeal to multiple markets, from high philosophy in the art-house cinemas of the academy through middlebrow multi-screen literary criticism and on to local fleapit sociology. If not exactly meaning all things to all people, the term obviously signified differently within different discourses: in short, it is at least as polysemic a sign as 'cultural studies' itself. But an apparently enduring postmodern trope was that of 'being after'. '*Post*modernism', wrote the late Ferenc Fehér, 'like many of its conceptual brethren, *post*-revolutionary or *post*-industrial society, *post*-structuralism and the like, understand themselves not in terms of what they are but in terms of what they come after' (Fehér, 1990, p. 87). But in this instance, after what, exactly? After modernism certainly: the earliest uses of the term, which date from Latin America in the 1930s and 1940s, deliberately counterposed postmodernist poetry and art, or *post-modernismo*, to an earlier *modernismo* (Anderson, 1998, pp. 3–4). After modernity too: the first Anglophone usages, from the 1950s, were either socio-historical, as in Arnold Toynbee's and C. Wright Mills' notions of a postmodern 'age', or they connected the socio-historical to the cultural, as in Charles Olson's sense of his own poetry as written for a new 'post-modern', post-western world (pp. 5–13).

After modernism

The shift within the 'high cultural' social subsector, from something recognisable as artistic 'modernism' to something different from and, in a sense, coming 'after' it, provided the 'postmodernist' debate with much of its initial vocabulary. The term 'modernism' was itself essentially an umbrella concept, used to refer to a whole series of early twentieth-century artistic movements, each of which sought in one way or another to challenge the predominantly 'realist' conventions of nineteenth-century European art. Where realist art had aimed at verisimilitude, that is, at the appearance of fidelity to 'real' life, modernist art tended to celebrate the materiality of its own existence as art, and hence its distance and difference from the real. Examples of modernist movements include Impressionism, Expressionism, Futurism, Dadaism and Surrealism. There is no consensus as to the date of modernism's beginnings: one standard academic text suggests 1890 (Bradbury & McFarlane, 1976); more interestingly, Virginia Woolf nominated December 1910 (Woolf, 1966, p. 321). But it is clear that the initial modernist impetus was a product of the late nineteenth century. This new modernism was characterised above all by its aesthetic self-consciousness, by a formalist experimentalism that recurred in painting and drama, poetry and music, the novel and sculpture. Some accounts also stress the importance of an avant-garde conception of the artist, where the role of the intellectual is understood as that of cultural leader, moving ahead of the wider society, much like the revolutionary vanguard in the Leninist view of politics. For the avant-garde, art stood in opposition to the dominant 'bourgeois' culture, as an essentially 'adversarial' force, aspiring to a positively 'redemptive' social function.

Bradbury and McFarlane see the presence of such cultural avant-gardes as integral to high modernism (Bradbury & McFarlane, 1976, p. 29). But Peter Bürger, Professor of Comparative Literature at the University of Bremen, takes issue with this conflation of modernism and the avant-garde, arguing for a more complex model of the avant-garde as a movement within and in some respects against modernism, rather than as coextensive with it (Bürger, 1984, p. 22). However we resolve such differences, it is clear that both modernist high culture in general and the avant-garde in particular were products of a specific geographical location as well as of a specific historical time. They were both creations of the great cities of continental Europe: Berlin and Vienna, Moscow and St Petersburg, above all Paris (cf. Bradbury,

1976). As such, they were fated to become direct casualties of the twin totalitarianisms of Nazism and Stalinism, both of which subscribed to a determinedly—not to say lethally—anti-modernist cultural politics. Driven into exile in the United States, what survived in New York was an increasingly successful commodification of avant-garde style, increasingly bereft of avant-garde social purpose. This was 'post-modernism' in the most obvious of senses, that of the 'high' culture that survived after modernism, a culture clearly dating from the 1940s. Relocated geographically from Europe to America and sociologically from the avant-garde to the mainstream, this was modernism as a commercial enterprise.

'Post-modernism' in this sense is grudgingly acknowledged even by those most hostile to the term's more generalising implications: Alex Callinicos, for example, agreed that the 'postwar stabilization of capitalism left the few still committed to avant-garde objectives beached' (Callinicos, 1989, p. 60); Perry Anderson that 'the Second World War . . . cut off the vitality of modernism' (Anderson, 1992, p. 37). As Fredric Jameson nicely observed of an earlier version of this last essay: 'whatever . . . Anderson . . . thinks of the utility of the period term—postmodernism—his paper demonstrates that . . . the conditions of existence of modernism were no longer present. So we are in something else' (Jameson, 1988, p. 359). As Anderson would later concede, this something else is postmodernism. As such, it is best understood neither as a distinctive style nor as a distinctive set of themes, but rather as a distinctive social relation between art and capitalism. In short, postmodernism is modernism stripped of its avant-garde redemptive functions. As we shall see, this change also implied a radical transformation in the relationship between modernism and what was variously described as the mass media, mass civilisation or popular culture.

After modernity

What, then, of postmodernity as distinct from postmodernism? Crucially 'postmodern' meant after the Second World War: the generations that attempted to theorise these many and varied postmodern conditions had grown up in a world that considered itself quite decisively 'postwar'. When Morris remarked that 'the postmodern era could be said to begin in 1945, at Hiroshima and Nagasaki' (Morris, 1988, p. 186), she unwittingly echoed Olson's own insistence that this act of nuclear terror had ended the modern age (Anderson, 1998, p. 7n). Such datings are by no means uncontroversial: the focus has sometimes fallen on the late 1950s and the early 1960s, as in Jameson's *Postmodernism, or, The Cultural Logic of Late Capitalism* (Jameson, 1991), or the 1970s and 1980s, as in the analyses of 'New Times' developed by Hall and such collaborators as Martin Jacques (Hall, 1996a; Hall & Jacques, 1989). These and other even later periodisations call attention to significant changes within postwar society and culture, such as the rise of the 'new social movements' or the development of new 'post-industrial' technologies. But the more fundamental shift is that registered by Morris and Olson, to a distinctively postwar world, the more general characteristics of which continue to structure our contemporary reality.

The historical fate of the avant-garde aside, at least four other features of contemporary politico-economic postmodernity date from the 1940s. The first is a prodigiously consumerist economy of affluence, initially confined to the United States, but later dispersed throughout the western world. The second is the increased centrality, within these consumerist economies, of the culture industries themselves, again initially in the United States, but later also more generally. At the international level, a third key structural novelty is provided by the rapid collapse of the older European empires and the development of new trans-national cultural and economic forms. All three of these were in turn overshadowed and underpinned, at a fourth level, by a dynamically expansionist global hypermilitarism, most visibly represented in nuclear weapons systems, but also seen in the more general growth of high-tech military and industrial capacities. This, then, is our starting point: a distinction between postmodernism as culture and postmodernity as political economy, a definition of postmodernism as the successor culture to a chronologically prior modernism, and a periodisation that specifies the postmodern era as coextensive with the postwar era.

Postmodernism, cultural politics and cultural theory

If postmodernism is not a specific type of cultural theory, then nor is it a specific type of politics. It is, rather, a particular cultural space available for analysis to many different kinds of contemporary cultural theory, and for intervention to many different kinds of contemporary cultural politics. As Michèle Barrett has observed: 'postmodernism is not something that you can be for or against: the reiteration of old knowledges will not make it vanish . . . it is a cultural climate as well as an intellectual position, a political reality as well as an academic fashion' (Barrett, 1999, p. 156). The term is best understood, then, as denoting a 'cultural dominant', in Jameson's phrase, or even, in Williams' terms, a 'structure of feeling'. At this most general of levels, it is quite simply the dominant culture of the postwar West. In this sense, Habermas' sustained polemic against the implied neo-conservatism of French post-structuralism (Habermas, 1987) can be read as an intervention within postmodernism as much as an argument against it. There was even less point, then, in Callinicos' argument *against* the very idea of postmodernism than in Lukács' earlier arguments against the substance of modernism. As Fehér asked, echoing Huyssen, 'who wants to become the Lukács of postmodernism?' (Fehér, 1990, p. 92; cf. Huyssen, 1988, p. 200).

Yet a complication appears to enter as we acknowledge not only that some cultural theory affects to be itself 'postmodernist', but also that some postmodernist art has been very much aware of postmodernist theory and has even sought to position itself in relation to the latter. Here we need to insist that it is perfectly possible to disagree with postmodernist theories of culture or of society, but to accept that important instances in our cultural life are indeed postmodern. Such disagreement remains tenable, moreover, even when postmodernist art has self-consciously sought to position itself in relation to postmodernist theory. Art is as able to make good use of bad theory as of what some would see as 'heretical' or 'idolatrous' religions, 'false' or 'incorrect' political doctrines. The mere fact that we live in a postmodern culture and enjoy postmodernist art does not in itself require us to agree with postmodernist cultural theory. Here we should register—if only in order to then reject—the commonplace conflation of post-modernism with post-structuralism. There is, of course, a certain 'fit' between the kind of post-structuralist theoretical relativism we explored in previous chapters and the kind of social and cultural pluralism many commentators find distinctive of our contemporary postmodern condition. But the two are by no means synonymous. Where post-structuralism represents a particular line of development from within semiology towards what we have termed 'difference theory', postmodernism is better understood as a much more specific attempt to define the novelty of our contemporary cultural condition. Indeed, the major post-structuralist thinkers were often quite uninterested in the latter debate. In general, French post-structuralism was far too pre-occupied with the high modernist canon to accord much serious attention to a contemporary culture that acquired an increasingly postmodern complexion: both Barthes' writerly texts and Kristeva's poetic revolution were modernist rather than post-modernist in character; insofar as Foucault could envisage a 'post-modern' episteme, it was that inaugurated by high struct-uralism itself (Foucault, 1973a, pp. 385–6); Guattari specifically rejected postmodernism because of its cynicism and conservatism (Guattari, 1986).

Andreas Huyssen, Professor of German and Comparative Literature at Columbia University, argued that 'rather than offering a *theory of postmodernity* and developing an analysis of contemporary culture, French theory provides us primarily with an *archaeology of modernity*, a theory of modernism at the stage of its exhaustion' (Huyssen, 1988, p. 209). Lash was surely right, then, in his early attempts at a sociology of postmodernism, to insist that there was no necessary parallel between post-structuralism and postmodernism, nor, conversely, between critical theory and anti-postmodernism (Lash, 1990, p. 153). Much of the debate over postmodernity was in fact conducted within an explicitly historicist theoretical framework, deriving at least as much from German critical theory, or its emigré American sub-variants, as from any kind of post-structuralism. This is true, for example, of writers as diverse as Zygmunt Bauman, Daniel Bell, Peter Bürger, Habermas, Huyssen himself, Jameson, Heller and

Fehér. It is even true, albeit to a lesser extent, of the two most famously postmodernist of cultural theorists: the late Jean-François Lyotard (1924–98), Professor of Philosophy at the University of Paris, Vincennes, and later of French at the University of California, Irvine, and, by turn, at Emory University; and Jean Baudrillard, for many years Professor of Sociology at Paris, Nanterre. We turn to their work very shortly. In the meantime, however, let us briefly explore the vexed question of the relationship between modernism, postmodernism and popular culture.

MODERNISM, POSTMODERNISM AND THE POPULAR

Thus far we have characterised modernism—and by extension postmodernism—primarily by way of their antithetical relationship to a predecessor culture of bourgeois realism. But we should note that modernism also stood in a similarly antagonistic relation to contemporary 'mass' or 'popular' culture. This is especially significant to our understanding of postmodernism, for however else we might care to characterise postmodernity, there is little doubt that postmodernist art typically attempted, or at least resulted from, precisely the collapse of this antithesis between high and low, elite and popular. This boundary, as much as any other, is what is transgressed in postmodern culture.

Elite and popular culture in pre-modern and early-modern societies

Relatively distinct elite and popular cultures almost invariably arise from the combination of structured social inequality and the cultural technology of writing. It is only in relatively classless, tribal societies that one finds relatively unitary oral cultures (and even these are internally differentiated by age and gender). Once writing becomes available, cultural differentiation becomes virtually unavoidable, since writing is, as Williams observed, 'wholly dependent on forms of specialized training, not only . . . for producers but also, and crucially, for receivers' (Williams, 1981, p. 93). Despite much literary-humanist and sociological speculation to the contrary, the historical and anthropological record actually provides very little evidence for the view that traditional, pre-modern, literate cultures were unitary. The literary canon was never, in fact, the expression of the spirit of a 'people', but rather the product and possession of an extremely small and socially exclusive cultural elite. As late as 1839, only 58.4% of those married in Britain were able to sign the marriage register (Williams, 1965, p. 187): it seems unlikely that many of this illiterate majority would have had much taste for Metaphysical poetry.

Truly popular, pre-modern cultures were primarily non-literate, oral and 'folkish', and the record we have of them is often both imprecise and patchy. That they were significantly differentiated from contemporaneous elite cultures seems, though, almost certain to be the case. We can be rather more definite about elite cultures. In pre-modern Europe, these were overwhelmingly defined, constructed and regulated either by the church or by the court. If the former had a popular dimension, the latter by and large did not. And even then, popular Catholicism was very often distinctly heretical and normally distinctly heterogeneous: it was never a part of the seamless web of some ideal Christian social organism. The new, more fully modern cultures of the eighteenth and nineteenth centuries—or at least what was distinctively modern about them—were quintessentially 'bourgeois' in form: democratic, realistic and prosaic. The exemplary instance here is the rise of the realist novel. Formally democratic though the realist novel might have been, it was not, however, a truly popular literary form: in the eighteenth century, the 'price of a novel . . . would feed a family for a week or two' (Watt, 1957, p. 43). Throughout the eighteenth century, and across Europe, print runs were generally still well below 2000; by way of contrast, Orwell's *Nineteen Eighty-Four* sold 360,000 copies in the United States and 50,000 in Britain during its first year of publication in 1949–50 (Febvre & Martin, 1976, p. 220; Crick, 1980, p. 393).

High modernism and mass popular culture

It is only in the late nineteenth century, in fact, that we are able to observe the more or less simultaneous emergence of the new modernist high culture and a new mass popular culture. The new modernism was characterised by aesthetic self-consciousness, the new mass culture by the rapid development of a whole range of technically novel cultural forms, each in principle near universally available (yellow journalism, penny dreadfuls and later paperback fiction, radio, cinema, and so on). Whenever we date the precise beginnings of modernism, there can be no doubt that high modernism and mass culture were roughly contemporaneous. However we characterise the cultural avant-garde, there can be little doubt that both modernism and the avant-garde stood in essentially adversarial relation, to bourgeois realism, and to mass culture.

Bürger himself argued that bourgeois art consisted of a celebration in form of the liberation of art from religion, from the court, and eventually even from the bourgeoisie (Bürger, 1984, pp. 46–9). Modernist art thus emerged as an autonomous social 'institution', the preserve and prerogative of an increasingly autonomous intellectual class, and thereby necessarily counterposed to other non-autonomous arts. As the memory of bourgeois realism receded, it was hostility to contemporary popular culture in particular that developed into perhaps the most characteristic of topoi, or stock themes, in twentieth-century intellectual life. Sometimes this hostility is explicit and overt, as in the Leavisite opposition between mass civilisation and minority culture (of which Eliot's modernism was a central instance) or the Frankfurt School's between the culture industries and autonomous art. Sometimes it is covert, as in the structuralist distinction between readerly and writerly texts, the text of *plaisir* and the text of *jouissance*. Whether as degraded culture for the conservative intelligentsia or as manipulated culture for the radical intelligentsia, mass culture remained the Other, or at least an Other, of modernist high culture.

Postmodernism and popular culture

Which brings us to postmodernism. For whatever else they might disagree about, almost all the available theorisations of postmodernism, whether celebratory or condemnatory, whether or not themselves postmodernist, agree on the centrality of the progressive deconstruction and dissolution of what was once, in Bourdieu's phrase, the 'distinction' between high and low culture. Indeed, Huyssen even went so far as to locate postmodernism quite specifically 'after the great divide' between modernism and mass culture. It operates in a field of tension, he argued, 'between tradition and innovation, conservation and renewal, mass culture and high art, in which the second terms are no longer automatically privileged over the first' (Huyssen, 1988, pp. 216–17).

A few brief examples will serve to illustrate the extent to which this view is echoed elsewhere. For Lyotard, the postmodern 'incredulity towards metanarratives', or grand stories, necessarily extended not only to the metanarratives of science and politics, but also to that of art as enlightenment. And if art is no longer necessarily enlightenment, then it has no special claim to make against mere popular culture. For Baudrillard, postmodernity is characterised by 'the disappearance of aesthetics and higher values in kitsch and hyperreality . . . the disappearance of history and the real in the televisual' (Baudrillard, 1988a, p. 101). For Bürger, postmodernism was initiated by the failure of the historical avant-garde to subvert from within the cultural institutions of high modernism, a failure that resulted in the final loss of criteria for determining the paradigmatic work of art (Bürger, 1984, p. 63) and, hence, in a loss of criteria for distinguishing between high art and popular non-art. For Lash, postmodernist 'de-differentiation' informed the transgression 'between literature and theory, between high and popular culture, between what is properly cultural and properly social' (Lash, 1990, pp. 173–4). For Jameson, postmodernism is characterised above all by 'an effacement of the older distinction between high and so-called mass culture' (Jameson, 1991, p. 63). For Huyssen, postmodernism had 'revitalized the impetus of the historical avant-garde', but only so as to deliver it over to a 'withering' quasi-populist critique (Huyssen, 1995, p. 17).

CELEBRATING POSTMODERNISM: LYOTARD AND BAUDRILLARD

As a major academic event, postmodernism dates from the late 1970s, from the first publication of Lyotard's *La Condition postmoderne*, prepared originally for the Conseil des Universités of the Government of Quebec (Lyotard, 1984). The concept was by no means an original coinage, however. To the contrary, Lyotard's argument had been quite deliberately inserted into an already existing North American discourse. As he explained: 'the word *postmodern* . . . is in current use on the American continent among sociologists and critics' (p. xxiii). The most important of Lyotard's American sources was Daniel Bell, then Professor of Sociology at Harvard University, whose *The Coming of Post-Industrial Society* (Bell, 1973) figured in the very first footnote. Bell had argued that modernism represented a radically 'adversary culture', opposed not merely to this particular society but to any and all conceivable societies. According to Bell, the development of the capitalist economic system had rendered its older Puritan values obsolete, thereby unleashing an increasingly unrestrained modernism, the simultaneous product of Hobbesian individualism and corporate economics (Bell, 1976, pp. 80–1, 84). The 'postmodernism' of the 1960s—and this was the term he used—had finally subverted all restraints: 'It is a programme to erase all boundaries, to obliterate any distinction between the self and the external world, between man and woman, subject and object, mind and body' (Bell, 1977, p. 243). 'In doctrine and cultural life-style', he concluded, 'the anti-bourgeois has won . . . The difficulty in the West . . . is that bourgeois society—which in its emphasis on individuality and the self gave rise to modernism—is itself culturally exhausted' (pp. 250–2).

Periodising postmodernism: Lyotard and Baudrillard

Bell's argument was in essence a translation into North American idiom of the cultural pessimism of German *Kulturkritik*. Translated back into French, the debate soon acquired a more optimistic tenor. For where Bell had found licence, Lyotard would soon cry liberty, both meaning in effect transgression, in the sense of a continuous disturbance or subversion of pre-existing cultural norms. For Lyotard this led to an essentially celebratory account of postmodernism as a technocratic liberal-individualist utopia. Baudrillard's reading of the postmodern contained similarly utopian elements, but was less unambiguously 'celebratory', even if on occasion it was described as such (Grossberg, 1996, p. 133). There is much in common, nonetheless, between their two accounts. Both Lyotard and Baudrillard commenced from a logic of periodisation, in which the 'postmodern' (for Lyotard) or the 'hyperreal' (for Baudrillard) had succeeded to and proceeded from a past understood as modern, industrial and capitalist. Both also sought to explain postmodern culture as the historical effect of changes in the system of economic production. For Lyotard, 'the status of knowledge is altered as societies enter . . . the postindustrial age' (Lyotard, 1984, p. 3). For Baudrillard, the shift from industrial production to the hyperreal 'simulations' of the media economy is an effect of '*capital itself*' (Baudrillard, 1993, p. 8).

Once the postmodern stage had been achieved, however, the cultural 'superstructures' became dominant over what had once been the economic 'base'. For Lyotard, 'flexible networks of language games' predominate over postindustrial postmodernity (Lyotard, 1984, p. 17), both in its 'normal' functioning and in the utopian possibilities immanent within it. Hence the aspiration to language games 'of perfect information at any given moment' (p. 67). For Baudrillard, the real economy has now been superseded by an 'order no longer of the real, but of the hyperreal' (Baudrillard, 1993, p. 3). Hence his conclusion that 'the real message . . . *lay in reproduction itself.* Production itself has no meaning: its social finality is lost' (p. 56).

Lyotard on the decline of the grand narrative

In *The Postmodern Condition* Lyotard had characterised modernism and modernity by the co-presence of science and a series of universalising and legitimating metanarratives, deriving ultimately from the Enlightenment. These metanarrative paradigms had run aground, he argued, in the period since the Second World

War: 'In contemporary society and culture—postindustrial society, postmodern culture—the . . . grand narrative has lost its credibility, regardless of what mode of unification it uses, regardless of whether it is a speculative narrative or a narrative of emancipation'. The postmodern incredulity towards metanarratives, whether in aesthetics or science or politics, was, for Lyotard, in part a consequence of the internal logic of the metanarratives themselves, which tended to proceed from scepticism to pluralism. But it was also a correlate of postindustrialism, since knowledge itself had now become a principal form of production, thereby, according to Lyotard, shifting emphasis 'from the ends of action to its means' (Lyotard, 1984, p. 37).

His slightly later essay, 'What is Postmodernism?', recapitulated much of this earlier analysis, but abandoned the initial attempt at cultural periodisation (p. 79). Here, the postmodern continued to be understood as that which 'denies itself the solace of good forms, the consensus of a taste which would make it possible to share collectively the nostalgia for the unattainable; that which searches for new representations . . . in order to impart a strong sense of the unpresentable' (p. 81). The postmodern, he declared, will 'wage a war on totality', that 'transcendental illusion' of the nineteenth century, the full price of which has proven to be 'terror' (pp. 81–2). For Lyotard, then, the nineteenth-century dream of 'totality' had given birth to the twentieth-century nightmare of totalitarianism.

Baudrillard on simulacra and simulation

Baudrillard uses the term 'simulacrum' to mean a sign without a referent, 'never exchanged for the real, but exchanged for itself'; and 'simulation' to mean the processual aspects of simulacra, or the non-referential equivalent of representation (Baudrillard, 1994, p. 6). He argued that there had been a succession of three orders of simulacra since the Renaissance—the natural, the productive, and 'the simulacra of simulation', respectively. The first of these need not concern us here. But the shift from the second order, which was founded on industrial manufacture, to the third, founded on information and characterised by hyperreality

(p. 121), provides the Baudrillardian counterpart to Lyotard's shift from modernity and postmodernity. In this new world of the mass media, wrote Baudrillard: 'Simulation is . . . the generation by models of a real without origin or reality: a hyperreal' (p. 1). The resulting 'implosion of meaning' implies the 'end of the social' and the decline of the political, since what is true of signs in general is true of political signs in particular. For Baudrillard, then, both the rational liberal individual subject and the class-conscious collective subject cease to function: 'there is no longer any social signified to give force to a political signifier' (Baudrillard, 1983, p. 19). The one still functional referent is 'the silent majority', or 'the masses'. But since their existence is merely statistical rather than social, they function only as an imaginary referent for the simulations of the media (pp. 19–20).

It follows that in the most fundamental of senses, the media and the masses imply each other: 'Mass(age) is the message' (p. 44). This mutual implication of masses and media is, for Baudrillard, a matter neither of manipulation nor of democratisation, a cause neither for hope nor for regret (Baudrillard, 1988, p. 207). To the contrary, the inertia of the masses is precisely their strength: '*the masses are a stronger medium than all the media*' (Baudrillard, 1983, p. 44). Hence his conclusion that since 'the system' itself aims to maximise speech, meaning and participation, the 'actual strategy of the masses', their strategic resistance, is that of 'the refusal of meaning and the refusal of speech' (Baudrillard, 1988, p. 219). The masses thereby become the repository of Baudrillard's hopes and expectations for 'a finally delusive, illusive, and allusive strategy', the 'correlative' of an 'ironic, joyful, and seductive unconscious' (p. 217). As with much in Baudrillard, it's not at all clear that this makes very much sense. What we can say, however, is that for all its apparently utopian gestures, this account actually gives rise to a developing political fatalism. The 'clearest result of the whole media environment', he concludes, is 'stupor . . . a radical uncertainty as to our own desire, our own choice, our own opinion, our own will' (p. 209). To suffer from stupor of this kind is to be a part of the 'masses', to be 'made up of . . . useless hyperinformation which claims to enlighten . . . when all it does is clutter up the space of the representable' (p. 211). It goes without saying that we are all, Baudrillard included, a part of the masses (p. 212).

By and large, contemporary cultural criticism has found Lyotard's celebration of postmodernity much more interesting than Bell's indictment. But note their common origins in a North American, rather than European, perception of the postmodern as at once uniquely contemporary and uniquely transgressive. Lyotard's various accounts of the postmodern were stories told by a Frenchman, it is true, but told in the first place to Canadians. These American connotations have persisted, most obviously in the sense of the American present as an anticipation of Europe's near future. So, for Baudrillard, the Americans 'were a marginal transcendence of that Old World', but 'are today its new, eccentric centre . . . It will do us no good to worry our poor heads over this. In Los Angeles, Europe has disappeared' (Baudrillard, 1988a, p. 81). Which suggests that no matter how French its theoretical accents, postmodernism remains peculiarly visible from a New World, extra-European vantage point. Lyotard's tales were also, however, grand narratives of dissolution, bespeaking a political and cultural history more fraught than those endured by the European colonies of settlement in the Americas and Australasia. Modernity was thus quite specifically European, its transcendental illusions explicitly those of Hegel and Marx, its terrors those of Stalin and Hitler. Postmodernity is thus to modernity as the New World is to the Old, as California is to France, but also as the Californianisation of France and the Disneyfication of Paris.

POSTMODERNISM AND THE INTELLIGENTSIA

Whichever account of postmodernism we adopt, we should note that what is being charted is primarily an endogenous transformation, internal to post-elite culture itself, rather than to any wider, mass or popular culture. Postmodernism has doubtless entered the vocabulary of popular style, much as did French existentialism, for example, in the years immediately after the Second World War (Heller, 1990). But such popular borrowings from elite or, in this case, 'quasi-elite' cultures are by no means in themselves peculiarly postmodernist: as we have seen, parodic borrowings from elite culture were a characteristic feature of the medieval 'carnivalesque' (Bakhtin, 1965). Postmodernism proper is neither a popular culture nor, in any sense that Leavis or even Williams might have understood, a common culture. Postmodernism might well 'quote' from mass culture, but it is not in itself a popular culture: Campbell's soup is indeed a mass commodity, but Andy Warhol's famous oil and silk-screen prints of Campbell's soup cans are not. What postmodernism provides us with, then, is an index of the range and extent of the western intelligentsia's own internal crisis, its collective crisis of faith in its own previously proclaimed redemptive functions, whether conservative or adversarial.

The social functions of intellectuals

Historically, most cultural institutions have been staffed by Gramscian 'traditional' intellectuals. But their pretensions to cultural authority have also been replicated by counter-cultural intelligentsias, such as those associated in the early twentieth century with both the literary and artistic avant-garde and the revolutionary political party. It is the collapse of such pretensions, whether traditional, avant-garde or vanguardist, that most clearly marks the moment of postmodernism. Certain aspects of this collective crisis of faith were no doubt very specific: to the European intellectual confronted by America; to the literary intellectual confronted by the mass media; to the male intellectual confronted by the rise of feminism. But their sum added up to a Jamesonian 'cultural dominant', rather than to any particular literary or artistic style. Indeed, the effort to define a distinctively postmodernist style serves only to remind us of the latter's deeply derivative relationship to high modernism. It is the general crisis of faith, rather than any particular set of cultural techniques, that is truly defining. Here, Zygmunt Bauman's distinction between the role of the intellectual as legislator and as interpreter, and his account of how the latter function progressively displaces the former, becomes instructive (Bauman, 1992, pp. 1–24). As

Bauman concluded: 'The postmodernity/modernity opposition focuses on the waning of certainty . . . grounded in the unquestioned hierarchy of values . . . and on the transition to a situation characterized by a coexistence or armistice between values' (p. 24).

The central social functions of the postwar, postmodern western intelligentsia have, then, become primarily interpretive rather than legislative. The novelty of this situation was registered both in Foucault's distinction between the 'universal' and 'specific' intellectual and in the only limited applicability of the Gramscian distinction between 'traditional' and 'organic' intellectuals to the cultural sociology of the postwar West. No doubt, there are still Gramscian traditional intellectuals at work within the clergy or the judiciary, perhaps even within academia. No doubt there are still Gramscian organic intellectuals: the bourgeoisie have their economists, engineers and accountants, the proletariat its trade union officials and labour politicians. Gramsci, however, clearly envisaged both kinds of intellectual as performing an essentially legislative or universal function, whereas the dominant role of each has become primarily interpretive and specific. If the changing role and self-perception of the western intelligentsia is indeed central to this postmodernist reorientation of cultural discourse, as Bauman argued, then the very generality of that reorientation suggests the possibility that postmodernist culture might have deep structural roots in some distinctively postmodern socio-political reality.

The sociological debate: postmodernism or late modernity?

In the dominant sociological theorisations of these deep structural roots there has been a tendency to subsume the rupture between modernism and postmodernism into some more gradual process by which an earlier modernity evolved into a later. Different variants of this formulation can be observed in the work of: Ulrich Beck, Professor of Sociology at the University of Munich; Anthony Giddens, Director of the London School of Economics; and Scott Lash, Director of the Centre for Cultural Studies at Goldsmiths College, London. For Beck, this latest stage is the 'risk society', a 'reflexive modernization', which also represents a 'radicalization of modernity' (Beck, 1994, pp. 2–3; cf. Beck, 1992). For Giddens, it is 'late modernity', a similarly reflexive 'post-traditional society', in which globalisation 'disembeds' the 'traditional contexts of action', so that 'lifestyle and taste' become 'as evident markers of social differentiation as position in the productive order' (Giddens, 1994, pp. 95–6; Giddens, 1994a, p. 143; cf. Giddens, 1991). More interesting than either is Lash's notion of aesthetic modernity as a 'second modernity', contemporaneous with the rationalism of the first, but based on reflexivity and difference, rather than the rationality of the same (Lash, 1999, pp. 3–4). The distinctively 'postmodern' moment—though this is not Lash's preferred term—arrived when both modernities were superseded, in the 'multimediatized cultural space' of the global information culture, by a new world order, at once post-national, post-human and even post-western, in which human subjectivities become equal with 'animals, things, machines, nature and other objects' (pp. 11–14). The result is not so much difference as *in*difference.

'This is the scenario ever repeated in turn-of-the-twenty-first-century popular culture', writes Lash: 'there is no longer a constitutive outside', only 'a swirling vortex of microbes, genes, desire, death, onco-mice, semiconductors, holograms, semen, digitized images, electronic money and hyperspaces in a general economy of indifference' (p. 344). As impressionistic description, this is suggestive. As evaluation, however, it is excessively melancholic; as explanation, near vacuous. As Bauman observed of a similar blend of melancholia and 'hyperreal' excess in Baudrillard: 'there is life after and beyond television', and for many, 'reality remains what it always used to be: tough, solid, resistant and harsh' (Bauman, 1992, p. 155). Bauman too is a sociologist, Emeritus Professor of Sociology at the Universities of Leeds and Warsaw in fact, but unlike Beck, Giddens and Lash, he has remained fully committed to the notion of a sociology of the postmodern. The problem here is with his overly individualised understanding of what the postmodern might comprise.

As we have seen, Bauman's early formulations had defined the opposition between modernity and postmodernity primarily in relation to the pluralisation of values. More recently, however, he has tended to gloss this pluralism as freedom. Postmodern men and women, he argues, have:

> *exchanged a portion of their possibilities of security for a portion of happiness.* The discontents of modernity arose from a kind of security which tolerated too little freedom in the pursuit of individual happiness. The discontents of postmodernity arise from a kind of freedom of pleasure-seeking which tolerates too little individual security (Bauman, 1997, p. 3).

That a Jewish exile from Communist Poland should read totalitarianism as 'thoroughly modern' (p. 12) is barely surprising (cf. Bauman, 1989). But, as with Adorno and Foucault, this understanding of modernity radically underestimates the difference between modern liberal democracies, no matter how flawed, and their totalitarian adversaries.

That Bauman should then read postmodernity as an ethical opportunity is similarly unsurprising. He is, of course, right to insist that '*postmodernity is the moral person's bane and chance at the same time*'; that '*which of the two faces of the postmodern condition will turn out to be its lasting likeness, is itself a moral question*' (Bauman, 1995, p. 8). But this was also true of modernity, and in both instances the question might be construed with equal plausibility to be political, rather than moral. The difference between modernity and postmodernity surely cannot be read as that between the differential availabilities either of moral choice or, still less, freedom and security. For security is a kind of freedom and freedom a kind of security. What changed was not so much the mix between the one and the other, but rather the social distribution of both, globally and nationally. At one level, Bauman knows this: he writes wisely that, as '*flawed consumers*', the poor 'are the new "impure" . . . redundant—"truly objects out of place"' (Bauman, 1997, p. 14). But he prefers to think in terms of patterns of individual choice, rather than in terms of the social structures that determine those patterns.

At this structural level, the crucial issues are surely globalisation, on the one hand, and universal commodification, on the other. The fate of the avant-garde, and the concomitant shift from modernist to postmodernist art, functioned historically as key early warning signals as to how these two processes would eventually combine to threaten what most people in the West had previously understood not only by 'culture', but also by 'society'. Which might help to explain why the most persuasive and influential account to date of the deep structural roots of postmodernism should have come, not from sociology at all, but from literary and cultural studies, in the shape of Fredric Jameson, Professor of Comparative Literature at Duke University. This has been so, we suspect, precisely because the sociologists had tended to underestimate the more general social significance of the specifically aesthetic aspects of post-*modernism*.

MAPPING POSTMODERNISM: JAMESON

Jameson is a key figure in contemporary cultural theory, the most important exponent of North American critical theory after Marcuse. Indeed, a good case could be made for his inclusion in our third chapter, alongside Habermas and Bourdieu. But despite a long and distinguished career as literary theorist and critic, Jameson is still best known for his theory of postmodernism. His various essays on the subject have become standard references (Jameson, 1984; Jameson, 1985; Jameson, 1988a; Jameson, 1994; Jameson, 1998); and his full-length study, *Postmodernism, or the Cultural Logic of Late Capitalism*, is for many the *locus classicus* of the postmodern debate. As Anderson rightly observes, Jameson's work has 'set the terms of subsequent debate' (Anderson, 1998, p. 78).

Jameson and cultural theory

Jameson's earliest intellectual interests were in existentialism and contemporary French literature, but he was attracted to the New Left during the 1960s and thence to German critical theory. His initial reputation as a critic was established by two books published in the early 1970s, both concerned at least as much with French as with German theory (Jameson, 1971; Jameson, 1972).

Over time, however, the German theorists, especially Lukács, Adorno and Brecht, came to occupy an increasingly prominent place in his thinking. For Jameson, the key concept in Hegelian dialectics, which distinguished western critical theory from Soviet Marxism, was what Lukács had termed 'totality', Sartre 'totalisation'. 'There is no content, for dialectical thought', Jameson wrote, 'but total content' (Jameson, 1971, p. 306).

His most influential work of literary criticism was *The Political Unconscious*, which prompted Hayden White to describe him as 'the best socially-oriented critic of our time'. This was Jameson's most Lukácsian work and also, perhaps, his most theoretically original. Here he developed a systematic outline of a 'totalising' critical method capable of subsuming other apparently incompatible critical methods by 'at once canceling and preserving them' (Jameson, 1981, p. 10). He argued that the object of inquiry for cultural analysis could be located at any of three analytically distinct levels: 'text', 'ideologeme' and 'ideology of form'. Each of these has its socio-historical corollary in an equivalent 'semantic horizon', respectively: 'political history', in the sense of a chronicle-like sequence of events; 'society'; and global 'history', in the sense of a sequence and succession of modes of production (pp. 75–6). By 'ideologeme', Jameson meant the kind of collective discourse in relation to which texts function as 'little more than . . . individual *parole* or utterance'. Since 'society' could be characterised for Jameson primarily in terms of class struggle, then it followed that the ideologeme should be defined as 'the smallest intelligible unit of the essentially antagonistic collective discourses of social classes' (p. 76). Class thus became one of the key analytical tools in his critical method, providing the occasion for a 'double hermeneutic', which simultaneously embraced both the negative hermeneutic of ideology-critique and the positive of a 'non-instrumental conception of culture' (p. 286). In short, all class consciousness is a matter both of ideology and of utopia.

Postmodernism and late capitalism

The range of Jameson's cultural reference, from architecture to video, from conceptual art to dystopian cinema, is at its most impressive in his writing on postmodernism. Here he applies a double hermeneutic of his own to postmodernism, understood as something very close to an ideologeme. Jameson posited a historical periodisation, deriving in part from Ernest Mandel's *Late Capitalism* (Mandel, 1975), according to which there were three main stages in the history of capitalism, each accompanied by a characteristic 'cultural dominant': aesthetic realism was the cultural dominant of nineteenth-century 'market capitalism'; modernism of early twentieth-century 'monopoly capitalism' and postmodernism of contemporary multinational 'late capitalism' (Jameson, 1991, pp. 35–6). For Jameson, class consciousness presupposed the 'narrative figurability' of class inequalities, their representability 'in tangible form' (Jameson, 1992, pp. 37–8). But the capacity for such representation becomes progressively attenuated, he would conclude, as monopoly capitalism evolved into global capitalism, modernism into postmodernism: 'In our own postmodern world there is no longer a bourgeois or class-specific culture . . . but rather a system-specific phenomenon: the various forms which reification and commodification and the corporate standardizations of media society imprint on human subjectivity and existential experience' (Jameson, 1992a, p. 131).

If late capitalism is 'the purest form of capital yet to have emerged, a prodigious expansion of capital into hitherto uncommodified areas' (Jameson, 1991, p. 36), then art itself is one of these hitherto largely uncommodified areas, postmodernism the form of its commodification. 'What has happened', Jameson wrote, 'is that aesthetic production . . . has become integrated into commodity production generally' (p. 4). Postmodernism is thus inherently a commodity culture, distinguishable from earlier modernisms as much by its 'resonant affirmation . . . of the market' as by any distinctive style (p. 305). Hence its aesthetic populism: one of its most fundamental features, he argued, is an 'effacement . . . of the older (essentially high modernist) frontier between high culture and so-called mass or commercial culture, and the emergence of new kinds of texts infused with the forms, categories and contents of that very Culture Industry so passionately denounced by all ideologues of the Modern'. Postmodernist art is thus 'fascinated by this whole "degraded" landscape of schlock and kitsch, of

TV series and Readers' Digest culture, of advertising and motels, of the late show and the grade-B Hollywood film' (p. 2).

As a thoroughgoing commodity culture, postmodernism can have no defining normative standards of its own: its value is what it will fetch in the market. It is therefore a 'field of stylistic and discursive heterogeneity without a norm'. In consequence, parody, which assumes such norms, has been progressively effaced by pastiche, which does not. Both involve imitation, Jameson explains, but pastiche is a 'neutral practice of such mimicry, without any of parody's ulterior motives, amputated of satiric impulse, devoid of . . . any conviction that alongside the abnormal tongue you have momentarily borrowed, some healthy linguistic normality still exists' (p. 17). In the absence of any truly distinct, contemporary style, postmodernism becomes 'the random cannibalization of all the styles of the past' (p. 18). The result is a 'waning of . . . historicity', so that 'the past as "referent" finds itself gradually bracketed, and then effaced altogether, leaving us with nothing but texts' (pp. 21, 18). Discussing contemporary cinema's use of earlier novels and films, Jameson argued that 'our awareness of the preexistence of other versions . . . is now a constitutive and essential part of the film's structure: we are now . . . in "intertextuality" as a deliberate, built-in feature of the aesthetic effect' (p. 20).

Globalisation and cognitive mapping

Jameson also stressed the radically internationalising nature of socio-economic postmodernity, that is, late capitalism's peculiarly global character. There is now a world capitalist system, he concluded, as distinct from the previous set of competing colonial empires. The new system and the new culture is thus simultaneously post-European, 'American' and global: 'it was the brief "American century" (1945–73)', he wrote, 'that constituted the hothouse, or forcing ground, of the new system, while the development of the cultural forms of postmodernism may be said to be the first specifically North American global style' (p. x). Moreover, Jameson was clear that there is something 'progressive' about this 'original new global space' that is 'the "moment of truth" of postmodernism' (p. 49). A fully contemporary version of what the young Lukács had meant by class consciousness would therefore need to apprehend precisely this moment of truth. But in a culture so commodified, so subject to the logic of the simulacrum, what becomes of class consciousness? At one level, the answer is obvious. If its emergence requires that the realities of class structure become representable, then the widening rift between sign and referent will tend to produce formidable structural inhibitors to its development: 'For a society that wants to forget about class . . . reification . . . is very functional indeed' (p. 315).

Since the emergence of class consciousness has been structurally pre-empted, the capacity to map or model 'the system' either disappears altogether or must temporarily lie elsewhere. That elsewhere is located somewhere between critical theory and a hypothetically postmodern political art. For this was Jameson's solution to the temporary absence of class consciousness from postmodern late capitalism: to posit the need for an 'aesthetic of cognitive mapping', through which to learn how to represent 'the truth of postmodernism—that is . . . the world space of multinational capital' and so 'again begin to grasp our positioning as individual and collective subjects' (Jameson, 1991, p. 54). Cognitive mapping, he explained, is in reality a 'code word' for class consciousness 'of a new and hitherto undreamed of kind', which has not yet come into being. Hence the sense of his own work as the anticipation in theory of what might eventually become class consciousness—as an experiment 'to see whether by systematizing something that is resolutely unsystematic, and historicizing something that is resolutely ahistorical, one couldn't outflank it and force a historical way at least of thinking about that' (p. 418).

Jameson and Adorno

At this point, Adorno's special significance for Jameson becomes apparent. For despite its American idiom, Jameson's rhetorical and theoretical strategy is clearly reminiscent of the Frankfurt School. Adorno and Horkheimer had initially imagined their critical theory as aligned with a proletarian opposition to fascism. But from the *Dialectic of Enlightenment*, at least, such emancipatory potential inhered in the immanent logic of critical theory itself. As Jameson noted, this eventually led Adorno to a kind of 'temperamental and cantankerous quietism' that proved a disabling liability at moments of popular politicisation (Jameson, 1990, p. 249). For Jameson himself, the 1960s had been 'the most politicized era in modern American social history' (Jameson, 1994, p. 68). But by the 1990s, Adorno 'in the postmodern' had become 'a joyous counter-poison and a corrosive solvent to apply to the surface of "what is"' (Jameson, 1990, p. 249). Like Adorno's, Jameson's critical theory functions by way of a great refusal, both of the increasingly totalised late-capitalist system and of the postmodernist ideologies that legitimate it. There is thus a certain grandeur to this intransigent resistance to the lures of commodity culture. And unlike Adorno, Jameson still clings to the formal certainty of an eventual return to class politics. In the meantime, however, class consciousness can exist only as cognitive mapping; that is, only *in theory*.

Jameson's central insight is contained in his dual emphasis on globalisation *and* commodification. Here he captured much of what is truly distinctive about contemporary culture. The more commodified that culture has become, the less plausible the intelligentsia's erstwhile pretensions to legislative cultural authority have appeared, both to themselves and to their prospective audiences. As Bauman observed: 'within the context of a consumer culture no room has been left for the intellectual as legislator. In the market, there is no one centre of power, nor any aspiration to create one . . . There is no site from which authoritative pronouncements could be made, and no power resources concentrated and exclusive enough to serve as the levers of a massive proselytizing campaign' (Bauman, 1987, p. 167). Nineteenth- and early twentieth-century conceptions, whether literary-critical, anthropological or sociological, had almost invariably envisaged culture not simply as distinct from economy and polity, but also as itself the central source of social cohesion: human society as such appeared inconceivable without culture. But it is so *now*: postmodern late capitalism is held together not by culture, understood as a normative value system, but rather by the market.

As Jameson writes: 'ideologies in the sense of codes and discursive systems are no longer particularly determinant . . . ideology . . . has ceased to be functional in perpetuating and reproducing the system' (Jameson, 1991, p. 398). In short, postmodern intellectual culture is at once both peculiarly normless and peculiarly hedonistic. The hedonism arises very directly from out of the commodity cultures of affluence, as they impinge on the wider society, and on the intelligentsia in particular. The normlessness, however, might well have its origins elsewhere: on the one hand, in a recurring apocalyptic motif within postwar culture, which must bear some more or less direct relation to the threat of nuclear extinction; and on the other, in the radically internationalising nature of postwar society and culture, which progressively detached erstwhile national intelligentsias from the national cultural 'canons' of which they had hitherto been the custodians.

THE POLITICS OF POSTMODERNISM

Early in 1996 the journal *Social Text* published 'Transgressing the Boundaries: Toward a Transformative Hermeneutics of Quantum Gravity', by Alan Sokal, Professor of Physics at New York University (Sokal, 1996). Supposedly a serious contribution to a special issue on 'Science Wars', the article was actually an elaborate hoax, intended to poke fun at postmodern epistemological relativism. A brief quotation should suffice to suggest its tone: 'The teaching of science and mathematics must be purged of its authoritarian and elitist characteristics, and the content of these subjects enriched by incorporating the insights of the feminist, queer, multiculturalist and ecological critiques' (p. 230). Sokal later collaborated with Jean Bricmont, Professor of Mathematics at the University of Louvain in Belgium, in a book-length critique of what they termed 'postmodern philosophers' abuse of science', published in French in 1997, in English a year later.

Sokal and Bricmont's *Intellectual Impostures*

Entitled *Intellectual Impostures*, this book made no distinction between postmodernism and post-structuralism, which were even defined so as to include structuralism (Sokal & Bricmont, 1998, pp. 11–12). It contained only a very brief discussion of Lyotard, whole chapters on Lacan, Kristeva, Irigaray, Baudrillard, Deleuze and Guattari, but nothing substantial on Lévi-Strauss or Barthes, Foucault or Derrida. Sokal and Bricmont's main target was the supposedly widespread notion among English-speaking devotees of French theory that 'modern science is nothing more than a "myth", a "narration" or a "social construction", among many others' (p. x). Their argument was not intended as a generalised polemic either against the humanities or against political radicalism. Indeed, they either acknowledged assistance from or quoted with approval such prominent humanities radicals as Bourdieu, Eagleton and Noam Chomsky, the anarchist Professor of Linguistics at the Massachusetts Institute of Technology (pp. xiii, 187, 189). Rather, their polemic took as its object something much more specific: 'intellectual confusion' (p. xii).

It is difficult to dispute these natural scientists' right to defend their disciplines against what they saw as a misappropriation of key terms and concepts. So, for example, they judged Baudrillard's use of chaos theory a 'gradual crescendo of nonsense . . . high density scientific and pseudo-scientific terminology . . . in sentences that are . . . devoid of meaning' (pp. 141–2). And they found Deleuze guilty, in turn, of deploying valid technical terms in the service of an argument 'devoid of both logic and sense' (p. 156). The nonsense is not always so obviously nonsensical, however; sometimes it is simply non-scientific. So, for example, when they take Irigaray to task for her view that Einstein's $E = Mc^2$ is masculinist for 'having privileged what goes the fastest', they miss the point that the equation might indeed be masculinist, even if it is 'experimentally verified' (p. 100): the social genealogy of a proposition has no logical bearing on its truth value. Moreover, their later objection that to 'link rationality and objectivity to the male, and emotion and subjectivity to the female, is to repeat the most blatant sexist stereotypes' (p. 112) is obviously political, rather than scientific, in character. In short, they simply disagree with Irigaray's version of radical feminist politics. Similarly, when they object to her belief that the female 'sexual economy' is attuned to 'cyclic and cosmic rhythms', they object not to her use of science, but to her mysticism *per se* (pp. 112–13). We are neither radical feminists nor mystics and would readily accept the argument against a deliberate misuse of scientific terms. But we would add that politics and mysticism might often be, not so much opposed to science, as different from it.

Postmodernism and political radicalism: Sokal v. Jameson

For Sokal and Bricmont, postmodernism is symptomatic of a disorientation of radical politics in a situation where 'the communist regimes have collapsed; the social-democratic parties . . . apply watered-down neo-liberal policies; and the Third World movements . . . have . . . abandoned any attempt at autonomous development' (p. 189). Hence the resort to relativism, by which the 'postmodern left' unintentionally deprives itself of 'a powerful instrument for criticizing the existing social order' (p. 191). Again this is a political rather than a scientific argument, though one with which we have some sympathy. Certainly, we have no wish to call into question their political radicalism: even Judith Butler has acknowledged, in an article originally published in *Social Text* itself, that 'the recent efforts to parody the cultural Left could not have happened if there were not this prior affiliation and intimacy' (Butler, 1999, p. 35). But we also note how the Sokal hoax has been transformed into an icon of conservative anti-intellectualism, no doubt against the intentions of its author, but nonetheless with a certain grim predictability. As Segal observed: 'few intellectual efforts are less politically productive, or more symptomatic of morbidity, than the attempts . . . to defend the supposedly "real" left against a phony "cultural" left' (Segal, 1999, p. 224).

When Sokal came to select the target for his hoax, it was perhaps unsurprising that the chosen journal should have been one Jameson helped found and co-edit. Yet there was an obvious irony in this. For if Jameson has indeed remained fascinated by the postmodern, there is no doubting the critical edge to that fascination, as registered at the very least in the distance between the appalled theorist and the 'extraordinarily demoralizing and depressing . . . new global space' he sought to theorise (Jameson, 1991, p. 49). Nor was there much doubting the critical vantage point from which this theorising had been mounted. One available response to the postmodernist insistence on the disconnectedness of social position and cultural identity is to treat it, not as an ontological or epistemological proposition, but as pertaining to the period culture of a specifically postmodern stage in human history. As Huyssen has it: 'the waning of historical consciousness is itself a historically explainable phenomenon' (Huyssen, 1995, p. 9).

This is exactly the view canvassed by Jameson. Hence the paradox that the work of this apparently postmodern thinker should have acquired an increasingly Adornian cast, as a kind of *Kulturpessimismus* for the 1990s. The paradox is more apparent than real, however, for if Jameson has been ready to concede the theoretical value of postmodernism and post-structuralism, it was only ever on the condition that critical theory 'must necessarily become true again when the dreary realities of exploitation . . . and the resistance to it in the form of class struggle . . . slowly reassert themselves' (Jameson, 1988a, p. 208). In the absence of an effective socialist movement, there was therefore an almost inescapable logic in Jameson's resort to Adorno and Horkheimer 'to restore the sense of something grim and impending within the polluted sunshine of the shopping mall' (Jameson, 1990, p. 248). This seems to us at least as honourably political a response to the postmodern condition as anything in Sokal and Bricmont.

The twin faces of postmodernism

Which takes us to the more general question of the politics of postmodernism. Bauman observes that the postmodern condition has two faces. This sense of Janus as the presiding god of postmodernity has been widespread in the postmodern debate, especially in discussions of cultural politics. Huyssen, for example, argued that postmodernist culture was at once both incorporated and oppositional, commodified and subversive, and concluded by invoking a 'postmodernism of resistance' against the 'postmodernism of the "anything goes" variety' (Huyssen, 1988, p. 220). Interestingly, he also noted how high modernism had established itself through an opposition to mass culture, which coded the latter 'as feminine and inferior' (p. 62). Hence feminism's contribution to an emergently postmodern 'problematic of "otherness"' (p. 219). Writing from a more explicitly feminist perspective, Ann Kaplan described these twin faces of postmodernism as, respectively, the 'commercial' and the 'utopian' (Kaplan, 1988, p. 4). In the first, the capitalist mass market deconstructed the binary opposition between elite and popular cultures; in the second, postmodern feminism that between masculinity and femininity. These vastly differing conceptions of the postmodern had coexisted in a single cultural space, she argued, because both responded to the cultural situation of the 1960s (p. 5).

Postmodernism and posthumanism

The Janus trope is evident, too, in the debates over posthumanism. For Lash is by no means alone in imagining the global information culture as potentially 'posthuman'. During the second half of the twentieth century, structuralist and post-structuralist semiologies and a range of new technologies for re-embodiment and dis-embodiment combined so as to radically decentre earlier humanist notions of the human. As Ihab Hassan observed a quarter of a century ago: 'five hundred years of humanism may be coming to an end, as humanism transforms itself into something that we must helplessly call posthumanism' (Hassan, 1977, p. 212). This has become an increasingly pressing theme in recent speculation located in the various theoretical spaces between cyberpunk and cyborgs, virtual reality and the Internet. The best-known of these is still *Simians, Cyborgs and Women* by Donna Haraway, Professor of History of Consciousness at the University of California at Santa Cruz. Claiming that we already live in a posthuman era, where machine and organism are already hybridised, she posited the 'cyborg' as a 'fiction mapping our social and bodily reality and as an imaginative resource' (Haraway, 1991, p. 150). 'The cyborg is a kind of disassembled and reassembled, postmodern collective and personal self', she argued: 'This is the self feminists must code' (p. 163). The feminist potential of such cyborg imagery should be readily apparent: 'The cyborg is a creature in a post-gender world', she wrote; its 'imagery can suggest a way out of the maze of dualisms in which we have explained our bodies and our tools to ourselves' (pp. 150, 181).

Like Huyssen and Kaplan, Haraway also noted the twin faces of posthumanism. 'From one perspective', she wrote, 'a cyborg world is about the final imposition of a grid of control on the planet, . . . about the final appropriation of women's bodies in a masculinist orgy of war'. But from another, she continued, it 'might be about lived social and bodily realities in which people are not afraid of their joint kinship with animals and machines, not afraid of permanently partial identities and contradictory standpoints'. No doubt she was right to conclude that 'each reveals both possibilities and dominations unimaginable from the other' (p. 154). And it is difficult not to be affected by her enthusiasm for the positive potential of science and technology. As she writes elsewhere: 'to "press enter" is not a fatal error, but an inescapable possibility for changing maps of the world . . . It's not a "happy ending" we need, but a non-ending' (Haraway, 1992, p. 327). Her alternative perspectives are not simply logical possibilities, however; they are also socio-historical potentials, the effectivity of which is conditioned by the balance of historical probabilities and social forces. And at this level, in the short term at least, endings do sometimes happen and they are as likely to be unhappy as happy.

Postmodernism and the collapse of traditional humanism

The coexistence of these twin faces of postmodernism is not so much a feature of the 1960s in particular as of the postwar period in general. It arose, moreover, as the effect of an absence rather than a presence. Where critical theorists have detected commodification and post-structuralists difference, we find both, connected to each other not by any positive content, such as the beneficence of the market, but by a negativity, that of the prior collapse of the high culture of the traditional intelligentsia. In itself this can easily be welcomed: neither traditional minority culture nor avant-garde modernism is in any obvious sense compatible with cultural democracy. But it remains an absence, or perhaps an opening, a space in which new options might be explored, others foreclosed, a problem rather than its resolution. When academic cultural theory bought into structuralism and post-structuralism, and into radically 'structuralist' versions of Marxism, it effectively gave up on its more traditionally 'culturalist' function of policing the boundaries of cultural authority. The relatively arcane language by which the manoeuvre was effected obscured its culturally populist import. But the import was real enough: the only boundaries academics tend to police these days are those of critical rigour itself, their only sacred texts theoretical ones.

At one level, all of this seems absolutely welcome. The older literary humanism had, by the time of its demise, ossified into an irredeemable elitism, its public face that of a near permanent sneer—at 'mass culture', at women's writing, at foreign literature, at creative writing, at community arts. Its version of a common culture can best be understood as an 'ideology', in the most pejorative of senses. But this is not the whole story. European Romanticism in general had developed by way of reaction against the European Enlightenment, British culturalism by way of reaction against utilitarian political economy. And in each case, it is the latter, rather than the former, that most properly characterises 'the dominant ideology'. The dominant classes and elites in societies like ours are still very much as Romanticism construed them: children of civilisation rather than culture, servants of utility rather than beauty, industry rather than art. By virtue of that very organicism that seems so reprehensibly monocultural to contemporary post-Marxist, post-structuralist, post-feminist, postmodernist sensibilities, these Romantic and post-Romantic conceptions of culture actually did set up deep resistances to the driving imperatives of a capitalist civilisation that was, in its dominant modes, utilitarian, competitive, acquisitive and individualistic.

Culture, economics and politics

Romantic and post-Romantic culturalisms envisaged culture not simply as separate from economy and polity, but also as in itself the central source of social cohesion: society was inconceivable without culture. They also, in one way or another, counterposed the claims of culture, understood as a repository of superior values, to utilitarian capitalist civilisation, understood as driven by the dynamics of profitable exchange. In these terms, postmodernism represents a triumph of civilisation over culture even in its utopian aspects. For it has been the commodity cultures of the market, rather than the alternative communities of the new social movements that have sustained the most explicitly commercial of postmodernisms and the radicalised cultures of difference. Let us be clear what is at stake here. Any society will possess some institutional arrangement or another for the regulation of symbolic artefacts and practices; in this sense, society is inconceivable without culture. But these institutions might themselves be either 'political', based on the ultimate threat of coercion wielded by the state; or 'economic', organised through commodity exchange in a more or less (normally less) competitive market; or 'cultural', in the 'culturalist' sense, based on theoretically (though often not actually) consensual arrangements for the generation of authoritative, but not in fact politically coercive, judgements of value.

Official Communist aesthetics provided us with an extreme instance of the first, contemporary postmodernism the second. But most cultures have been much more properly 'cultural'. The old literary humanist common culture was neither common nor consensual: most people were very effectively excluded from its deliberations on grounds of lack of taste. But its rhetoric did capture an important part of what many of us still experience as the most basic of truths about our culture: that our art, our religion, our morals, our knowledge, our science, are not simply matters of private revealed preference, but rather possess an 'objectivity' the validity of which is ultimately 'social'; in short, that we belong to our culture very much more than it belongs to us. The problem with any radical commodification of culture, such as has been entailed in postmodernism, is not simply the perennial failing of all markets—that they confer the vote not on each person, but on each dollar, and thereby guarantee undemocratic outcomes—but also a more specific failing: that the market undermines precisely what it is that is most cultural about culture—its sociality. The danger remains, then, that such deconstructions of the elite/popular boundary will unwittingly confirm the incorporative dynamics of commercial postmodernism, of multinational late capitalism. Hence, Zizek's disturbingly astute comparison between the compulsive speech of the obsessional neurotic and 'all the talk about new forms of politics': both are 'frantically active', he concludes, 'precisely in order to ensure that something—what *really matters*—will *not* be disturbed'. For the latter, he continues, this something is 'the inexorable logic of Capital' (Zizek, 1999a, p. 354).

THE ILLUSIONS OF POSTMODERNISM

Whatever the appeal either of postmodernist sensibility in general or of post-structuralist theory in particular, their refusal of history remains both disabling and debilitating. For, as Jameson quite rightly insisted, history is not a text, though it is nonetheless inaccessible to us except in textual form (Jameson, 1981, p. 35). 'History is what hurts', he wrote, 'it . . . sets inexorable limits to individual as well as collective praxis . . . we may be sure that its alienating necessities will not forget us, however much we might prefer to ignore them' (p. 102). History is also often progress, although it is currently unfashionable to admit as much. This, too, Jameson recognised: the mystery of the cultural past can be re-enacted, he observed, 'only if the human adventure is one'—only if its apparently long-dead issues can be 'retold within the unity of a great collective story; only if, in however disguised and symbolic form, they are seen as sharing a single fundamental theme . . . the collective struggle to wrest a realm of Freedom from a realm of Necessity' (p. 19). Orwell's 'struggle of the gradually awakening common people against the lords of property' (Orwell, 1970, p. 305) is but one local instance of this same single human adventure. So too was Williams' long revolution, simultaneously an industrial revolution, a democratic revolution, a revolution in the social relations of class, and in the extension of culture.

Williams on postmodernism

In his original formulations, Williams almost certainly erred on the side of evolutionism, in the sense of both an excessive reliance on the inevitability of gradualism and an over-confident expectation of continuing progress. But the dismal political failings of the British Labour governments of the 1960s and 1970s, and the darkly utilitarian rationalisms of the Conservative governments that succeeded them, provoked a growing awareness that: 'If there are no easy answers there are still available and discoverable hard answers' (Williams, 1983, pp. 268–9). Williams' two major works of the 1980s, his 1983 reworking of the long revolution analysis, *Towards 2000*, and his last unfinished work, *The Politics of Modernism*, both quite explicitly addressed the cultural politics of postmodernity. They both attempted to reformulate the original culturalist project, its aspiration to community and culture as a whole way of life, by way of a critique both of modernism and of postmodernism, a critique that rejected—in principle, in theory and in practice—the antithesis between mass civilisation and minority culture without becoming trapped in the cultural logic of commodification.

In *The Long Revolution* itself, as in *Culture and Society*, Williams had respectfully but determinedly aired his differences with the guardians of the old minority culture. By *Towards 2000*, he had become much more dismissive: 'There are very few absolute contrasts left between a "minority culture" and "mass communications"'; 'many minority institutions and forms have adapted, even with enthusiasm, to modern corporate capitalist culture' (pp. 134, 140). Moreover, Williams was insistent that the older modernisms, which once threatened to destabilise the certainties of bourgeois life, had become transformed into a new '"post-modernist" establishment' which 'takes human inadequacy . . . as self-evident'; and that its deep structures had already been transferred into effectively popular cultural forms in film, TV and fiction (p. 141). The work of monopolising both corporations and elite intellectuals, 'these debased forms of an anguished sense of human debasement . . . have become a widely distributed "popular" culture that is meant to confirm both its own and the world's destructive inevitabilities' (pp. 141–2). That there are resistances to this culture went without saying for a thinker as fundamentally optimistic as Williams. But these are more obviously present in popular life itself, in the 'very general area of jokes and gossip, of everyday singing and dancing, of occasional dressing-up and extravagant outbursts of colour' (p. 146), than in the mass media.

A second site of cultural resistance was, of course, the radical intelligentsia. But as early as 1983, Williams was already deeply sceptical of the type of 'pseudo-radical' intellectual practice in which a nominally revolutionary radicalism is turned back into the confusions of 'bourgeois subjectivism' by 'the negative structures of post-modernist art' (p. 145). In *The Politics of Modernism* he would state the case much more forcefully:

> Are we now informed enough, hard enough, to look for our own double edges? Should we not look, implacably, at those many formations, their works and their theories, which are based practically only on their negations and forms of enclosure against an undifferentiated culture and society beyond them? . . . Can theory not help in its refusal of the rationalizations which sustain the negations, and in its determination to probe actual forms, actual structures of feeling, actually lived and desired relationships, beyond the easy labels of radicalism which even the dominant institutions now incorporate or impose? (Williams, 1989, pp. 175–6).

To affirm as much, it is clear, would be to break decisively with the predominantly postmodernist cultural forms, and their variously post-structuralist and post-Marxist theoretical legitimations, which still construct much of the radical intelligentsia in the image of Williams' 'New Conformists'.

Eagleton on postmodernism

These and related themes have been taken up in Eagleton's more recent work on postmodern culture and politics, especially *The Illusions of Postmodernism*. Here he gives rather more credence to postmodernism's radical credentials than did Williams in *Against the New Conformists*. But the conclusions remain remarkably similar: 'Postmodern end-of-history thinking does not envisage a future . . . much different from the present', Eagleton writes, 'a prospect it oddly views as a cause for celebration'. What if the future turns out to be different, he continued, what if it witnessed a revival of fascism, for example? The answers are as damning as anything in Williams:

> its cultural relativism and moral conventionalism, its scepticism, pragmatism, and localism, its distaste for ideas of solidarity and disciplined organization, its lack of any adequate theory of political agency: all these would tell heavily against it . . . the left . . . has need of strong ethical and anthropological foundations . . . And on this score, postmodernism is . . . part of the problem rather than of the solution (Eagleton, 1996b, pp. 134–5).

He also identified Williams's notion of a common culture as one possible source of these strong foundations (pp. 84–5). But as we noted in chapter 2, the idea is even more explicitly foregrounded in Eagleton's recent *The Idea of Culture*. Here, he again takes postmodernism as his target; he again argues for the theoretical superiority of Williams' notion of commonality over more recent theories of difference (Eagleton, 2000, pp. 122–3).

To speak or to write of actually lived and desired relationships among real human beings, as Williams did and Eagleton does, is necessarily to appeal to some kind of 'solidarity effect'. For the vast majority of human beings still live out considerable portions of their lives through face-to-face networks of kinship and community, identity and obligation, friendship and love. Indeed, this is what most of us mean by 'life'. Williams' own understanding of the common culture was neither inherently reactionary nor inherently utopian. Rather, it represented the only practical alternative, within the space of postmodernity, to that radical commodification that now threatens to absorb the cultural into the economic. At one level, it registered little more than the truth of an already existing commonality, evident in language and in the most fundamental of moral proscriptions. But at another, it registered the 'ideals' of community and solidarity, as standards against which to measure the actual deficiencies of our culture and our society. As Williams himself concluded: 'If we are to break out of the non-historical fixity of *post*modernism, then we must search out and counterpose an alternative tradition . . . which may address itself . . . to a modern *future* in which community can be imagined again' (Williams, 1989, p. 35).

7

Cultural criticism and cultural policy

The subject matter of this book was provided, in the first instance, by a cluster of cultural theories that had derived their initial inspiration from three major academic disciplines (literary criticism, sociology and linguistics); from three intellectual traditions (culturalism, critical theory and structuralism); and from three national intellectual cultures (British, German and French). The fit between discipline, tradition and national culture was by no means exact—there were French critical theorists, German literary humanists and British semioticians. And there was much—the British Marxist historians, for example, or the French structural anthropologists—that escaped these over-neat classifications. But if the Caesarean cliché about Gaul having three parts works anywhere, it is probably here. That said, it has all been much complicated by the cultural politics of difference inaugurated by the new social movements and by the postmodernisation—which is also, in some important aspects, the Americanisation—of both culture and cultural theory. Chapters 2 to 4 sketched out the basic models, chapters 5 and 6 added in the complications.

An additional complication, however, was broached in chapter 1: that of the status of cultural studies itself. Cultural theory is still powerfully informed by the legacy of the three predecessor disciplines and it continues to be important to them. How, after all, can you have a literary criticism or a sociology that doesn't have a theory of culture? But we have also traced the emergence of this new discipline, or maybe proto-discipine, cultural studies. Where culture is a part only, albeit an important part, of sociology, it has become the subject matter for cultural studies. Where literary criticism focuses on one particular kind of culture—'high' literature—cultural studies is concerned in principle with all kinds. Whatever the origins of cultural theory in these other disciplines, we do now have to add cultural studies into the equation. What kind of discipline is this? Indeed, is it really a discipline at all?

In chapter 1 we canvassed four different versions of what cultural studies might be: an inter- or post-discipline; a political intervention into the existing academic disciplines; a new discipline, defined in terms of a new subject matter; and a new discipline, defined in terms of a new theoretical paradigm. We concluded by arguing for an understanding of cultural studies as a loosely 'social-scientific' approach to the study of all textualised meanings, both elite and popular, literary and non-literary. This will have important extra-textual aspects—the study of cultural production and reception, for example—but it also retains a distinctly textual moment as central to the entire enterprise. It is all well and good to discover who writes what, how it is distributed and how read, but there is a certain pointlessness to the exercise if no attempt is made to analyse what it is that has actually been written, distributed and read. Which poses the question of what methods cultural studies should deploy in its study of 'texts', using this latter term very loosely to refer to any semantic unit of meaning, whether written, spoken, cinematic, televisual, or whatever. In chapter 1, we also noted Mulhern's distinction between, in his phrase, '*Kulturkritik*' and 'Cultural Studies'—the criticism of elite and of popular texts, respectively, in each case for the purposes of demonstrating their supposed value. These are both models for textual analysis. Indeed, as Mulhern astutely observes, despite their reversed valorisations of the elite and the popular, they are in essence the same model, insofar as they each reproduce the same 'metacultural' discursive form and fulfil the same 'metapolitical' function: the symbolic resolution of real social contradictions. In short, they are each instances of 'criticism'.

CULTURAL STUDIES AND CULTURAL CRITICISM

However we define cultural studies, whether as the study of all texts, or only of popular texts, it is clear that it opted for a very different subject matter from that originally identified by culturalist literary criticism. But in some important manifestations it has retained the notion of criticism, if not exactly that of literature. But what exactly is criticism? The classic nineteenth-century statement of the case is Matthew Arnold's 'The Function of Criticism at the Present Time', first published in his *Essays in Criticism* in 1865. Here he had defined it as *'a disinterested endeavour to learn and propagate the best that is known and thought in the world'* (Arnold, 1980, p. 265). Here, as elsewhere in his work, disinterestedness had meant 'steadily refusing to lend [oneself] to any . . . ulterior, political, practical considerations about ideas' (p. 248). But this disinterested criticism certainly had its own social purpose: 'to learn and propagate the best that is known and thought in the world, and thus to establish a current of fresh and true ideas'. It was by 'communicating fresh knowledge, and letting his own judgement pass along with it', Arnold wrote, 'that the critic will generally do most good to his readers' (p. 264).

Arnold's notion that criticism should evaluate and pass on its evaluations, so as to do good to its readers, remained powerfully influential in literary studies, through to the Leavises and beyond. However, there are important objections to this notion of criticism. Most obviously, it attributes an entirely false 'objectivity' to the notion of value itself, as if Arnold's 'the best', the 'fresh' and the 'true' were simple matters of fact. These and the other distinctions that define the different versions of the humanist literary canon—for example, between more or less authentic and more or less inspired texts—are judgements of value, rather than statements of fact. But insofar as literary studies understands itself as the study of 'great' literature, or cultural studies as the study of 'really' popular culture, then such value judgements enter into the definition of the subject matter and take on the quasi-objectivity of pseudo-facts. In the specific case of literary studies, moreover, the focus normally falls not simply on valued writing, but on how to value or 'appreciate' it. Given that the texts chosen for study are already deemed valuable, this amounts in practice to little more than an indoctrination into a particular set of pre-existing values. The logic of the process was nicely caught in Baldick's conclusion that: 'The title of "criticism" was usurped by a literary discourse whose entire attitude was at heart uncritical. Criticism in its most important and most vital sense had been gutted and turned into its very opposite' (Baldick, 1983, p. 234).

Neither the 'literariness' of literature nor the 'popularity' of the popular is an inherent property of a certain type of text; each is a function of how different kinds of text are socially processed by cultural producers, distributors, critics, audiences, and so on. As Eagleton argued: 'There is no such thing as a literary work or tradition which is valuable *in itself*, regardless of what anyone might have said or come to say about it. "Value" is a transitive term: it means whatever is valued by certain people in specific situations, according to particular criteria and in the light of given purposes' (Eagleton, 1996, p. 11). Such valuations are not random for, as Eagleton also insisted, 'they have their roots in deeper structures of belief' (p. 16). Whatever else the literary and the popular might be, they are also social constructions.

Williams' move from literary into cultural studies had been occasioned, in part, by an aversion to criticism of this sub-Arnoldian kind. In *Keywords*, for example, he had indicted criticism as 'ideological' on the grounds that it 'actively prevents that understanding of response which does not assume the habit (or right or duty) of judgement' (Williams, 1976, p. 76). In *Communications*, he insisted that we 'have to learn confidence in our own real opinions, and this depends on a kind of openness and flexibility . . . which much that is called "criticism" does nothing to help' (Williams, 1976a, p. 147). At one point in a discussion of radical realist television, he even went so far as to describe contemporary British society as 'rotten with criticism', insisting that 'we need not criticism but analysis . . . the complex seeing of analysis rather than . . . the abstractions of critical classification' (Williams, 1989b, p. 239).

But there is more to Williams' work than mere descriptive sociology. Indeed, part of the point of what Williams 'came to say' was always, as with Arnold, to do some 'good' for his readers.

Perhaps more interestingly, this is true also of neo-Marxists such as Eagleton, most obviously so in the book that takes its title from Arnold, *The Function of Criticism*. Following Habermas, Eagleton analyses seventeenth- and eighteenth-century criticism as a discourse of the early liberal public sphere. He stressed the unusually consensual form taken by the English variant of eighteenth-century criticism: unlike its continental counterparts, it functioned so as to facilitate a fusion of aristocratic and bourgeois—that is, Cavalier and Puritan—values. Nonetheless, early English criticism had reproduced all the essential features of the early bourgeois public sphere. 'A polite, informed public opinion pits itself against the arbitrary diktats of autocracy', wrote Eagleton:

> within the translucent space of the public sphere it is supposedly no longer social power, privilege and tradition which confer upon individuals the title to speak and judge, but the degree to which they are constituted as discoursing subjects by sharing in a consensus of universal reason (Eagleton, 1996a, p. 9).

This bourgeois public sphere was progressively undermined during the nineteenth century, according to Eagleton, first, by the expansion of the literary market and the concomitant rise of an anonymous public and, second, by the eruption into the public sphere of social interests opposed to its rational norms, in particular the working class, radicalism, feminism and dissent. Criticism was thus increasingly faced with the choice between a general cultural humanism, which became necessarily increasingly amateur as capitalist society developed, and an expert professionalism, which could only achieve intellectual legitimacy at the price of social relevance. The eventual outcome was the institutionalisation of criticism within the universities. Leavisism was thus the guilty conscience of this academicism, 'nothing less than an attempt to reinvent the classical public sphere, at a time when its material conditions had definitively passed' (p. 75).

Eagleton clearly aspires to reverse both the Leavisite specialisation of criticism to 'Literature' and the substitution of essentially uncritical celebration for negative critique. Criticism, he wrote, 'was only ever significant when it engaged with more than literary issues—when . . . the "literary" was . . . foregrounded as the medium of vital concerns deeply rooted in the general intellectual, cultural and political life of an epoch' (p. 107). Hence his concluding aspiration to 'recall criticism to its traditional role' (p. 123), in effect to reinvent a non-academic counter-public sphere. 'Modern criticism was born of a struggle against the absolutist state', Eagleton insisted: 'unless its future is now defined as a struggle against the bourgeois state, it might have no future at all' (p. 124). This is an argument for a more generally cultural, rather than specialist literary criticism, but for a criticism nonetheless, and a critical, or negative, criticism at that. It would be neither disinterested nor merely celebratory of the 'best' (nor was eighteenth-century criticism), but in some respects it would indeed be Arnoldian. Clearly, Eagleton's version of criticism did aspire to use critical commentary on contemporary culture to change people's minds. The rhetoric was, of course, extreme and interested, but the logic not so different from that of Arnold. This idea recurs elsewhere, most obviously in Frankfurt School critical theory, but also in the kind of comparative literary studies pursued by Said or Jameson. When Said insisted that the proper business of intellectuals is 'to speak the truth to power', for example, he places the stress above all on their critical function (Said, 1994, p. 71). And even if Jameson maintains that 'cognitive mapping' is really class consciousness, it might just as plausibly be understood as critique.

Such criticism differs from Arnold and Leavis in at least two crucial aspects: it is concerned with culture in general, rather than merely with the 'best' that has been known, thought, said, written, filmed or recorded; and it combines hostile as well as celebratory moments into something very close to what Jameson had meant by a double hermeneutic. Thus reformed, criticism is neither *Kulturkritik* nor 'Cultural Studies', in Mulhern's sense, but rather something closer to Williams, and it seems to us an essential aspect, a necessary moment, in any cultural studies worth the name. But it has been by no means unchallenged. The most important counter-argument, written from well within the 'true' of cultural studies, is almost certainly Tony Bennett's *Outside Literature*. Starting from very similar premises to those in Williams, Bennett argued for a wholesale rejection of the notion of criticism. Philosophical aesthetics had misconstrued literary and artistic judgement as universal modes of cognition, he observed, rather than as socially specific applications of the particular rules of value shared by particular valuing communities. The aestheticians thereby 'fetishise the objects of value and deploy a discourse of disqualification in relation to those subjects who do not . . . conform to their edicts' (Bennett, 1990, p. 160). In aesthetic discourse, therefore, the relative intolerance characteristic of all discourses of value effectively 'becomes absolute' (p. 165). Hence Bennett's rejection of all such notions of aesthetic value, whether Arnoldian, Leavisite, or whatever.

As it happened, however, this 'whatever' turned out to be precisely the kind of neo-Marxist criticism advocated by Eagleton. Marxism's central failure in cultural studies, Bennett argued, was its enduring loyalty to the 'idealist concerns of bourgeois aesthetics' (p. 33). Here it becomes clear that his central objection was to neither the exclusive stress on high culture nor the unremitting positivity of Arnold's hermeneutic, but to the way criticism aspired to have an effect on its readers. Critics like Eagleton, Said and Jameson had replicated the original Arnoldian, and Leavisite, sense of the 'function of criticism', Bennett complained: they tended 'to re-align criticism with a totalising conception of social and cultural critique' (p. 194); and they hoped to secure a political relevance for it only 'by going back to being what it once was—a set of interpretive procedures oriented towards the transformation of the consciousness of individual subjects' (p. 195). To such idealism Bennett sought to counterpose a thoroughgoing 'cultural materialism', though one that derived from Foucault rather than from Williams. Spurning the vocation of the 'universal intellectual' as critic, he insisted that the role of the 'specific intellectual' now demanded 'more specific and localised assessments of the effects of practices of textual commentary conducted in the light of the institutionally circumscribed fields of their social deployment' (p. 10). In short, rather than aim directly to transform the consciousnesses of individual readers, cultural studies should aim to adjust the social institutions that shape those consciousnesses.

Like Williams, Bennett envisaged criticism's supersession by a kind of cultural studies that would be essentially sociological in character. Their different understandings of sociality, though, pointed towards very different kinds of cultural sociology. As Williams made clear, his own objections to criticism were levelled not so much at judgement *per se*, which seemed to him 'inevitable', but at the peculiar 'pseudo-impersonality' of literary-critical judgement (Williams, 1979, pp. 334–6). Indeed, his generally humanist reading of the importance of social agency and of social consciousness, and his continuing sense of class loyalty, actually required non-specialist value judgements of a more or less explicit kind. For if the long revolution was to be continued, then everyday arguments, about culture and society, politics and letters, must succeed in changing people's minds, that is, in 'transforming' the 'consciousness of individual subjects', to translate the proposition from humanist into post-structuralist terms. This is exactly what Bennett objected to: the attempt to change people's minds through rational debate. There is no other way to proceed, of course, for a politics that is both democratic and, as it were, inspired 'from below'. For Bennett, however, the specific intelligentsia should aim at a very different type of politics, at once both micropolitical and 'from above'. In short, he aimed to examine 'the truth/power symbiosis that characterises particular regions of social management—with a view . . . to [not only] undoing that symbiosis but also . . . installing a new one in its place' (p. 270). The term used for this kind of work is 'cultural policy studies'.

CULTURAL STUDIES AND CULTURAL POLICY

Since the Second World War, most western governments have tended to regard cultural policy of one kind or another as a necessary, albeit often relatively minor, contribution to the maintenance of 'national identity'. In the first instance, then, these policies were developed in relation to essentially national frameworks. But over the last 30 years or so, feminism, anti-racism and gay activism have forced issues of minority cultural representation into the national arena in many societies. Moreover, the roughly contemporaneous development of digitalised mass-communication media, globalised systems of trade and large refugee and diaspora populations have resulted in far-reaching and qualitative changes in conceptions of cultural identity and representation. Cultural practices were increasingly shaped in unforeseen ways by new social alignments that problematised most hitherto taken-for-granted assumptions about nationality and culture. As a result, cultural policy and funding are now increasingly discussed in terms of such issues as the relations between local and international content, national and ethnic identities, settler and aboriginal cultures, cosmopolitan and traditional or urban and rural cultural practices. This terrain forms the background against which cultural policy studies was developed and expanded.

The last two decades of the twentieth century witnessed the creation of institutionalised centres for the study of cultural policy in a number of 'First World' societies. Obvious examples include the Institute of Policy and Cultural Studies at Chuo University, Tokyo; the Centre for Cultural Policy Studies at the Royal School of Library and Information Science in Copenhagen; the Australian Key Centre for Cultural and Media Policy at Griffith University in Brisbane; the Centre for the Study of Cultural Policy at the University of Warwick; the Center for Cultural Policy Studies at the University of Chicago; the Cultural Policy and Production Project in the Mexican Center of the University of Texas at Austin; the Princeton University Center for Arts and Cultural Policy Studies; the Privatization of Culture Project at New York University; and so on.

In most western societies, cultural policy was overwhelmingly a matter of government funding and regulation of the arts. The only obvious exception was the United States, where funding came primarily from individual philanthropy and corporate sponsorship or patronage, at least until the Johnson Administration set up the National Endowment for the Arts. Even then, public funding paled into insignificance by comparison with that provided by the Ford, Carnegie, Rockefeller and Mellon Foundations or by large private corporations such as Exxon and Philip Morris. But insofar as the role of government did indeed predominate elsewhere, then cultural policy studies tended to shift intellectual focus away from texts and towards the politico-social processes that drove their funding, control, distribution and consumption. Such questions were inextricably connected to often highly politicised debates over the problematic and contradictory relations between culture and 'national community'—over democratic access and minority representation, for example. In both respects, cultural policy studies tended, therefore, to share many of the characteristic concerns of contemporary cultural theory. Policy analysts were unavoidably concerned, for example, with exactly those questions—how different cultural forms, images and practices either comply with or contest the institutionalised relations of power—that were of such theoretical centrality to Williams' cultural materialism, Foucault's genealogy and Bourdieu's cultural sociology.

Cultural policy studies had its origins in radical politics, such as Nicholas Garnham's work for the left-wing Greater London Council during the early 1980s. Now Professor of Media Studies and Founding Director of the Centre for Communication and Information Studies at the University of Westminster, Garnham has long insisted on the need for media analysts 'both as citizens and scholars' to decide 'which side they are on' (Garnham, 1983, p. 329). The journal he co-edits, *Media, Culture and Society*, has defined its distinctive contribution as a stress on media and communication policy viewed not from a technical or administrative vantage point, but from that of a 'critical intelligentsia', serving a 'democratic public interest' (Collins et al., 1986, pp. 4–5). As we noted in chapter 2, Garnham regards himself as a cultural materialist after the fashion of Williams. But the move into policy studies required him to distance himself from the tradition of 'idealist' cultural analysis he describes as 'delineated' in *Culture and Society* (Garnham, 1987, p. 24), a book some would see as itself also a significant contribution to that tradition. For all the obvious respect Garnham accorded to Williams' work on the mass media, he clearly found the latter's continuing interest in literary criticism perplexing: witness the complaint that Williams' key insights should be 'hidden in a book of literary theory' (Garnham, 1990, p. 20). The aversion to criticism would become even more endemic as cultural policy studies began to take shape as an academic sub-discipline.

This sub-discipline's most theoretically articulate mission statement—informed simultaneously by less radical political affiliations and a much greater suspicion of criticism—would be that formulated by Bennett, in his former role as director of the Institute for Cultural Policy Studies at Griffith University and his present as successor to Hall in the chair of sociology at Britain's Open University. There is no denying the practical significance of the empirical work done either by Bennett or under his auspices. To cite the best-known example, the cultural development strategy devised by Bennett and Colin Mercer for the city of Brisbane is widely regarded internationally as a pathbreaking exercise. The theoretical sophistication of the larger project is the most distinctive feature, however, of the work done at Griffith by Bennett and colleagues such as Mercer, Ian Hunter and Stuart Cunningham. They made extensive and elaborate use of contemporary cultural theory: Bennett himself happily acknowledged a debt to Williams and even cited the latter's role in the British Arts Council as prefiguring his own interest in policy (Bennett, 1989, pp. 86–7; Bennett, 1998, p. 36); he quite explicitly connected the shift towards policy studies to the 'Foucault effect' (Bennett, 1998, pp. 82–4); and his more recent work on cultural taste cites Bourdieu as its 'main source of inspiration' (Bennett et al., 1999, p. 3).

Outside Literature included a preliminary sketch of an underlying theoretical rationale for cultural policy studies. It no longer seemed 'fruitful', Bennett explained, to regard neo-Marxism of the Eagletonian variety as 'adequate to the theorisation of social phenomena' (Bennett, 1990, p. 7). Literary criticism of this kind reflected 'a fundamental failure', he concluded, 'to pose questions of literary politics' in ways 'sufficiently precise and focused to make a sustained difference to the functioning of literary institutions' (p. 286). These were exactly the questions pursued in Hunter's *Culture and Government*, which had sought to analyse popular literary education, in Foucauldian terms, as productive of 'an ethical technology directed to forming the moral attributes of a citizenry' (Hunter, 1988, p. 152). Rather than denounce the world in the hope of changing their readers' minds, Bennett and his colleagues set out to reform both the university itself and as much else of the culture industries as seemed practically reformable. Their version of cultural policy studies would thus stand in much the same relation to cultural studies as had British Fabian social engineering to sociology. *Outside Literature* was essentially a work of negative critique, however: its positive corollary, the case for cultural policy studies—as distinct from that against post-literary criticism—was to be outlined in a series of shorter essays written during the early 1990s and then, at greater length, in *Culture: A Reformer's Science*, first published in 1998.

FROM CULTURAL CRITICISM TO CULTURAL ENGINEERING

Bennett's essays argued that cultural studies should re-orient itself towards policy formation and the production of what he termed 'useful' knowledge, making itself socially and politically relevant by abandoning both Romanticism and the history of ideas. The 'cultural critic' should become a 'cultural engineer', he argued. The proper function of cultural studies would thus become 'the training of cultural technicians'; their role, in turn, was to be 'less committed to cultural critique' as an instrument for changing consciousness than to 'modifying the functioning of culture by means of technical adjustments to its governmental deployment' (Bennett, 1992, p. 406). Bennett rejected Gramscian-inspired cultural studies both as too preoccupied with textual analysis and as paying 'insufficient attention to the institutional conditions that regulate different fields of culture' (Bennett, 1992a, p. 25). These would be better addressed, he concluded, by way of Foucault's notion of 'governmentality', treating culture not in the anthropological sense, as had Williams, but rather as a form of moral regulation, 'a historically specific set of institutionally embedded relations of government' through which the thought and conduct of 'extended populations' are 'targeted for transformation', in part by way of the 'forms, techniques, and regimens of aesthetic and intellectual culture' (p. 26).

In *Culture: A Reformer's Science*, Bennett argued that culture had become 'so deeply governmentalised' that it now no longer made sense to think of it 'as a ground situated outside the domain of government . . . through which that domain might be resisted' (Bennett, 1998, p. 30). The early New Left's understanding of higher and secondary education, as more or less freely available to the political projects of groups of intellectuals, was simply politically naive, he cautioned: 'the institutions and spaces of public education are . . . contexts which necessarily confer their own logic and social direction on the work that is conducted within them' (p. 49). It follows, then, that cultural studies must set aside cultural critique in order to lay claim to some definite set of 'knowledge claims and methodological procedures' convertible into practically utilisable 'clearly defined skills and trainings' (p. 52). In practice, he concluded, these skills and trainings will need to be policy-oriented: 'intellectuals working in cultural studies needed to begin to "talk to the ISAs"—that is Althusser's famous Ideological State Apparatuses' (p. 33). This, then, is what Bennett means by 'disciplining' cultural studies: 'allowing everyday life and cultural experience to be fashioned into instruments of government via their inscription in new forms of teaching and training' (p. 51).

Bennett is right to insist that the changing norms and practices of secondary school English teaching were more important than the New Left as a primary 'conditioning context' of British cultural studies (p. 49). But it was the New Left's intervention into this context that provided cultural studies with both its initial subject matter and its founding texts. Bennett is also right to define the object of study in cultural studies as 'the relations of culture and power' (p. 53). But these relations can be critiqued, as well as studied or serviced. Any institutionalised pedagogy must, it's true, have something in particular to offer to its students, but the inference Bennett draws, that the relevant skills and trainings must be policy-oriented, is unwarranted. Hunter is right to insist that public education had developed historically as an amalgam of two earlier educational projects, the 'bureaucratic' and the 'pastoral', concerned with, respectively, 'social training' and 'individual salvation', or 'self-realising personhood', as the latter eventually became secularised (Hunter, 1994, pp. 61, 92). But there is no good reason to suppose that the bureaucratic ethos must necessarily take precedence over the pastoral.

To the contrary, and as both Bennett and Hunter knew well, it is a matter of historical record that English Literature was able to function both without any such policy-orientation and as a predominantly pastoral discipline, specialising in self-expressivity, within the more general pedagogic amalgam of the bureaucratic and the pastoral (cf. Hunter, 1994, pp. 80–1; Hunter, 1988). There is no good reason, then, to suppose that this option shouldn't be available to cultural studies, that its primary business will be teaching and the training of teachers, in higher and secondary education, in a version of literary studies so reformed as to make it more directly relevant to the concerns and interests of the students of the early twenty-first century.

Neither Bennett nor Hunter was at all willing to embrace this possibility: Bennett because he remained determined that cultural studies should not become 'the heir of literary studies in its English formation', a prospect he found positively 'depressing' (Bennett, 1998, p. 52); Hunter because he deemed the resultant 'refurbishment of literature departments' likely to result in a parallel renovation of the kind of 'fundamentally aesthetic critique' cultural studies inherited from Romanticism by way of Leavis and Williams (Hunter, 1993, p. 172; cf. Hunter, 1992). These are reasons, but not necessarily good ones. Depressing or not, and turning Bennett's 'tough-mindedness' against itself, it seems to us that cultural studies is actually more likely to evolve in a post-literary than a sub-sociological direction. And this is so for reasons they might both accept: because 'Literature', constructed as the antithetical 'Other' of print and other 'fictions', is already a theoretically indefensible category; and because state education systems will still be required to educate the subjectivities of their populations.

In *The Politics of Modernism*, Williams had asked exasperatedly of cultural theory: 'Is there never to be an end to petit-bourgeois theorists making long-term adjustments to short-term situations?'

(Williams, 1989, p. 175). We doubt he can have had Bennett in mind here, but the shift from cultural critique to cultural policy studies can indeed be read as such an adjustment. Bennett is clearly sensitive to the possibility and addresses it directly. In the societies where cultural studies has 'made some headway', he writes, Williams' 'long-term vision' has now lost 'its coherence and purchase'. 'For this particular petit-bourgeois theorist', he continues, the issue is, rather, one 'of making long-term adjustments because the long-term situation itself now has to be thought in new ways' (Bennett, 1998, p. 37). The matters at issue here seem to devolve into two analytically distinct questions: the relative cultural significance attaching to common culture, solidarity and social class on the one hand; 'difference' and the new social movements on the other; and the role of the state in cultural management. In Bennett's view, the new situation is such that the business of cultural studies must now be to negotiate and facilitate the relations between these various social interests and the state bureaucracies (pp. 37, 30).

But he is surely mistaken on both counts. The new global 'anti-capitalist' movements serve to remind us that the aspiration to commonality and the effects of social class are of greater long-term political and cultural significance than 1990s' notions of difference tended to suggest. And neither culture in general nor higher education in particular is anything as 'governmentalised' as Bennett assumes. His notion of 'governmentality' refers to a far more explicitly 'statist' process than that identified in Foucault himself (Bennett, 1998, p. 144; cf. Foucault, 1991). But if governmentality is the work of the state in particular, rather than of power in general, then the most striking feature of post-modern late capitalism is its opposite: the commodification and consequent 'de-governmentalisation' of cultural texts, practices and institutions.

CULTURAL STUDIES AND CULTURAL CHANGE

Bennett has claimed that his work in policy studies was indebted to distinctly 'Australian traditions of government', which 'have historically tended to be more strongly directive and utilitarian—more Benthamite, even—than those associated with British forms of liberal government' (Bennett, 1998, p. 7). There is some warrant for this: a society that invented industrial arbitration and gave the world the word 'femocrat' probably did provide unusually fertile soil for the transformation of cultural studies into cultural policy studies. But we should also note the anxieties about the earliest formulations of the case for neo-Foucauldian policy studies from within Australian cultural studies itself, notably from Tom O'Regan and Meaghan Morris. O'Regan had a long-standing interest in policy and is now Professor and Director of the Key Centre at Griffith; Morris is perhaps the best known of all Australian cultural critics and had long insisted on the need for a 'critical vocabulary available to people . . . to theorise the discriminations . . . they make in relation to . . . popular culture' (Morris, 1988a, p. 25).

O'Regan objected to the false dichotomy set up by Bennett and his colleagues between between policy analyst and cultural critic. The term 'policy' gestures towards two broadly different activities, he commented: 'participation as an actor in policy administration and development'; and 'promotion of policy as a privileged focus of critical attention' (O'Regan, 1992, p. 520). The latter he found questionable, especially in its 'language of "rationalities", "strategies" and "governmentality"', which appeared to license speaking as a privileged policy agent 'endowed with regulatory vision and authorization' (p. 529). O'Regan also pointed to the misrepresentation of Foucault in Bennett: 'By contrast with Foucault's own emphasis', he wrote, 'the pro-policy polemic proposes a reading . . . that supports a policy of acting in the social on behalf of governmental agencies' (pp. 529–30). Morris herself described the so-called 'policy debate' as little more than 'a one-sided head-kicking exercise' (Morris, 1992, p. 546). The dichotomy between 'Criticism and Policy' would not focus the debate realistically, she argued, because its framework could not admit a 'multivariate' critical strategy. The counter-example she cites was that of Sneja Gunew, 'who produces specialized cultural criticism for an international audience, engages locally in public debate, and works for national policy outcomes in the field of multiculturalism'. To make an effective case for subordinating 'criticism' to 'policy', Morris wryly observed, policy studies would need 'to show why such a critic should make her policy work both the *content* and the *goal* of her criticism—and why the resulting loss of readership would be worth while' (p. 548).

These early Australian responses to Bennett should alert us to the possibility that the issue here might not be between criticism and policy, but between different conceptions of both While Bennett had imagined criticism in essentially Arnoldian terms as authoritatively prescriptive and policy as an exercise applied to populations by experts, O'Regan and Morris were inclined to think of both as part of a more democratic process of debate and discussion containing significant inputs from 'below'. In this respect, they were closer to Williams and Eagleton, Said and Jameson, than to Bennett and Hunter. This is barely surprising: in the increasingly globalised and totalising space of postmodern late capitalism, distinctive national traditions of government, such as those to which Bennett refers, have become increasingly subject to the international logics of cultural commodification. Like Garnham and Williams before him, Bennett had initially imagined cultural policy studies as in the service of left-of-centre governments committed to some kind of public intervention into the arts. The reality has been quite otherwise, however: much closer in fact to that anticipated by critics like Jameson than by these would-be policy advisers.

The cultural logic of commodification has not simply been one of privatisation, although this has been important in most western countries, especially in the English-speaking world. Arguably as significant, however, is the introduction of utilitarian practices and principles into the still sometimes substantial government sector. In Britain, for example, Jim McGuigan, at Loughborough University, has tracked what he describes as 'the emergence and dissemination of a pervasive managerialist and market reasoning in the public sector itself' (McGuigan, 1996, p. 2). He concludes that policy debate in the cultural field is framed by 'economic reductionisms and technological determinisms' and that these often inform even supposedly 'critical political economy of the media' (p. 28). George Yúdice, Professor of American Studies at New York University, has tracked more or less the same process in the United States. He argues that the overt 'struggle between the Right and the Left' over funding issues involving the National Endowment for the Arts actually obscured a much deeper and more insidious process: not so much privatisation as a shift of the entire 'partnership between government, the corporate sector, and the nonprofit sector' towards a 'primarily competitive and entrepreneurial' corporate 'ethos' (Yúdice, 1998, p. 2).

Yúdice identifies a 'triangulation' of government, corporate and non-profit involvement in arts funding, in which it 'no longer makes sense to speak of public and private, for they have been pried open to each other' (p. 26). He sees the transformation of both the arts and education since the late 1980s as driven by a utilitarian, neo-liberal ideology in which the public legitimations for art and culture have veered away from the humanist rhetoric 'that they provide uplift' towards 'profitable outcomes' from practices such as cultural tourism (p. 29). There is a new consensus between the corporate right and the cultural left, he observes, that quite explicitly downgrades the value of art as oppositional cultural critique. It has arisen quite specifically in a context where 'progressives' no longer believe in class struggle or anti-imperialism and the sectors of capital involved in 'cultural marketing and point of purchase politics' now espouse environmentalism, antiracism and antisexism (p. 31). If the 1980s was 'the decade of the curator', Yúdice suggests that the 1990s might be that of the 'arts administrator'. The conservative attacks on multiculturalism, antiracism and feminism, which have so enraged the Left, were actually less important than this 'new governmentalization', he concludes, since it will increasingly require the direct subordination of the arts to 'administrators, planners, managers, and entrepreneurs', irrespective of any individual 'ideological proclivities' (p. 32).

This is the process to which 'governmentalised' policy studies now seems irreparably committed. The problem is not, as O'Regan had feared, that policy analysts might usurp a privileged position within the policy process, but rather that they occupy this position only at the behest of the corporate interests that increasingly dominate the entire process. As O'Regan himself recently observed: 'Cultural policy and by implication cultural policy studies is becoming less its own sui generis domain and more part of a variety of other governmental processes, spheres, knowledges and domains'. 'In these several encounters with industry', he continues, 'cultural policy risks losing not only a sense of common identity of purpose and orientation but also its sense of its own coordinating and facilitating role' (O'Regan, 2001). This might not be such a bad thing, of course, were it not for the fact that corporatisation threatens to be so much worse.

CRITICISM AND GLOBALISATION

The way out of the dilemma seems to us to have a dual aspect: first, a rehabilitation of the critical impulse itself; and, second, a theoretical interrogation of the technological determinism evident in much of the rhetoric of globalisation. As to the first, the threatened absorption and incorporation of policy studies into the state apparatuses has already prompted widespread interest in applying Habermasian critical theory to policy analysis. This is apparent, for example, in recent developments in and around *Media, Culture and Society*. In 1992, three of Garnham's colleagues had defined the journal's 'project' in terms of a defence of Enlightenment reason against postmodern irrationalism and of the 'public sphere' against the globalisation of the cultural market (Scannell et al., 1992, pp. 3, 13). In 1995, a lead article by Garnham himself, introducing a special issue on intellectuals, cited the role of the 'critical intellectual' in opposition to the 'widespread defenestration of the intellectual' in postmodernism (Garnham, 1995, pp. 371–3). McGuigan too has adopted what he sees as a 'broadly Habermasian perspective', seeking to follow a middle path 'between theoretical critique and practical policy'; between Habermas' own overly idealised communicative speech pragmatics and Foucault's over-determined notion of power-saturated human activity. Hence the commitment to a cultural policy studies based on 'critical and communicative rationality'. Thus understood, cultural studies is about the 'politics of culture': 'the clash of ideas, institutional struggles and power relations in the production and circulation of symbolic meanings' (McGuigan, 1996, p. 1).

But neither McGuigan nor Garnham seems able to appreciate the significance of (literary or philosophical) textual criticism, as distinct from social critique. This isn't simply a matter of ideology-critique, in the sense of Jameson's negative hermeneutic, but of the double hermeneutic, including its positively Arnoldian moment. The point to note here is how literature figured in Williams as a site for what Jones terms '"emancipatory" ideology critique': the immanent analysis of the 'emancipatory promise' inherent in the utopian claims of ideologies, a promise that can turn them into a 'court of critical appeal' rather than an ideological legitimation (Jones, 1999, pp. 43–4). This is the procedure Garnham had found objectionable in *Culture and Society*. But it was of quite fundamental importance, not only to Williams, but also to Adorno and Marcuse. Garnham's own commitments to social critique are indisputable, but his work tends to underestimate the intimate connection between critique and criticism. There is an irony here, furthermore, given his own recent interest in the role of the 'aesthetic' as a counterweight to postmodern relativism: Garnham's *Emancipation, the Media and Modernity* makes impressive use of discourse ethics to ground a non-relativist aesthetic, at one point oddly reminiscent of Leavis (Garnham, 2000, p. 162). Its conclusion, that we need to move towards 'the development of a common culture' and a respect for 'cultural differences' that 'have been tested in comparison with alternative interpretations and evaluations', surely requires that these interpretations and evaluations be tested precisely by criticism.

As to the question of technology, let us begin by noting how powerfully the economic reductionisms and technological determinisms identified by McGuigan do indeed inform the debates over globalisation. The best argument for the new corporatisation seems often little better than Mrs Thatcher's 'There Is No Alternative'. To cite a particularly sad example as representative of a much wider genre, observe how Scott Lash, an erstwhile 'critical sociologist', who in 1990 still insisted on taking Marxism and the socialist tradition 'very seriously indeed' (Lash, 1990, p. 3), now seeks to define the post-postmodern condition. 'The rise of the global information culture', he writes:

> seems to be irreversible. It cannot be wished away no matter how great the longing for a much kinder age of mass trade unionism, socialist parties, a formidable welfare state, full employment, comparative income and wealth equality, and the now seemingly gemütlich charms of print culture and the first media age (Lash, 1999, p. 14).

The implication that everything millions of people have worked for, hoped for, fought for, has simply been swept aside by an irreversible technological logic isn't so much sociological explanation as damagingly suasive politicised rhetoric.

What Williams wrote of television remains equally true for the new information systems:

> When there has been such heavy investment in a particular model of social communications, there is a restraining complex of financial institutions, of cultural expectations and of specific technical developments, which though it can be seen, superficially, as the effect of a technology is in fact a social complex of a new and central kind (Williams, 1974a, p. 31).

The point is not that the global information culture can simply be wished away, but that it must be understood as a human creation, a social complex, formed to serve some interests and not others, not as a technological inevitability, but as a site of contest. The key question for Williams was that of the radical incompatibility of large-scale capitalism with democracy; and of how, in the face of a capitalism as hubristic as any in the history of modernity, to create and strengthen the institutions of political, economic and cultural democracy. This is still our problem. Its solution will require all the resources we can muster—from critique and policy, from protest and advocacy, and, yes, from criticism too.

Glossary

More detailed and comprehensive glossaries of key terminology can be found in Raymond Williams' *Keywords*, Peter Brooker's *A Concise Glossary of Cultural Theory* and O'Sullivan, Hartley, Saunders, Montgomery and Fiske's *Key Concepts in Communication and Cultural Studies* (Williams, 1976; Brooker, 1999; O'Sullivan et al., 1994).

Aesthetics A branch of philosophy concerned with the nature and judgement of artistic beauty. Developed in the late eighteenth and early nineteenth centuries as part of a more general 'middle-class' interest in the valorisation of taste and discernment.

Alienation In philosophy, theology, psychology and sociology, the separation or estrangement from each other of elements that are normally connected. In Hegel, humanity's separation from its own spirituality; in Marx, the worker's separation from and lack of control over production in a market economy.

Archaeology Literally, the study of human antiquities through the analysis of their material remains. In Foucault, by analogy, the study of past and present *epistemes*, or ways of knowing—relatively large-scale and systematic conceptual-discursive frameworks, understood as defining the truth criteria by which particular knowledge problems are resolved, and as embedded in and implying particular institutional arrangements.

Aura In Benjamin, the combination of uniqueness, authenticity and authority that gave the traditional work of art its aesthetic power. Undermined by 'mechanical reproduction'.

Avant-garde Late nineteenth- and early twentieth-century radically experimentalist movements in literature and the arts, which imagined themselves as in some sense ahead of society. In Bürger and in Habermas, more precisely, movements of protest against the autonomous institutionalisation of modern art, which attempted (unsuccessfully) to force a new reconciliation between art and life (for example, Surrealism, Dadaism and Futurism).

Base/superstructure In Marx, a metaphor to suggest that the relationship between the economy and the politico-legal system is analogous to that between the foundations and the superstructure of a building. In later Marxisms, expanded to include art and culture as superstructures and to insist that the base somehow 'determined' the superstructures.

Big Other/little other In Lacan, the big Other is everything that the subject desires to know and bond with, in plenitude and full presence, but which necessarily remains forever at a remove. The little other is whatever this frustrated desire is transferred towards. In later theorisations, the big Other is redefined as the Real.

Canon Originally, those Christian religious texts considered divinely inspired by the Church. In secular aesthetics, literary and other texts accorded a privileged status, within some version or another of a 'great tradition', as embodying the core values of a culture.

Capitalism In economics and sociology, an economic system where goods and services are produced only in order to be sold as commodities in the market; and where production is organised by the owners of 'capital' (whether as plant or finance) for the maximisation of profit.

Carnivalesque In Bakhtin, a form of cultural transgression, entailing a temporary inversion of social and linguistic hierarchies.

Class In general, a particular group or category identifiable within a system of classification. In sociology, a social group, conceived as located within a hierarchical order of such groups, whose identity, membership and relationships with other such social groups are primarily governed by economic considerations. Examples include the 'working class' and the 'middle class'.

Cognitive mapping In Jameson, the attempt to 'map' or conceptualise the postmodern global space, so as to endow the individual with a heightened sense of place within it.

Commodity culture A set of cultural practices in which cultural products are produced primarily for sale in a more or less competitive market. A commodity is a product produced in order to be sold for profit.

Commodity fetishism In Marx, and in Marxist and post-Marxist critical theory, the process by which human relations in a market economy tend to take on the appearance of relations between things, that is, between commodities or between money and commodities.

Condensation/displacement In Freud and in psychoanalysis, 'condensation' refers to the fact that dreams carry more than one meaning, 'displacement' to the process by which they are projected onto a seemingly unrelated object.

Counter-culture Various social and cultural movements from the 1960s and 1970s, originally in opposition to the Vietnam War, but later to conventional middle-class morality more generally.

Critical theory A type of cultural theory associated with the 'Frankfurt School', especially Adorno, Horkheimer, Marcuse and Benjamin, but also Habermas and Honneth, and with the thinkers from whom they derived inspiration, especially Marx and Freud. Its goal is 'emancipation from slavery' rather than knowledge *per se*.

Culturalism A 'literary-humanist' tradition of speculation about the relationship between culture and society, mainly German or British, which conceived of culture as an organic whole and as a repository of values superior to those of material civilisation.

Cultural materialism In Williams and his followers, an approach to cultural theory that sees art and culture as socially and materially productive processes.

Cultural policy studies A branch of cultural studies concerned with the practical administration of cultural funding, as distinct from the analysis of cultural texts and performances.

Cultural capital In Bourdieu, a metaphor to suggest that acquired cultural knowledges, skills and credentials function socially in ways analogous to economic capital, providing individuals with a kind of 'wealth' that can be used to secure social and economic advantage.

Cultural imperialism In radical criticism, used to describe how the characteristic values, styles and cultural products of a politically and economically dominant society displace or 'colonise' their local equivalents.

Cultural studies The academic study of culture. Used to refer to: interdisciplinary studies of culture, based primarily in the older disciplines of literary criticism, anthropology, history and sociology; radical political interventions into existing academic disciplines; a new discipline devoted to the study of popular culture; and a loosely 'social-scientific' theoretical paradigm for the study of all systems of textualised meaning—literary and non-literary, elite and popular.

Cultural theory Theory used in the academic study of culture. Neither philosophy nor discipline-specific theory, it is often understood as a new and distinctly 'postmodern' type of 'trans-disciplinary' post-structuralist theorising. Others argue that earlier forms of systematic speculation about cultural modernisation and postmodernisation are similarly theoretical and, by implication at least, similarly transdisciplinary.

Culture Originally, the cultivation of organic material, later, by extension and analogy, the cultivation of human beings. In the humanities, the term tends to denote the arts; in the social sciences, the way of life of a people. The two sets of meaning are connectable through the notion that the former express the latter. More generally, the word refers to the entire range of institutions, artefacts and practices that make up our symbolic universe. It tends to include art and religion, science and sport, education and leisure, but not normally economics and politics.

Culture industries In Adorno and Horkheimer, a derogatory term for the way capitalist mass culture is manufactured by quasi-industrial techniques. More recently, a more neutral (or uncritical) description of private or state-owned institutions that produce, sell or distribute cultural products and services, normally on a mass scale.

Culture wars In the United States, the bitter political debates of the 1980s and 1990s that resulted from the more forceful projection of minority cultural issues such as feminism, gay activism, AIDS awareness, anti-racism and multiculturalism into the national cultural arena.

Cyborg A 'cybernetic organism', composite of human and machine. In posthumanist cultural theory, the literal and/or metaphorical shape of the human condition after humanism.

Deconstruction In Derrida and his followers, textual analysis that pushes textualised meaning to its limits, so as to discover the differences within a text, the way it fails to say what it means to say.

Defamiliarisation In Russian Formalism, the way new art and literature 'makes strange' both previous art and literature and the world itself.

Denotation/connotation In semiotics, a distinction between the primary and secondary functions of the sign. Denotation refers to the primary function, its most obvious and literal meaning; connotation to its further associative meanings. Thus the word 'lion' denotes an animal, but also connotes bravery.

Dialectics In Plato, a form of philosophical reasoning or argumentation in which contrary positions are resolved into a higher synthesis. In Hegel, history itself proceeds according to a dialectical logic in which the spirit of one age contradicts that of another. In Marx, this 'idealist' dialectic is given 'materialist' redefinition as the contradiction between the social relations of production (the class structure) and the forces of production (the available technology).

Dialogism In Bakhtin, the open-ended multiplicity and dialogue between discourses, especially in literary texts, which arises from the nature of the speech situation itself. He argues that although speaker and addressee share a patterned speech situation, which conditions what can be communicated, this situation is itself conditioned by such dialogue. As a result, speech situations are open-ended and subject to inflection according to class, profession, generation, region and so on.

Différance In Derrida, a neologism coined to stress the double meaning of the French verb, *différer*, as both to differ and to defer. Difference is thus always also deferral, since meaning is continually displaced from signifier to signifier, in an endless chain of signification precluding fixed or stable meaning. The idea was taken up by a whole range of late twentieth-century cultural theories, inspired in whole or in part by the 'politics of difference' of the 'new social movements'.

Discourse In Foucault and his followers, a rule-governed group of statements operating in a field of power relations.

Distinction In Bourdieu, the role of cultural 'taste' as a marker of class position.

Écriture féminine In Cixous and feminist cultural theory more generally, the idea that women's writing articulates the female body.

Empiricism In philosophy, the theory according to which knowledge proceeds from experience.

Enlightenment A seventeenth- and eighteenth-century European philosophical and intellectual movement characterised by its rationalist, scientific basis and by its opposition to theological explanation. Among the key ideals were progress, science, the rule of law, the social contract and the free market.

Essentialism A normally derogatory term to describe and criticise the view that human beings, cultural texts and other objects possess a 'true' nature, defined by their underlying 'essence'. In Spivak and Showalter, used 'strategically' on behalf of subaltern groups.

Ethnicity The characteristic of belonging to a particular subnational and often subordinate group, defined in terms of some shared cultural, religious or linguistic characteristic. The term suggests a quasi-racial sense of 'belonging' to a tribe or clan.

Eurocentrism In postcolonial and other radical criticism, the conception, widespread among Europeans during the nineteenth and twentieth centuries, of Europe as the moral, intellectual and cultural centre of the world.

Feminism A political movement defined in opposition to 'patriarchal' social structures and the systematic domination of women and children by men.

Gaze In Lacan and his followers, the notion that humans seek confirmation of self in the gaze of others. Where Freud had viewed 'scopophilia', the pleasure of looking, as at the root of narcissism, voyeurism and masochism, Lacan extended its relevance into the formation of subjectivity itself.

Gender In feminist cultural theory, the culturally constructed, rather than biological, aspects of sexual difference.

Genealogy Literally, ancestry, lineage or pedigree. In Nietzsche and Foucault, by extension and analogy, the study of how particular discourses are formed historically and how they are imbricated with relations of power.

Globalisation A key feature of late capitalism, the processes by which corporations, capital and information (and to a lesser extent people) acquired an increasingly global reach during the last decades of the twentieth century.

Gynocritics In Showalter and other feminist cultural theory, a woman-centred approach to the study of women's culture and writing.

Habitus In Bourdieu, the framework within which the cultural norms or models of behaviour and action that are specific to a particular social group are unconsciously internalised during socialisation. These 'dispositions' function as a form of pre-reflective background to subsequent action.

Hegemony In Gramsci, the construction and permeation throughout the whole of society of a system of values and beliefs supportive of an existing ruling class. In later reformulations the term is extended to include the values and beliefs of other socially dominant groups.

Hermeneutics Theories of 'interpretation' taking as their central problem that of how to understand the more or less intended meanings of others. Contemporary hermeneutics has been concerned with the differences between truth in the humanities and in the natural sciences and with how pre-understandings, or 'prejudices', provide the preconditions without which understanding cannot take place.

Heteroglossia/polyphony In Bakhtin, the multiplicity of interacting discourses or 'voices', especially in novels, which stand in opposition to the monological discourse of authority or the author figure.

Historicism Originally, the view that historical events can be understood only in the immediate context of their occurrence, rather than as instances of some abstract theory. In some later reformulations, the view that history itself has a logic that shapes such contexts.

Humanism A philosophical view of the world, beginning with the Renaissance, centred on humanity and human reason, rather than God and divine reason.

Hyperreality In Eco, Baudrillard and postmodernism more generally, the idea that in a mass-mediated world reality becomes less real than its media 'simulations'.

Id/ego/super-ego In Freud, the tripartite structure of the mind. The id is the location and source of libidinal desire and pyschic energy and is inaccessible to the waking mind. The ego is our sense of self and conscious perception. The super-ego is formed through the internalisation of parental and societal restraint and is what we loosely describe as 'conscience'.

Idealism In philosophy, especially German philosophy, the view that the most fundamental level of reality consists in ideas.

Ideological state apparatuses (ISAs) In Althusser, institutions that function to reproduce the system of structured social inequality, or the relations of production, by interpellating the subject. Althusser names these as the religious ISA, the educational ISA, the family ISA, the legal ISA, the political ISA, the trade union ISA, the communications ISA and the cultural ISA.

Ideology Originally, in de Tracy, the study of ideas. In Marx, a term used to denote the connectedness of ideas and beliefs with social position. Marx argued that rival classes produce rival systems of ideas in their struggle for social leadership. But he also argued that the ruling ideas are normally the ideas of the ruling class and thus, in a sense, an instrument of social domination. More recent accounts tend to understand ideology less as a tool of the ruling class than as the discursive precondition for participation in social discourse. In Marx occasionally and Althusser almost invariably, science is troped against ideology as truth to falsehood.

Imaginary/Symbolic/Real In Lacan, the tripartite model of the pyscho-social world. The Imaginary refers to the Freudian pre-Oedipal stage of infant development; the Symbolic, to the world of language, social communication and culture; the Real, to all that lies outside and inside the subject, but which is never directly accessible.

Interpellation In Althusser, the way ideology 'hails' the subject, so that individual subjectivity is formed by pre-existent ideological structures.

Intertextuality In semiology, a concept that denotes how all texts are embedded in a network of texts, so that each text is inextricably a composite of other texts; also, how a text implicitly or explicitly 'cites' other texts, including its own prior contextualisation or reception.

Jouissance Originally, the French word for extreme pleasure or joy, especially of a sexual kind. In Barthes, by analogy and extension, the kind of extreme pleasure produced by those texts that position the reader as their active co-author, rather than as passive consumer. In Cixous and some feminists, a distinctly female realm of sexual and textual enjoyment beyond patriarchal control.

Langue/parole In Saussure, the distinction between the social and systemic rules of language (*langue*) and the individual and particular instances of speech or utterance (*parole*).

Late capitalism In Jameson, a third stage in the history of capitalism, dating from some time after the Second World War, when national monopolies were transformed into global corporations, and market values became dominant in practically every sphere of human activity.

Legitimation In Weber, the process by which social subordinates come to believe in their superordinates' right to give commands and be obeyed. Weber argued that there were three main types of legitimate authority: 'traditional', 'charismatic' and 'rational/legal'. The latter is the most significant for modernity and rests on belief in the 'legality' of normative rules.

Liberalism In general, a political doctrine that values individual liberty and autonomy in opposition to the state. More narrowly, an economic theory according to which governments should not interfere in the workings of the market.

Literariness Literally, whatever endows 'literature' with its own distinctive properties. In Russian Formalism, this is synonymous with a text's capacity for defamiliarisation.

Logocentrism Literally, word-centredness or speech-centredness and, by extension, God-centredness. In Derrida, a pejorative term to describe the notion of language as prior 'voice' and writing as mere technology. He believes the entire western philosophical tradition to be 'metaphysical' insofar as it imagines some real 'presence' prior to discourse. In Cixous and other feminists, and in Derrida's own later work, the notion has been reconceptualised as 'phallogocentrism'.

Mass culture/mass civilisation/mass media Mass culture and mass civilisation are generally derogatory terms used to describe and decry subcultures associated with mass media audiences. Mass media is more neutral, denoting those mainly twentieth-century communication systems (especially paperback fiction, newspapers and magazines, cinema, radio and television) that combine mechanical reproduction with commodity production. Media audiences are often treated as masses both by media critics such as Adorno and Leavis and by media corporations. For Williams and his followers, the problem was not in the masses, but in seeing people as masses.

Mechanical reproduction In Benjamin, the relatively large-scale replication of cultural artefacts by means of machine technologies, where each replica is neither any more nor any less 'original' than any other.

Mediation In general, any process by which some factor intervenes between two elements so as facilitate their relations. In cultural theory, first, the way human relations are 'mediated' by social conventions, ideology, class, gender, etc., and, second, the way the mass media 'mediate' and thus filter and shape the transmission of information.

Modernism The late nineteenth- and early twentieth-century art and literature that sought to break with the conventions of nineteenth-century realism.

Modernity In sociology and history, the social condition of being 'modern', variously connected to industrialisation, capitalism and progress, democracy, nationalism and the nation-state, liberalism, socialism and communism, Protestantism, the Enlightenment, science, technology and, of course, modernism.

Multiculturalism The extension and institutionalisation of (primarily 'ethnic') cultural diversity into the nation-state, through such avenues as the legal system, the education system, government policy towards health and housing, and respect for culture-specific linguistic, communal and religious practices and customs.

New historicism In Greenblatt and his followers, a neo-Foucauldian approach to cultural theory aiming to show how social power and historical conflict permeate the textuality of a society's culture.

Oedipus complex In Freud, and in psychoanalysis more generally, the most fundamental of repressed desires. Freud argued that for all children the first sexual impulse is an early attraction to the mother as love object, the first hatred for the father as erotic rival. Through the fear of castration, the male child eventually identifies with the authoritarian father figure and ceases to desire the mother. Lacking a penis, the female child is unable to do this and therefore redirects her desire from mother to father. She nonetheless continues to suffer from 'penis envy', which finds resolution only in giving birth to a child of her own.

Orientalism In Said, and in postcolonial criticism more generally, the system of ideological fictions by which the European 'Occident' constructed the Asiatic, especially Middle Eastern, 'Orient' (and by extension the whole non-European world) as 'Other'. It functions by way of binary oppositions in which the West, its possessions, attributes and ethnicities are valorised positively against the inferior status of non-western peoples.

Pastiche In literature, film and other arts, the open borrowing of a style in an essentially incongruous context. In Jameson, 'blank parody', that is, parody devoid of satirical intent, or distortion without derision.

Patriarchy Literally, the rule of the fathers. In feminist social and cultural theory, the systems of interlocking politico-economic, cultural and social structures through which men dominate women.

Performativity In semiology and linguistics, the property shared by some speech acts of performing that which they signify, for example when a judge announces 'I sentence you . . .' or a bride and bridegroom say 'I do'. In feminist, gay and lesbian cultural theory, by extension and analogy, the performed or socially constructed nature of sexual identities.

Phallocentrism Literally, centred on the 'phallus'. In feminist cultural theory, male-centredness, a near-synonym for androcentrism, but often associated with logocentrism.

Phallus Literally, a symbolic representation of the penis used in ancient Greek and other religions and variously seen as signifying fertility, virility and patriarchal power. In Lacan, the entry of the father and the subsequent socialisation and gendering of the child is symbolised by the phallus, understood as the Law of the Father. Lacan calls the phallus the 'transcendental signifier', or that which grounds the social order.

Pluralism In philosophy, any system of thought and belief that acknowledges more than one ultimate principle, the antonym of monism. More loosely, the acceptance of theoretical, political, social and cultural difference.

Polymorphous perversity In Freud and psychoanalysis more generally, a stage of infant pan-sexuality where both male and female sexuality is dispersed, uninhibited and as yet not centred on genitality.

Polysemy In semiology, the property (shared by all signs) of being able to signify multiple meanings.

Popular culture Literally, the culture of the people, often not made by them, but made for them and identified as theirs by the culture industries. In humanist literary criticism, a generally pejorative term used to denote inferior kinds of work or work deliberately setting out to win favour. More recently and more neutrally, work consumed and well liked by many people. In populist cultural studies, a celebratory term denoting that which is commercially viable and free from cultural elitism. The sense of people making their own culture is often displaced to the past or to the 'Third World' as 'folk culture'.

Positivism In Comte, and in philosophy and the social sciences more generally, the view that all valid knowledge claims should proceed according to the logic of the natural sciences.

Postcolonialism In cultural theory, an approach that attempts to 'decentre' white, metropolitan, European cultures so as to valorise the margin against the metropolis and the periphery against the centre.

Posthumanism In cultural theory, a term referring to the combined effects of the decentring of the liberal humanist subject in structuralist and post-structuralist theory and the 'cyborg' merging of human and machine in a range of technologies for re-embodiment and dis-embodiment. Where humanism displaced God from the centre of world, posthumanism promises or threatens to displace the human.

Postmodernism Literally, the art that came after modernism, the non-realist and non-traditional arts of the post-Second World War period. More generally, the commodity cultures of the late twentieth-century western world and the cultural, social and philosophical conditions that accompanied them. In Lyotard, a condition characterised by and celebrated for its loss of faith in Enlightenment-inspired 'meta-narratives', or grand stories. In Jameson, characterised and critiqued as 'the cultural dominant of late capitalism'.

Post-structuralism In cultural theory, the kinds of (mainly French) theory that developed after, in relation to and in reaction against structuralist semiology: Derridean 'deconstruction', Foucauldian 'genealogy', Lacanian psychoanalysis and Deleuzian 'rhizomatics', for example.

Psychoanalysis In Freud and his followers, the science of the human mind, organised around the concept of the psychic unconscious.

Public sphere In Habermas, the institutions of organised public opinion. He uses the term to describe the emergence in

Europe, during the seventeenth and eighteenth centuries, of a middle-class public opinion, relatively independent of the absolute monarchy and made up of formally free, equal, rational individuals.

Queer Historically, a pejorative term for homosexuality, subsequently appropriated by the gay community and given positive redefinition. In cultural theory, an approach concerned with the identity claims of non-normative sexualities and with a radical deconstruction of the categories of 'gender' and 'sexuality'.

Racism Vilification, discrimination, harassment or persecution directed at people perceived to be 'racially' different. Such racial difference is typically associated, at least rhetorically, with phenotypical characteristics (skin colour, hair, physique, etc.). But 'race' (usually written in inverted commas) is a notoriously controversial term, which founders on the impossibility of drawing definitive boundaries between one 'race' and another.

Rationalisation In Weber, the underlying logic of modernity and of modernisation, by which 'rational/legal' cultural norms tend to displace 'traditional'.

Readerly/writerly In Barthes, the distinction between texts that position their reader as passive consumer (readerly texts), and those that demand that the reader actively participate as their co-author (writerly texts). Later reformulated as the distinction between the text of *plaisir* and that of *jouissance*.

Realism In art, literature and aesthetics, the notion that art factually does or ideally should represent reality 'as it really is'. More precisely, the kind of art that produces 'reality effects', that is, represents itself as if it were an accurate reflection of some reality external to itself.

Reification Literally, the treatment of non-things (processes, relations, human beings) as things or objects. In Lukács, a term carrying much the same meaning as 'commodity fetishism' does in Marx. Lukács generalised the notion beyond the commodity relation, however, insisting that the whole of capitalist reality was reified.

Representation The use of one thing to stand in for another in order to transmit meaning; the construction of meaning through the use of signs and concepts.

Rhizome In botany, a horizontal or subterranean root-like system. In Deleuze and Guattari, by extension and analogy, a 'deterritorialised' or non-hierarchical form of writing and thinking in which no overarching narrative or system predominates. They posit 'rhizomatics' in direct opposition to the dominant 'arborescent' mode in western thought, which is seen as based on vertical, hierarchised and systematic principles.

Romanticism In the arts and philosophy, during the eighteenth and early nineteenth centuries, a broad international movement in reaction against the Enlightenment. Important thematics included a view of the artist as uniquely creative and a belief in the superiority of art, as *Kultur*, over everyday civilisation.

Russian Formalism In Shklovsky, Jakobson and their co-thinkers, a proto-structuralist approach to literary theory that sought to establish the study of literature on scientific and systematic foundations.

Semiology In Saussure, Barthes and more generally, the science of the study of signs. Also known as semiotics.

Semiotic In Kristeva, a roughly equivalent concept to the 'Imaginary' in Lacan. But unlike Lacan, Kristeva sees it as persisting into adulthood as an alternative mode of signification.

Sign/signifier/signified/referent In Saussure, and in semiology more generally, a sign is a relatively simple token of some other more complex reality. It is formed by the union of a 'signifier', that is, the sign's perceptible aspect (for example, the marks *dog* written on a page), and the 'signified', that is, the idea or mental concept the signifier symbolises (here, the idea of 'a dog' held by the communicators, which might incorporate notions as diverse as 'man's best friend' or 'exquisite delicacy'). The referent is the real object in the material world to which the sign refers (here, a particular furry animal with paws).

Simulacrum/simulation Literally, a simulacrum is a specious likeness, simulation a false pretence. In Baudrillard, a 'simulacrum' is a sign without a referent, a copy without an original, 'simulation' its processual aspect, the non-referential equivalent of representation. He argues that in contemporary culture the dominant order of simulacra consists of 'simulacra of simulation', that is, 'hyperreal' simulacra founded on information.

Species-being In Marx, the humanness of humanity, constituted by our capacity for conscious, collective, creative production.

Structuralism Loosely, an approach to the study of human culture centred on the search for constraining patterns or 'structures'. More specifically, an approach that applies the methods of structural linguistics to all aspects of human culture.

Structure of feeling In Williams and his followers, a mediating term between 'art' and 'culture' denoting the patterned 'articulation' of different texts and sign-systems. The word 'feeling' is intended to draw attention to the felt sense of the quality of life in a particular place at a particular time. The concept was meant to embrace both the immediately experiential and the generationally specific aspects of artistic process. In some formulations, structures of feeling are represented as quite specifically 'counter-hegemonic'.

Subaltern Literally, a person of inferior rank, a vassal or a junior officer. In Gramsci and in later postcolonial theory, the largely unorganised underclasses and, by extension, subordinated groups more generally.

Subjectivity In general, consciousness of being, especially of being an acting subject. In structuralist and post-structuralist cultural theory, the unconscious effect of a 'subject position', a sense of identity constructed and conditioned by pre-existing social, cultural and linguistic frameworks.

Sublimation In Freud, the process by which unconscious and unfulfilled desires and drives are channelled into socially useful activities. If these can be neither expressed in perversion nor sublimated into socially acceptable activities such as work, sport, art or intellectuality, they become manifest as neurosis.

Synchronic/diachronic In Saussure, and in structuralism more generally, the distinction between analysis of a structure at a given point in time (synchronic) and analysis of changes over time (diachronic).

System/life-world In Habermas, the distinction between society viewed from the perspective of economy and state (the 'system'), which functions through the logic of instrumental reason, and viewed as the world of everyday experience, social discourse, cultural values, science, politics and art (the 'life-world').

Unconscious In general, psychic operations not present to, but nonetheless able to influence, the conscious mind. In Freud, and in psychoanalysis more generally, seen as the product of psychic repression.

Utilitarianism In British philosophy, especially Bentham and Mill, and in the social sciences, especially economics, a view of the social world as comprising a plurality of discrete, rational individuals, each motivated by the pursuit of pleasure (or 'utility') and the avoidance of pain. Just policy and right conduct therefore lead to the greatest happiness of the greatest number, by least inhibiting individuals in pursuit of their pleasures. Closely associated with liberalism.

Appendix: The institutionalisation of academic cultural studies

The best-known cultural studies programme is probably still that of the Department of Cultural Studies and Sociology at the University of Birmingham in England, a successor institution to the pioneering Centre for Contemporary Cultural Studies. Elsewhere in the United Kingdom one could cite: the School of Communication Studies at Westminster University, which houses a research Centre for Communication and Information Studies and one of the leading journals in the area, *Media, Culture and Society*; the School of Journalism, Media and Cultural Studies at Cardiff University in Wales, which is home to the Tom Hopkinson Centre for Media Research and, since 1998, the *International Journal of Cultural Studies*; the School of Cultural and Community Studies at the University of Sussex; the Department of Cultural Studies at the University of East London; and the increasingly prestigious Centre for Cultural Studies at Goldsmiths College, London. Even where such formal institutional autonomy doesn't exist, the subject is still often taught, but as part of sociology, English literature or visual arts. At Nottingham Trent University, for example, both cultural studies itself and *Theory, Culture and Society*, another leading journal in the field, are located in the Department of English and Media Studies. At the University of Leeds, by contrast, the Centre for Cultural Studies, which publishes the journal *Parallax*, is attached to the Department of Fine Art.

There are academic journals and associations, both national and international, devoted to the subject. The Third International Crossroads in Cultural Studies Conference, convened in June 2000 at Birmingham, appropriately enough, witnessed the foundation of an International Association of Cultural Studies. There is a *European Journal of Cultural Studies* co-edited from Cultural Studies at Birmingham, the School for Cultural Analysis, Theory and Interpretation at the University of Amsterdam in the Netherlands, and the Department of Sociology and Social Psychology at the University of Tampere in Finland. There is an International Research Center for Cultural Studies loosely associated with the University of Vienna. Elsewhere in Europe, institutionalised 'cultural studies' is less common, but it is clear that roughly similar kinds of work are conducted in France (Forbes & Kelly, 1995; Reynolds & Kidd, 2000), Italy (Forgacs & Lumley, 1996; Benedetti et al. 1996) and Germany (Berman, 1993; Burns, 1995; Denham et al. 1997).

In North America, an analogous list would include at least two Canadian institutions: the Cultural Studies Program at Trent University, Peterborough, and the Centre for Cultural Studies at the University of Guelph. In the United States itself, cultural studies has developed at such a pace as to leave Stuart Hall, a former director of the Birmingham Centre, 'completely dumbfounded' (Hall, 1992, p. 285). Here, a short list of institutions would include: the Program in Cultural Studies at the University of North Carolina at Chapel Hill, where the internationally prestigious journal *Cultural Studies* is now edited; the work in cultural studies of the English Institute and the old Center for Literary and Cultural Studies at Harvard; both the Center for Cultural Studies and the History of Consciousness Program at the University of California at Santa Cruz; the school of 'new historicist' cultural criticism in the Department of English at the University of California, Berkeley; the Department of Cultural Studies and Comparative Literature at the University of Minnesota; and the Graduate Program in Visual and Cultural Studies at the University of Rochester. For Australia, one would list the School of Communication and Cultural Studies at Curtin University; the Centre for Critical and Cultural Studies at the University of Queensland; the School of Film, Media and Cultural Studies at Griffith University, with its Key Centre for Cultural and Media Policy; the Department of English with Cultural Studies at the University of Melbourne; and the Centre for Comparative Literature and Cultural Studies at Monash University. There are similar or cognate institutions and programmes at the Federal University of Rio de Janeiro in Brazil, Lingnan University in Hong Kong and the University of Natal in South Africa. For similar programmes in India, Taiwan and Korea, see Guha & Spivak, 1988; Lal, 1996; Stratton & Ang, 1996, pp. 386–8.

Bibliography

Adorno, T. 1980, 'Letters to Walter Benjamin', trans. J. Zohn, in E. Bloch et al., *Aesthetics and Politics*, Verso, London, pp. 110–34.

—— 1980a, 'Reconciliation Under Duress', trans. R. Livingstone, in E. Bloch et al., *Aesthetics and Politics*, Verso, London, pp. 151–77.

—— and Horkheimer, M. 1979, *Dialectic of Enlightenment*, trans. J. Cumming, Verso, London.

Ahmad, A. 1992, *In Theory: Classes, Nations, Literatures*, Verso, London.

Althusser, L. 1971, *Lenin and Philosophy and Other Essays*, trans. B. Brewster, New Left Books, London.

——1977, *For Marx*, trans. B. Brewster, New Left Books, London.

—— and É. Balibar 1970, *Reading Capital*, trans. B. Brewster, New Left Books, London.

Anderson, B. 1991, *Imagined Communities: Reflections on the Origins and Spread of Nationalism*, Verso, London.

Anderson, P. 1976, *Considerations on Western Marxism*, New Left Books, London.

—— 1992, *A Zone of Engagement*, Verso, London.

—— 1998, *The Origins of Postmodernity*, Verso, London.

Anzaldúa, G. (ed.) 1990, *Making Face, Making Soul, Haciendo caras: Creative and Critical Perspectives by Women of Color*, Auntlute Foundation, San Francisco.

Aparicio, F. and Chávez-Silverman, S. (eds) 1997, *Tropicalizations: Transcultural Representations of Latinidad*, University Press of New England, Hanover, New England.

Arnold, M. 1966, *Culture and Anarchy*, (ed.) J.D. Wilson, Cambridge University Press, Cambridge.

—— 1980, 'The Function of Criticism at the Present Time', in *The Portable Matthew Arnold*, (ed.) L. Trilling, Penguin, Harmondsworth.

Ashcroft, B. et al. 1989, *The Empire Writes Back: Theory and Practice in Post-Colonial Literatures*, Routledge, London.

Bakhtin, M. 1965, *Rabelais and His World*, trans. Helen Iswolsky, MIT Press, Cambridge, Mass.

—— 1981, *The Dialogic Imagination*, (ed.) Michael Holquist, trans. Caryl Emerson and Michael Holquist, University of Texas Press, Austin.

—— 1984, *Problems of Dostoevsky's Poetics*, trans. Caryl Emerson, University of Minnesota Press, Minneapolis.

Baldick, C. 1983, *The Social Mission of English Criticism 1848–1932*, Oxford University Press, Oxford.
Barrett, M. 1988, *Women's Oppression Today: The Marxist/Feminist Encounter*, Verso, London.
—— 1991, *The Politics of Truth: From Marx to Foucault*, Stanford University Press, Stanford.
—— 1999, *Imagination in Theory: Essays on Writing and Culture*, Polity Press, Cambridge.
Barthes, R. 1968, *Elements of Semiology*, trans. A. Lavers and C. Smith, Hill and Wang, New York.
—— 1970, 'To Write: An Intransitive Verb?', trans. R. Macksey and E. Donato, in *The Languages of Criticism and the Sciences of Man*, (eds) R. Macksey and E. Donato, Johns Hopkins University Press, Baltimore.
—— 1973, *Mythologies*, trans. A. Lavers, Paladin, St Albans.
—— 1974, *S/Z*, trans. R. Miller, Hill and Wang, New York.
—— 1975, *The Pleasure of the Text*, trans. R. Miller, Hill and Wang, New York.
—— 1977, *Image-Music-Text*, trans. S. Heath, Hill and Wang, New York.
—— 1983, *The Fashion System*, trans. M. Ward and R. Howard, Hill and Wang, New York.
Baudrillard, J. 1983, *In the Shadow of the Silent Majorities, or, The End of the Social and Other Essays*, trans. P. Foss, J. Johnston and P. Patton, Semiotexte, New York.
—— 1988, 'The masses: the implosion of the social in the media', trans. M. Maclean, in *Selected Writings*, (ed.) M. Poster, Polity Press, Cambridge.
—— 1988a, *America*, trans. C. Turner, Verso, London.
—— 1993, *Symbolic Exchange and Death*, trans. I.H. Grant, Sage, London.
—— 1994, *Simulacra and Simulation*, trans. S.F. Glaser, University of Michigan Press, Ann Arbor.
Bauman, Z. 1987, *Legislators and Interpreters: On Modernity, Post-Modernity and Intellectuals*, Polity Press, Cambridge.
—— 1989, *Modernity and the Holocaust*, Polity Press, Cambridge.
—— 1992, *Intimations of Postmodernity*, Routledge, London.
—— 1995, *Life in Fragments: Essays in Postmodern Morality*, Blackwell, Oxford.
—— 1997, *Postmodernity and its Discontents*, New York University Press, New York.
Beck, U. 1992, *Risk Society: Towards a New Modernity*, trans. M. Ritter, Sage, London.
—— 1994, 'The Reinvention of Politics: Towards a Theory of Reflexive Modernization', trans. M. Ritter, in U. Beck et al., *Reflexive Modernization: Politics, Tradition and Aesthetics in the Modern Social Order*, Polity Press, Cambridge.
Bell, D. 1973, *The Coming of Post-Industrial Society*, Basic Books, New York.
—— 1976, *The Cultural Contradictions of Capitalism*, Heinemann, London.

—— 1977, 'Beyond Modernism, Beyond Self', in *Art, Politics and Will: Essays in Honour of Lionel Trilling*, (eds) Q. Anderson et al., Basic Books, New York.

Belsey, C. 1985, *The Subject of Tragedy: Identity and Difference in Renaissance Drama*, Methuen, London.

Benedetti, L., Hairston, J.L. and Ross, S.M. 1996, *Gendered Contexts: New Perspectives in Italian Cultural Studies*, Peter Lang, New York.

Benjamin, W. 1973, *Understanding Brecht*, trans. A. Bostock, NLB, London.

—— 1973a, 'The Work of Art in the Age of Mechanical Reproduction' in *Illuminations*, trans. H. Zohn, Fontana, Glasgow.

—— 1999, *The Arcades Project*, trans. H. Eiland and K. McLaughlin, Belknap Press, Cambridge, Mass.

Bennett, T. 1989, 'Holding Spaces', *Southern Review*, 22, 2.

—— 1990, *Outside Literature*, Routledge, London.

—— 1992, 'Useful Culture', *Cultural Studies*, 6, 3.

—— 1992a, 'Putting Policy into Cultural Studies', in *Cultural Studies*, (eds) L. Grossberg, C. Nelson and P. Treichler, Routledge, London.

—— 1998, *Culture: A Reformer's Science*, Allen & Unwin, Sydney.

—— et al. 1999, *Accounting for Tastes: Australian Everyday Cultures*, Cambridge University Press, Cambridge.

—— and Woollacott, J. 1987, *Bond and Beyond: The Political Career of a Popular Hero*, Macmillan, London.

Bentham, J. 1962, *The Works of Jeremy Bentham*, Vol. II, Russell and Russell, New York.

Berman, R.A. 1993, *Cultural Studies of Modern Germany: History, Representation and Nationhood*, University of Wisconsin Press, Madison.

Best, S. and Kellner, D. 1991, *Postmodern Theory: Critical Interrogations*, Guilford Press, New York.

Bhabha, H.K. 1990, 'DissemiNation: Time, Narrative, and the Margins of the Modern Nation', in *Nation and Narration*, (ed.) H.K. Bhabha, Routledge, London.

—— 1994, *The Location of Culture*, Routledge, London.

Bloom, H. 1994, *The Western Canon: The Books and School of the Ages*, Harcourt Brace and Co, New York.

—— et al. 1979, *Deconstruction and Criticism*, Seabury Press, New York.

Bondanella, P.E. 1997, *Umberto Eco and the Open Text: Semiotics, Fiction, Popular Culture*, Cambridge University Press, Cambridge.

Bourdieu, P. 1977, *Outline of a Theory of Practice*, trans. R. Nice, Cambridge University Press, Cambridge.

—— 1984, *Distinction: A Social Critique of the Judgement of Taste*, trans. R. Nice, Routledge and Kegan Paul, London.

—— 1988, *Homo Academicus*, trans. P. Collier, Polity Press, Cambridge.

—— 1989, 'The Corporatism of the Universal: The Role of Intellectuals in the Modern World', trans. C. Betensky, *Telos*, 81.

—— 1993, *Sociology in Question*, trans. R. Nice, Sage, London.

—— 1993a, 'The Field of Cultural Production, or: the Economic World Reversed', trans. R. Nice, in *The Field of Cultural Production: Essays on Art and Literature*, (ed.) R. Johnson, Polity Press, Cambridge.
—— 1996, *The Rules of Art: Genesis and Structure of the Literary Field*, trans. S. Emanuel, Polity Press, Cambridge.
—— 1996a, *The State Nobility; Elite Schools in the Field of Power*, trans. L.C. Clough, Polity Press, Cambridge.
—— 1998, *Acts of Resistance: Against the New Myths of Our Time*, trans. R. Nice, Polity Press, Cambridge.
—— 1998a, 'Pour une gauche de gauche', *Le Monde*, 8 April.
—— et al. 1999, *The Weight of the World: Social Suffering in Contemporary Society*, trans. P.P. Ferguson et al., Polity Press, Cambridge.
—— 2000, *Pascalian Meditations*, trans. R. Nice, Polity Press, Cambridge.
Bradbury, M. 1976, 'The Cities of Modernism', in *Modernism 1890–1930*, (eds) M. Bradbury and J. McFarlane, Penguin, Harmondsworth.
Bradbury, M. and McFarlane, J. (eds), 1976, *Modernism 1890–1930*, Penguin, Harmondsworth.
Brooker, P. 1999, *Cultural Theory: a glossary*, Oxford University Press, London.
Bürger, P. 1984, *Theory of the Avant-Garde*, trans. M. Shaw, University of Minnesota Press, Minneapolis.
Burns, R. 1995, *German Cultural Studies: An Introduction*, Oxford University Press, Oxford.
Butler, J. 1990, *Gender Trouble: Feminism and the Subversion of Identity*, Routledge, London.
—— 1993, *Bodies That Matter: On the Discursive Limits of 'Sex'*, Routledge, London.
—— 1999, 'Merely Cultural', *New Left Review*, 227.
Callinicos, A. 1989, *Against Postmodernism: A Marxist Critique*, Polity Press, Cambridge.
Carbey, H. 1987, *Reconstructing Womanhood: The Emergence of the Afro-American Woman Novelist*, Oxford University Press, New York.
Cevasco, M.E. 2000, 'Whatever Happened to Cultural Studies: Notes from the Periphery', *Textual Practice*, 14, 3.
Chakrabarty, D. 2000, *Provincializing Europe: Postcolonial Thought and Historical Difference*, Princeton University Press, Princeton.
Cixous, H. 1981, 'The Laugh of the Medusa', trans. K. Cohen and P. Cohen, in *New French Feminisms: An Anthology*, (eds) E. Marks and I. de Courtivron, Harvester, Brighton.
—— and Clément, C. 1986, *The Newly Born Woman*, trans. B. Wing, University of Minnesota Press, Minneapolis.
Collini, S. 1994, 'Escape from DWEMsville', *The Times Literary Supplement*, 27 May, pp. 3–4.
Collins, R. et al. 1986, 'Introduction', in (eds) R. Collins et al., *Media, Culture and Society: A Critical Reader*, Sage, London.
Crick, B. 1980, *George Orwell: A Life*, Secker & Warburg, London.

Daly, M. 1978, *Gyn/Ecology: The Metaethics of Radical Feminism*, Beacon Press, Boston.

Darder, A. and Torres, R.D. (eds) 1998, *The Latino Studies Reader*, Blackwell, Oxford.

de Beauvoir, S. 1972, *The Second Sex*, trans. H.M. Parshley, Penguin, Harmondsworth.

de Lauretis, T. 1978, 'Semiotics, Theory and Social Practice: A Critical History of Italian Semiotics', *Cine-tracts*, 2, 1.

Deleuze, G. and Guattari, F. 1983, *Anti-Oedipus: Capitalism and Schizophrenia*, trans. R. Hurley et al., University of Minnesota Press, Minneapolis.

—— 1986, *Kafka: Toward a Minor Literature*, trans. D. Polan, University of Minnesota Press, Minneapolis.

—— 1987, *A Thousand Plateaus: Capitalism and Schizophrenia*, trans. B. Massumi, University of Minnesota Press, Minneapolis.

—— 1994, *What is Philosophy?*, trans. H. Tomlinson and G. Burchell, Columbia University Press, New York.

Denham, S. et al. (eds) 1997, *A User's Guide to German Cultural Studies*, University of Michigan Press, Ann Arbor.

Derrida, J. 1970, 'Structure, Sign and Play in the Discourse of the Human Sciences', trans. R. Macksey, in *The Languages of Criticism and the Sciences of Man*, (eds) R. Macksey and E. Donato, Johns Hopkins University Press, Baltimore.

—— 1973, *Speech and Phenomena, and Other Essays on Husserl's Theory of Signs*, trans. D. B. Alison, Northwestern University Press, Evanston.

—— 1976, *Of Grammatology*, trans. G.C. Spivak, Johns Hopkins University Press, Baltimore.

—— 1978, *Writing and Difference*, trans. A. Bass, University of Chicago Press, Chicago.

—— 1982, *Margins of Philosophy*, trans. A. Bass, University of Chicago Press, Chicago.

—— 1983, 'The Principle of Reason: The University in the Eyes of Its Pupils', trans. C. Porter and E.P. Morris, *Diacritics*, 13, 3.

—— 1984, 'No Apocalypse, Not Now (Full Speed Ahead, Seven Missiles, Seven Missives)', trans. C. Porter and P. Lewis, *Diacritics*, 14, 2.

—— 1987, *The Truth in Painting*, trans. G. Bennington and I. McLeod, University of Chicago Press, Chicago.

—— 1992, *Acts of Literature*, (ed.) D. Attridge, Routledge, London.

—— 1994, *Specters of Marx: The State of the Debt, the Work of Mourning, and the New International*, trans. P. Kamuf, Routledge, London.

—— 1996, *Archive Fever: a Freudian Impression*, trans. E. Prenowitz, University of Chicago Press, Chicago.

—— 1997, *Politics of Friendship*, trans. G. Collins, Verso, London.

—— 1998, *Resistances of Psychoanalysis*, trans. P. Kamuf, P.A. Brault and M. Naas, Stanford University Press, Stanford.

—— 1999, 'Forgiving the Unforgivable', Lecture, Monash University Centre

for Comparative Literature and Cultural Studies, Melbourne, 6 August.
Dollimore, J. 1991, *Sexual Dissidence: Augustine to Wilde, Freud to Foucault*, Oxford University Press, Oxford.
—— 1994, 'Introduction: Shakespeare, Cultural Materialism and the New Historicism', in *Political Shakespeare: Essays in Cultural Materialism*, (eds) J. Dollimore and A. Sinfield, Manchester University Press, Manchester.
Dollimore, J. and Sinfield, A. (eds) 1994, *Political Shakespeare: Essays in Cultural Materialism*, Manchester University Press, Manchester.
During, S. 1990, 'Postmodernism or Post-Colonialism Today?', in *Postmodern Conditions*, (ed.) A. Milner et al., Berg, Oxford.
—— 1990a, 'Literature—Nationalism's Other? The Case for Revision', *Nation and Narration*, (ed.) H.K. Bhabha, Routledge, London.
—— 1999, 'Introduction', *The Cultural Studies Reader*, 2nd edition, Routledge, London.
Durkheim, E. 1964, *The Rules of Sociological Method*, trans. S.A. Solovay and J.H. Mueller, Free Press, New York.
—— 1976, *The Elementary Forms of the Religious Life*, trans. J.W. Swain, George Allen & Unwin, London.
Dworkin, A. 1974, *Woman Hating*, Dutton, New York.
Eagleton, T. 1968, 'The Idea of a Common Culture', in *From Culture to Revolution: The Slant Symposium 1967*, (eds) T. Eagleton and B. Wicker, Sheed and Ward, London.
—— 1975, *Myths of Power: A Marxist Study of the Brontës*, Macmillan, London.
—— 1976, *Criticism and Ideology*, New Left Books, London.
—— 1981, *Walter Benjamin or Towards Revolutionary Criticism*, Verso, London.
—— 1982, *The Rape of Clarissa: Writing, Sexuality and Class Struggle in Samuel Richardson*, Basil Blackwell, Oxford.
—— 1989, 'Base and Superstructure in Raymond Williams', in *Raymond Williams: Critical Perspectives*, (ed.) T. Eagleton, Polity Press, Cambridge.
—— 1989a, 'Bakhtin, Schopenhauer, Kundera', in *Bakhtin and Cultural Theory*, (eds) K. Hirschkop and D. Shepherd, Manchester University Press, Manchester.
—— 1990, *The Ideology of the Aesthetic*, Basil Blackwell, Oxford.
—— 1990a, 'Nationalism: Irony and Commitment', in T. Eagleton et al., *Nationalism, Colonialism and Literature*, University of Minnesota Press, Minneapolis.
—— 1992, 'A Culture in Crisis', *The Guardian* 3, 27 November.
—— 1995, *Heathcliff and the Great Hunger*, Verso, London.
—— 1996, *Literary Theory: An Introduction*, 2nd edition, Blackwell, Oxford.
—— 1996a, *The Function of Criticism: From 'The Spectator' to Post-Structuralism*, Verso, London.
—— 1996b, *The Illusions of Postmodernism*, Blackwell, Oxford.
—— 1999, 'In the Gaudy Supermarket', *London Review of Books*, 21, 10.
—— 2000, *The Idea of Culture*, Blackwell, Oxford.

Easthope, A. 1988, *British Post-Structuralism Since 1968*, Routledge, London.
—— 1991, *Literary Into Cultural Studies*, Routledge, London.
Eco, U. 1976, *A Theory of Semiotics*, Indiana University Press, Bloomington.
—— 1981, *The Role of the Reader: Explorations in the Semiotics of Texts*, Hutchinson, London.
—— 1989, *The Open Work*, trans. A. Cancogni, Harvard University Press, Cambridge, Mass.
—— 1994, *The Name of the Rose Including Postscript to 'the Name of the Rose'* trans. W. Weaver, Harcourt Brace, San Diego.
Eder, K. 1993, *The New Politics of Class: Social Movements and Cultural Dynamics in Advanced Societies*, Sage, London.
Eliot, T.S. 1962, *Notes Towards the Definition of Culture*, Faber, London.
—— 1963, *Selected Essays*, Faber, London.
Elliot, A. (ed.) 2000, *Freud 2000*, Melbourne University Press, Melbourne.
Erlich, V. 1955, *Russian Formalism: History-Doctrine*, Mouton, The Hague.
Febvre, L. and Martin, J. 1976, *The Coming of the Book: The Impact of Printing 1450–1800*, trans. D. Gerard, G. Nowell-Smith and D. Wootton, New Left Books, London.
Fehér, F. 1990, 'The Pyrhhic Victory of Art in its War of Liberation: Remarks on the Postmodernist Intermezzo', in *Postmodern Conditions*, (eds) A. Milner et al., Berg, Oxford.
Felperin, H. 1990, *The Uses of the Canon: Elizabethan Literature and Contemporary Theory*, Oxford University Press, Oxford.
Fischer, M. 1986, 'Ethnicity and the Post-Modern Arts of Memory', in *Writing Culture: The Poetics and Politics of Ethnography*, (eds) J. Clifford et al., University of California Press, Berkeley.
Flores, J. 2000, *From Bomba to Hip-Hop*, Columbia University Press, New York.
Forbes, J. and Kelly, M. (eds) 1995, *French Cultural Studies: An Introduction*, Oxford University Press, Oxford.
Forgacs, D. and Lumley, R. 1996, *Italian Cultural Studies: An Introduction*, Oxford University Press, Oxford.
Foucault, M. 1965, *Madness and Civilisation: A History of Insanity in the Age of Reason*, trans. R. Howard, Vintage Books, New York.
—— 1972, *The Archaeology of Knowledge*, trans. A.M. Sheridan, Tavistock, London.
—— 1972a, *Histoire de la folie á l'âge classique*, Éditions Gallimard, Paris.
—— 1973, *The Birth of the Clinic*, trans. A.M. Sheridan, Tavistock, London.
—— 1973a, *The Order of Things: An Archaeology of the Human Sciences*, Vintage Books, New York.
—— 1977, *Language, Counter-Memory, Practice*, (ed.) D.F. Bouchard, trans. D.F. Bouchard and S. Simon, Cornell University Press, Ithaca.
—— 1978, *The History of Sexuality. Volume 1: An Introduction*, trans. R. Hurley, Random House, New York.
—— 1979, *Discipline and Punish: The Birth of the Prison*, trans. A.M. Sheridan, Penguin, Harmondsworth.

—— 1980, *Power/Knowledge: Selected Interviews and Other Writings, 1972–1977*, (ed.) C. Gordon, Harvester Press, Brighton.
—— 1983, 'Introduction', in G. Deleuze and F. Guattari, *Anti-Oedipus*, University of Minnesota Press, Minneapolis.
—— 1987, *The Use of Pleasure. The History of Sexuality: Volume Two*, trans. R. Hurley, Penguin, Harmondsworth.
—— 1990, *The Care of the Self. The History of Sexuality: Volume Three*, trans. R. Hurley, Penguin, Harmondsworth.
—— 1991, *The Foucault Effect: Studies in Governmentality, with Two Lectures by and an Interview with Michel Foucault*, (eds) G. Burchell et al., University of Chicago Press, Chicago.
Fraser, N. 1984, 'The French Derrideans: Politicizing Deconstruction or Deconstructing the Political?', *New German Critique*, 33.
—— 1997, *Justice Interruptus: Critical Reflections on the 'Postsocialist Condition'*, Routledge, London.
Freud, S. 1973, *New Introductory Lectures on Psychoanalysis*, trans. J. Strachey, Penguin, Harmondsworth.
—— 1976, *The Interpretation of Dreams*, trans. J. Strachey, Penguin, Harmondsworth.
—— 1985, *The Origins of Religion*, trans. J. Strachey, Penguin, Harmondsworth.
—— 1985a, *Civilization, Society and Religion*, trans. J. Strachey, Penguin, Harmondsworth.
Frosh, S. 1999, *The Politics of Psychoanalysis*, 2nd edition, New York University Press, New York.
Gadamer, H.G. 1990, *Truth and Method*, trans. J. Weinsheimer and D. G. Marshall, Crossroad, New York.
Gallagher, C. 1996, 'Marxism and the New Historicism', in *New Historicism and Cultural Materialism: A Reader*, (ed.) K. Ryan, Arnold, London.
Gallagher, C. and Greenblatt, S. 2000, *Practicing New Historicism*, University of Chicago Press, Chicago.
Garnham, N. 1983, 'Towards a theory of Cultural Materialism', *Journal of Communication*, 33, 3.
—— 1987, 'Concepts of Culture: Public Policy and the Cultural Industries', *Cultural Studies*, 1, 1.
—— 1988, 'Raymond Williams, 1921–1988: a Cultural Analyst, a Distinctive Tradition', *Journal of Communication*, 38, 4.
—— 1990, *Capitalism and Communication: Global Culture and the Economics of Information*, Sage, London.
—— 1995, 'The Media and Narratives of the Intellectual', *Media, Culture and Society*, 17, 3.
—— 2000, *Emancipation, the Media and Modernity: Arguments about the Media and Social Theory*, Oxford University Press, Oxford.
Gates Jr, H.L. 1987, *Figures in Black*, Oxford University Press, Oxford.

—— 1988, *The Signifying Monkey: A Theory of Afro-American Literary Criticism*, Oxford University Press, Oxford.

Geertz, C. 1973, 'Thick description', in *The Interpretation of Cultures*, Basic Books, New York.

Gellner, E. 1964, *Thought and Change*, Weidenfeld & Nicolson, London.

—— 1997, *Nationalism*, New York University Press, New York.

Giddens, A. 1971, *Capitalism and Modern Social Theory*, Cambridge University Press, Cambridge.

—— 1991, *Modernity and Self-Identity: Self and Society in the Late Modern Age*, Stanford University Press, Stanford University Press.

—— 1994, 'Living in a Post-Traditional Society', in U. Beck et al., *Reflexive Modernization: Politics, Tradition and Aesthetics in the Modern Social Order*, Polity Press, Cambridge.

—— 1994a, *Beyond Left and Right: The Future of Radical Politics*, Polity Press, Cambridge.

Gilbert, S.M. and Gubar, S. 1988, *No Man's Land: The Place of the Woman Writer in the Twentieth Century, Vol. 1: The War of the Words*, Yale University Press, New Haven.

Gilmour, I. 2001, 'Little Mercians', *London Review of Books*, 23, 13.

Gilroy, P. 1992, *There Ain't No Black in the Union Jack*, Routledge, London.

—— 1993, *The Black Atlantic: Modernity and Double Consciousness*, Harvard University Press, Cambridge, Mass.

—— 2000, *Between Camps: Nations, Cultures and the Allure of Race*, Penguin, Harmondsworth.

—— et al. (eds) 2000, *Without Guarantees: In Honour of Stuart Hall*, Verso, London.

Gitlin, T. 1995, *The Twilight of Common Dreams: Why America is Wracked by Culture Wars*, Henry Holt, New York.

Goethe, J.W. 1973, 'Some Passages Pertaining to the Concept of World Literature', in *Comparative Literature: The Early Years*, (eds) H.-J. Schulz and P.H. Rhein, University of North Carolina Press, Chapel Hill.

Goldmann, L. 1964, *The Hidden God*, trans. P. Thody, Routledge and Kegan Paul, London.

Goldthorpe, J.H. 1990, 'A Response', in *John H. Goldthorpe: Consensus and Controversy*, (eds) J. Clark, C. Modgil and S. Modgil, Falmer Press, London.

Gómez-Peña, G. 1993, *Warrior for Gringostroika*, Greywolf Press, Saint Paul, Minn.

Goodchild, P. 1996, *Deleuze and Guattari: An Introduction to the Politics of Desire*, Sage, London.

Gorak 1988, *The Alien Mind of Raymond Williams*, University of Missouri Press, Columbia.

Gramsci, A. 1971, *Selections from Prison Notebooks*, trans. Q. Hoare and G. Nowell Smith, Lawrence and Wishart, London.

—— 1977, *Selections from Political Writings 1910–1920*, trans. J. Mathews, Lawrence and Wishart, London.

Greenblatt, S. 1980, *Renaissance Self-Fashioning: From More to Shakespeare*, University of Chicago Press, Chicago.
—— 1982, 'Introduction', in *The Power of Forms in the English Renaissance*, (ed.) S. Greenblatt, Pilgrim Books, Norman.
—— 1990, *Learning to Curse: Essays in Early Modern Culture*, Routledge, London.
—— 1994, 'Invisible Bullets: Renaissance Authority and its Subversion, Henry IV and Henry V', in *Political Shakespeare: Essays in Cultural Materialism*, (eds) J. Dollimore and A. Sinfield, Manchester University Press, Manchester.
Gross, E. 1986, 'Conclusion: What is Feminist Theory?', in *Feminist Challenges: Social and Political Theory*, (eds) C. Pateman and E. Gross, Allen & Unwin, Sydney.
Grossberg, L. 1996, 'On Postmodernism and Articulation: an Interview with Stuart Hall', in *Stuart Hall: Critical Dialogues in Cultural Studies*, (eds) D. Morley and K.-H. Chen, Routledge, London.
—— et al. 1988, *It's a Sin: Essays on Postmodernism, Politics and Culture*, Power Publications, Sydney.
Grosz, E. 1989, *Sexual Subversions: Three French Feminists*, Allen & Unwin, Sydney.
—— 1990, *Jacques Lacan: A Feminist Introduction*, Routledge, Allen & Unwin, Sydney.
—— 1990a, 'Feminism and Anti-Humanism', in *Discourse and Difference: Post-Structuralism, Feminism and the Moment of History*, (eds) A. Milner and C. Worth, Centre for General and Comparative Literature, Monash University, Melbourne.
—— 1994, 'Experimental Desire: Rethinking Queer Subjectivity', in *Supposing the Subject*, (ed.) J. Copjec, Verso, London.
—— 1994a, *Volatile Bodies: Toward a Corporeal Feminism*, Allen & Unwin, Sydney.
Guattari, F. 1986, 'The Postmodern Dead End', *Flash Art*, 128.
Guha, R. and Spivak, G.C. (eds) 1988, *Selected Subaltern Studies*, Oxford University Press, Oxford.
Gunew, S. 1985, 'Australia 1984: A Moment in the Archaeology of Multiculturalism', in *Europe and Its Others*, Vol. I, (eds) F. Barker et al., University of Essex, Colchester.
—— 1990, 'Denaturalizing Cultural Nationalisms: Multicultural Readings of "Australia"', in *Nation and Narration*, (ed.) H.K. Bhabha, Routledge, London.
—— 1994, *Framing Marginality: Multicultural Literary Studies*, Melbourne University Press, Melbourne.
Habermas, J. 1971, *Knowledge and Human Interests*, trans. Jeremy Schapiro, Beacon Press, Boston.
—— 1975, *Legitimation Crisis*, trans. T. McCarthy, Beacon Press, Boston.
—— 1979, 'Conservatism and Capitalist Crisis', *New Left Review*, 115.

—— 1984, *The Theory of Communicative Action*, Vol. I, *Reason and the Rationalisation of Society*, trans. T. McCarthy, Beacon Press, Boston.

—— 1985, 'Modernity—An Incomplete Project', in *Postmodern Culture*, (ed.) H. Foster, Pluto Press, London.

—— 1987, *The Philosophical Discourse of Modernity*, trans. F. Lawrence, Polity Press, Cambridge.

—— 1987a, *The Theory of Communicative Action*, Vol. II, *Lifeworld and System: A Critique of Functionalist Reason*, trans. T. McCarthy, Polity Press, Cambridge.

—— 1988, 'Law and Morality', trans. K. Baynes, in *The Tanner Lectures on Human Values*, 8, (ed.) S.M. McMurrin, Cambridge University Press, Cambridge.

—— 1989, *The Structural Transformation of the Public Sphere: An Inquiry into a Category of Bourgeois Society*, trans. T. Burger, Polity Press, Cambridge.

—— 1990, 'What Does Socialism mean Today? The Rectifying Revolution and the Need for New Thinking on the Left', *New Left Review*, 183.

—— 1994, *The Past as Future*, (ed.) and trans. M. Pensky, Polity Press, Cambridge.

—— 1998, *A Berlin Republic: Writings on Germany*, trans. S. Rendall, Polity Press, Cambridge.

—— 1998a, 'There Are Alternatives', *New Left Review*, 231.

—— 2001, *The Postnational Constellation: Political Essays*, (ed.) and trans. M. Pensky, Polity Press, Cambridge.

—— and Michnik, A. 1994, 'Overcoming the Past', trans. D. Fernbach, *New Left Review*, 203.

Hall, S. 1980, 'Cultural Studies: Two Paradigms', *Media, Culture and Society*, 2, 1.

—— 1980a, 'Cultural Studies and the Centre: Some Problematics and Problems', in *Culture, Media, Language*, (eds) S. Hall et al., Hutchinson/Centre for Contemporary Cultural Studies, London.

—— 1982, 'The Battle for Socialist Ideas in the 1980s', in *The Socialist Register 1982*, (eds) R. Miliband and J. Saville, Merlin Press, London.

—— 1983, 'The Great Moving Right Show', in *The Politics of Thatcherism*, (eds) S. Hall and M. Jacques, Lawrence and Wishart, London.

—— 1988, 'The Toad in the Garden: Thatcherism among the Theorists', in *Marxism and the Interpretation of Culture*, (eds) C. Nelson and L. Grossberg, Macmillan, London.

—— 1989, 'The Meaning of New Times', in *New Times: The Changing Face of Politics in the 1990s*, (eds) S. Hall and M. Jacques, Lawrence and Wishart, London.

—— 1992, 'Cultural Studies and its Theoretical Legacies', in *Cultural Studies*, (eds) L. Grossberg, C. Nelson and P. Treichler, Routledge, London.

—— 1993, 'Culture, Community, Nation', *Cultural Studies*, 7, 3.

—— 1996, 'New Ethnicities', in *Stuart Hall: Critical Dialogues in Cultural Studies*, (eds) D. Morley and K.-H. Chen, Routledge, London.

—— 1996a, 'The Meaning of New Times', in *Stuart Hall: Critical Dialogues in Cultural Studies*, (eds) D. Morley. and K.-H. Chen, Routledge, London.
—— (ed.) 1997, *Representations: Cultural Representations and Signifying Practices*, Sage, London.
—— 1999, 'Encoding/Decoding', in *The Cultural Studies Reader*, (ed.) S. During, Routledge, London.
—— 2000, 'Conclusion: the Multi-Cultural Question', in *Un/Settled Multiculturalisms: Diasporas, Entanglements, Transruptions*, (ed.) B. Hesse, Zed Books, London.
—— 2000a, 'Questioning Multiculturalism', Plenary Address, *Third International Crossroads in Cultural Studies Conference*, University of Birmingham, Birmingham.
—— and Chen, K.-H. 1996, 'Cultural Studies and the Politics of Internationalization: an Interview with Stuart Hall', in *Stuart Hall: Critical Dialogues in Cultural Studies*, (eds) D. Morley and K.-H. Chen, Routledge, London.
—— and Jacques, M. (eds) 1989, *New Times: The Changing Face of Politics in the 1990s*, Lawrence and Wishart, London.
—— and Jefferson, T. (eds) 1976, *Resistance Through Rituals: Youth Subcultures in Post-War Britain*, Hutchinson, London.
—— et al. 1978, *Policing the Crisis: Mugging, the State, and Law and Order*, Macmillan, London.
Halperin, D. 1995, *Saint Foucault: Towards a Gay Hagiography*, Oxford University Press, Oxford.
Haraway, D. 1991, *Simians, Cyborgs, and Women: The Reinvention of Nature*, Free Association Books, London.
—— 1992, 'The Promises of Monsters: A Regenerative Politics for Inappropriate/d others' in *Cultural Studies*, (eds) L. Grossberg, C. Nelson and P. Treichler, Routledge, London.
Hartley, J. 1998, 'Editorial (with goanna)', *International Journal of Cultural Studies*, 1, 1.
Hartman, G. 1997, *The Fateful Question of Culture*, Columbia University Press, New York.
Hassan, I. 1977, 'Prometheus as Performer: Toward a Posthumanist Culture? A University Masque in Five Scenes', in *Performance in Postmodern Culture*, (eds) M. Benamou and C. Caramello, Coda, Madison.
Hegel, G.W.F. 1956, *The Philosophy of History*, trans. J. Sibtree, Dover, New York.
Heller, A. 1990, 'Existentialism, Alienation, Postmodernism: Cultural Movements as Vehicles of Change in the Patterns of Everyday Life', in *Postmodern Conditions*, (eds) A. Milner et al., Berg, Oxford.
—— and Fehér, F. (eds) 1986, *Reconstructing Aesthetics: Writings of the Budapest School*, Blackwell, Oxford.

Herder, J.G. von 1968, *Reflections on the Philosophy of the History of Mankind*, trans. T.O. Churchill, (ed.) F.E. Manuel, University of Chicago Press, Chicago.

Higgins, J. 1999, *Raymond Williams: Literature, Marxism and Cultural Materialism*, Routledge, London.

Hirschkop, K. 1989, 'Introduction: Bakhtin and Cultural Theory', in *Bakhtin and Cultural Theory*, (eds) K. Hirschkop and D. Shepherd, Manchester University Press, Manchester.

Hoggart, R. 1958, *The Uses of Literacy*, Penguin, Harmondsworth.

—— 1970, *Speaking To Each Other: Vol. 2 About Literature*, Penguin, Harmondsworth.

—— 1995, *The Way We Live Now*, Chatto & Windus, London.

Honneth, A. 1996, *The Struggle for Recognition: The Moral Grammar of Social Conflicts*, trans. J. Anderson, MIT Press, Cambridge, Mass.

hooks, b. 1981, *Ain't I A Woman?: Black Women and Feminism*, South End Press, Boston.

—— 1990, 'Postmodern Blackness', *Postmodern Culture*, 1, 1.

—— 1994, *Outlaw Culture: Resisting Representations*, Routledge, London.

Horkheimer, M. 1972, *Critical Theory: Selected Essays*, trans. M.J.O. O'Connell, Seabury Press, New York.

—— 1989, 'The State of Contemporary Social Philosophy and the Tasks of an Institute of Social Research', trans. P. Wagner, in *Critical Theory and Society: A Reader*, (eds) S.E. Bronner and D. Kellner, Routledge, London.

Howe, S. 1998, *Afrocentrism: Mythical Pasts and Imagined Homes*, Verso, London.

Hull, G., Scott, P. and Smith, B. (eds) 1982, *All the Women are White, All the Blacks are Men, But Some of Us Are Brave: Black Women's Studies*, The Feminist Press, New York.

Hume, D. 1965, *Of the Standard of Taste and Other Essays*, Bobbs-Merrill, Indianapolis.

Hunter, I. 1988, *Culture and Government: The Emergence of Literary Education*, Macmillan, London.

—— 1992, 'Aesthetics and Cultural Studies', in *Cultural Studies*, (eds) L. Grossberg et al., Routledge, London.

—— 1993, 'Mind Games and Body Techniques', *Southern Review*, 26:14, pp. 172–85.

—— 1994, *Rethinking the School: Subjectivity, Bureaucracy, Criticism*, Allen & Unwin, Sydney.

Hutcheon, L. 1988, *A Poetics of Postmodernism*, Routledge, London.

Huyssen, A. 1988, *After the Great Divide: Modernism, Mass Culture and Postmodernism*, Macmillan, London.

—— 1995, *Twilight Memories: Marking Time in a Culture of Amnesia*, Routledge, London.

Irigaray, L. 1985, *This Sex Which Is Not One*, trans. C. Porter with C. Burke,

Cornell University Press, Ithaca.
Jakobson, R. 1960, 'Closing Statement: Linguistics and Poetics', in *Style in Language*, (ed.) T.A. Sebeok, MIT Press, Cambridge, Mass.
Jameson, F. 1971, *Marxism and Form*, Princeton University Press, Princeton.
—— 1972, *The Prison-House of Language*, Princeton University Press, Princeton.
—— 1981, *The Political Unconscious: Narrative as a Socially Symbolic Act*, Methuen, London.
—— 1984, 'Postmodernism, or the Cultural Logic of Late Capitalism', *New Left Review*, 146, 53–92.
—— 1985, 'Postmodernism and Consumer Society', in *Postmodern Culture*, (ed.) H. Foster, Pluto Press, London.
—— 1988, 'Discussion', in *Marxism and the Interpretation of Culture*, (eds) C. Nelson and L. Grossberg, Macmillan, London.
—— 1988a, *The Ideologies of Theory: Essays 1971–1986; Volume 2: The Syntax of History*, Routledge, London.
—— 1990, *Late Marxism: Adorno, or, the Persistence of the Dialectic*, Verso, London.
—— 1991, *Postmodernism, or The Cultural Logic of Late Capitalism*, Verso, London.
—— 1992, *Signatures of the Visible*, Routledge, London.
—— 1992a, *The Geopolitical Aesthetic: Cinema and Space in the World System*, Indiana University Press, Bloomington.
—— 1994, *The Seeds of Time*, Columbia University Press, New York.
—— 1995, 'Marx's Purloined Letter', *New Left Review*, 209.
—— 1998, *The Cultural Turn: Selected Writings on the Postmodern, 1983–1998*, Verso, London.
—— 1998a, *Brecht and Method*, Verso, London.
JanMohamad, A. and Lloyd, D. 1990, 'Introduction', in *The Nature and Context of Minority Discourse*, (eds) A. JanMohamad and D. Lloyd, Oxford University Press, New York.
Jauss, H.R., 1982, *Toward an Aesthetic of Reception*, trans. T. Bahti, Harvester, Brighton.
Johnson, B. 1987, *A World of Difference*, Johns Hopkins University Press, Baltimore.
Johnson, R. 1979, 'Histories of Culture/Theories of Ideology: Notes on an Impasse', in *Ideology and Cultural Production*, (eds) M. Barrett et al., Croom Helm, London.
Jones, P. 1999, '"The Problem is Always One of Method . . .": Cultural Materialism, Political Economy and Cultural Studies', *Key Words*, 2.
—— 2000, 'Williams's Critical Sociology of Culture', *Raymond Williams: After 2000 Conference*, Overland, Melbourne.
Kaplan, E.A. 1988, 'Introduction', in *Postmodernism and Its Discontents: Theories, Practices*, (ed.) E.A. Kaplan, Verso, London.

Klor de Alva, J. 1997, 'Aztlán, Borinquen, and Hispanic Nationalism in the United States', in *Tropicalizations*, (eds) F. Aparicio and S. Chávez-Silverman, University Press of New England, Hanover, N.J.

Kristeva, J. 1984, *Revolution in Poetic Language*, trans. M. Waller, Columbia University Press, New York.

Lacan, J. 1977, *The Four Fundamental Concepts of Psycho-Analysis*, trans. Alan Sheridan, Hogarth Press, London.

—— 1977a, *Écrits: A Selection*, trans. Alan Sheridan, W.W. Norton, New York and London.

Laclau, E. and Mouffe, C. 1985, *Hegemony and Socialist Strategy: Towards a Radical Democratic Politics*, Verso, London.

—— 1987, 'Post-Marxism without Apologies', *New Left Review*, 166.

Lal, V. 1996, *South Asian Cultural Studies*, Manohar, Delhi.

Lash, S. 1990, *Sociology of Postmodernism*, Routledge, London.

—— 1999, *Another Modernity, A Different Rationality*, Blackwell, Oxford.

Leavis, F.R. 1933, *For Continuity*, Minority Press, Cambridge.

—— 1938, *New Bearings in English Poetry*, Chatto & Windus, London.

—— 1948, *Education and the University: A Sketch for an 'English School'*, Chatto & Windus, London.

—— 1962, *Two Cultures?*, Chatto & Windus, London.

—— 1972, *Nor Shall My Sword: Discourses on Pluralism, Compassion and Social Hope*, Chatto & Windus, London.

—— and Thompson, D. 1960, *Culture and Environment*, Chatto & Windus, London.

Lévi-Strauss, C. 1963, *Structural Anthropology*, Vol. 1, trans. C. Jacobson and B. G. Schoepf, Basic Books, New York.

—— 1966, *The Savage Mind*, trans. G. Weidenfeld and Nicholson Ltd., University of Chicago Press, Chicago.

—— 1969, *The Elementary Structures of Kinship*, trans. J.H. Bell, J. Richard von Sturmer and R. Needham, Beacon Press, Boston.

—— 1976, *Structural Anthropology*, Vol. 2, trans. M. Layton, Basic Books, New York.

—— 1981, *The Naked Man, Vol. 4 of Mythologiques*, trans. J. and D. Weightman, Harper & Row, New York.

—— 1985, *The View From Afar*, trans. S. Modelski, Basic Books, New York.

Lovell, T. 1987, *Consuming Fiction*, Verso, London.

Lukács, G. 1963, *The Meaning of Contemporary Realism*, trans. J. and N. Mander, Merlin Press, London.

—— 1971, *History and Class Consciousness*, trans. R. Livingstone, Merlin Press, London.

Lyotard, J.-F. 1984, *The Postmodern Condition: A Report on Knowledge*, trans. G. Bennington and B. Massumi, University of Minnesota Press, Minneapolis.

Macherey, P. 1978, *A Theory of Literary Production*, trans. G. Wall, Routledge and Kegan Paul, London.

Maclean, M. 1990, 'Revolution and Exclusion: The Other Voice', in *Discourse and Difference: Post-Structuralism, Feminism and the Moment of History*, (eds) A. Milner and C. Worth, Centre for General and Comparative Literature, Melbourne.
Macpherson, C.B. 1962, *The Political Theory of Possessive Individualism: Hobbes to Locke*, Oxford University Press, Oxford.
Mandel, E. 1975, *Late Capitalism*, trans. J. De Bres, New Left Books, London.
Marcuse, H. 1966, *Eros and Civilization: A Philosophical Inquiry into Freud*, Beacon Press, Boston.
—— 1967, 'The Question of Revolution', *New Left Review*, 45.
—— 1968, *Negations*, trans. J.J. Shapiro, Beacon, Boston.
—— 1972, *One-Dimensional Man: Studies in the Ideology of Advanced Industrial Society*, Abacus, London.
Marx, K. 1970, *Capital: A Critique of Political Economy*, Vol. I, trans. S. Moore and E. Aveling, Lawrence and Wishart, London.
—— 1975, *Early Writings*, Penguin, Harmondsworth.
—— and Engels, F. 1967, *The Communist Manifesto*, trans. S. Moore, Penguin, Harmondsworth.
—— and Engels, F. 1970, *The German Ideology*, Part One, trans. W. Lough, C. Dutt and C.P. Magill, (ed.) C.J. Arthur, Lawrence and Wishart, London.
Marxist-feminist Literature Collective, 1978, 'Women's Writing: Jane Eyre, Shirley, Villette, Aurora Leigh', in *1848: The Sociology of Literature*, (eds) F. Barker et al., University of Essex, Colchester.
McGuigan, J. 1996, *Culture and the Public Sphere*, Routledge, New York.
Merleau-Ponty, M. 1974, *Adventures of the Dialectic*, trans. J. Bien, Heinemann, London.
Mill, J.S. 1962, *Utilitarianism*, Fontana, Glasgow.
Millett, K. 1977, *Sexual Politics*, Virago, London.
Milner, A. 2002, *Re-Imagining Cultural Studies: The Promise of Cultural Materialism*, Sage, London.
Mitchell, J. 1974, *Psychoanalysis and Feminism*, Penguin, Harmondsworth.
—— 1984, *Women: The Longest Revolution. Essays in Feminism, Literature and Psychoanalysis*, Virago, London.
Moers, E. 1978, *Literary Women*, Women's Press, London.
Moraga, C. and Anzaldúa, G. (eds), 1981, *This Bridge Called My Back: Writings by Radical Women of Color*, Persephone Press, Watertown, Mass.
Morris, M. 1988, *The Pirate's Fiancée: Feminism, Reading, Postmodernism*, Verso, London.
—— 1988a, 'Banality in Cultural Studies', *Block*, 14.
—— 1992, 'A Gadfly Bites Back', *Meanjin*, 51, 3.
Mulhern, F. 2000, *Culture/Metaculture*, Routledge, London.
Mullan, B. 1996, *Sociologists on Sociology*, 2nd edition, Avebury, Aldershot.
Nairn, T. 1977, *The Break-up of Britain*, New Left Books, London.
—— 1997a, *Faces of Nationalism: Janus Revisited*, Verso, London.

Noland, R.W. 1999, *Sigmund Freud Revisited*, Twayne, New York.
O'Regan, T. 1992, 'Some Reflections on the Policy Moment', *Meanjin*, 51, 3.
—— 2001, 'Cultural Policy: Rejuvenate or Wither?', Professorial Lecture, Griffith University, Brisbane.
Orwell, G. 1970, *Collected Essays, Journalism and Letters: Vol. 2*, Penguin, Harmondsworth.
Parsons, T. 1949, *The Structure of Social Action*, Free Press, New York.
Rex, J. 1996, *Ethnic Minorities in the Modern Nation State*, Macmillan, Basingstoke.
Reynolds, S. and Kidd, W. (eds) 2000, *Contemporary French Cultural Studies*, Arnold, London.
Robey, D. 1973, 'Introduction', in *Structuralism: An Introduction*, (ed.) D. Robey, Oxford University Press, Oxford.
Roudinescou, E. 1997, *Jacques Lacan*, trans. B. Bray, Columbia University Press, New York.
Rushdie, S. 1991, *Imaginary Homelands: Essays and Criticism 1981–1991*, Granta Books, London.
Ruthven, K.K. 1984, *Feminist Literary Studies: An Introduction*, Cambridge University Press, Cambridge.
Ryan, K. (ed.) 1996, *New Historicism and Cultural Materialism: A Reader*, Arnold, London.
Said, E.W. 1979, *The Question of Palestine*, Pantheon Books, New York.
—— 1986, *After the Last Sky: Palestinian Lives*, Faber, London.
—— 1993, *Culture and Imperialism*, Chatto & Windus, London.
—— 1994, *Representations of the Intellectual: The 1993 Reith Lectures*, Vintage, London.
—— 1995, *Orientalism*, Pantheon Books, New York.
Salomon, A. 1945, 'German Sociology', in *Twentieth Century Sociology*, (eds) G. Gurvitch and W.E. Moore, Philosophical Library, New York.
Sartre, J.-P. 1976, *Critique of Dialectical Reason*, trans. A. Sheridan-Smith, New Left Books, London.
Saussure, F. de 1974, *Course in General Linguistics*, trans. W. Baskin, Fontana, Glasgow.
Scannell, P. et al. 1992, 'Introduction', in *Culture and Power: a Media, Culture and Society Reader*, (eds) P. Scannell et al., Sage, London.
Schleiermacher, F.D.E. 1985, 'General Hermeneutics', trans. J. Duke and J. Forstman, in *The Hermeneutics Reader: Texts of the German Tradition from the Enlightenment to the Present*, (ed). K. Mueller-Vollmer, Continuum, New York.
Schlesinger, A. 1991, *The Disuniting of America*, Whittle Direct Books, Knoxville, Tenn.
Segal, L. 1999, *Why Feminism?*, Columbia University Press, New York.
Shelley, P.B. 1931, *A Defence of Poetry (with P. Sidney, An Apology for Poetry)*, (ed.) H.A. Needham, Ginn and Co., London.
Shklovsky, V. 1965, 'Art as Technique', trans. L. Lemon and M. Reis, in

Russian Formalist Criticism: Four Essays, (eds) L. Lemon and M. Reis, University of Nebraska Press, Lincoln.
Showalter, E. 1978, *A Literature of Their Own: British Women Novelists from Brontë to Lessing*, Virago, London.
—— 1985, 'Feminist Criticism in the Wilderness', in *The New Feminist Criticism: Essays on Women, Literature, and Theory*, (ed.) E. Showalter, Pantheon Books, New York.
—— 1989, 'A Criticism of Our Own: Autonomy and Assimilation in Afro-American and Feminist Literary Theory', in *The Future of Literary Theory*, (ed.) R. Cohen, Routledge, London.
Sinfield, A. 1992, *Faultlines: Cultural Materialism and the Politics of Dissident Reading*, Oxford University Press, Oxford.
—— 1994, *The Wilde Century: Effeminacy, Oscar Wilde and the Queer Moment*, Cassell, London.
—— 1994a, *Cultural Politics, Queer Reading*, Routledge, London.
—— 1997, *Literature, Politics and Culture in Postwar Britain*, 2nd edition, Athlone Press, London.
Sokal, A. 1996, 'Transgressing the Boundaries: Towards a Transformative Hermeneutics of Quantum Gravity', *Social Text*, 46/47.
—— and J. Bricmont, 1998, *Intellectual Impostures: Postmodern Philosophers' Abuse of Science*, Profile Books, London.
Sparks, C. 1996, 'Stuart Hall, Cultural Studies and Marxism', in *Stuart Hall: Critical Dialogues in Cultural Studies*, (eds) D. Morley and K.-H. Chen, Routledge, London.
Spender, D. 1980, *Man Made Language*, Routledge and Kegan Paul, London.
Spivak, G.C. 1987, *In Other Worlds: Essays in Cultural Politics*, Methuen, London.
—— 1988, 'Can the Subaltern Speak?', in *Marxism and the Interpretation of Culture*, (eds) C. Nelson and L. Grossberg, Macmillan, London.
—— 1999, *A Critique of Postcolonial Reason: Toward A History of the Vanishing Present*, Harvard University Press, Cambridge, Mass.
Stallybrass, P. and White, A. 1986, *The Politics and Poetics of Transgression*, Methuen, London.
Storey, J. 1997, *An Introduction to Cultural Theory and Popular Culture*, Prentice Hall, New York.
Stratton, J. and Ang, I. 1996, 'On the Impossibility of a Global Cultural Studies: "British" Cultural Studies in an "International" Frame', in *Stuart Hall: Critical Dialogues in Cultural Studies*, (eds) D. Morley and K.-H. Chen, Routledge, London.
Thompson, E.P. 1955, *William Morris: Romantic to Revolutionary*, Laurence and Wishart, London.
—— 1963, *The Making of the English Working Class*, Victor Gollancz, London.
—— 1978, *The Poverty of Theory and Other Essays*, Merlin Press, London.
—— 1980, 'Notes on Exterminism, the Last Stage of Civilization', *New Left Review*, 121.

Todorov, T. (ed.) 1965, *Théorie de la littérature: textes des formalistes russes*, Éditions du Seuil, Paris.
Torres, C.A. 1998, *Democracy, Education, and Multiculturalism: Dilemmas of Citizenship in a Global World*, Rowman and Littlefield, Lanham, MD.
Touraine, A. 1981, *The Voice and the Eye: An Analysis of Social Movements*, trans. A. Duff, Cambridge University Press, Cambridge.
Turner, G. 1996, *British Cultural Studies: An Introduction*, Routledge, Sydney.
Volosinov, V. N. 1973, *Marxism and the Philosophy of Language*, trans. L. Matejka and I. R. Titunik, Seminar Press, New York.
Watt, I. 1957, *The Rise of the Novel: Studies in Defoe, Richardson amd Fielding*, Penguin, Harmondsworth.
Weber, M. 1930, *The Protestant Ethic and the Spirit of Capitalism*, trans. T. Parsons, Unwin, London.
—— 1948, *From Max Weber: Esssays in Sociology*, (eds) H.H. Gerth and C. Wright Mills, Routledge and Kegan Paul, London.
—— 1949, *The Methodology of the Social Sciences*, trans. E.A. Shils and H.A. Finch, Free Press, New York.
—— 1958, *The Rational and Social Foundations of Music*, trans. D. Martindale, J. Riedel and G. Neuwirth, Southern Illinois University Press, Carbondale.
—— 1964, *The Theory of Social and Economic Organization*, trans. A. M. Henderson and T. Parsons, Free Press, New York.
—— 1968, *Economy and Society*, Vol. 3, trans. E. Fischoff et al., Bedminster, New York.
Weedon, C. 1987, *Feminist Practice and Post-Structuralist Theory*, Basil Blackwell, Oxford.
West, C. 1993, *Race Matters*, Beacon, Boston.
—— 1999, 'The New Cultural Politics of Difference' in *The Cornel West Reader*, (ed.) C. West, Basic Books, New York.
—— 1999a, 'On Black-Brown Relations' in *The Cornel West Reader*, (ed.) C. West, Basic Books, New York.
Williams, R. 1962, *Communications*, Penguin, Harmondsworth.
—— 1963, *Culture and Society 1780–1950*, Penguin, Harmondsworth.
—— 1964, *Second Generation*, Chatto & Windus, London.
—— 1965, *The Long Revolution*, Penguin, Harmondsworth.
—— 1973, *The Country and the City*, Oxford University Press, New York.
—— 1974, *The English Novel: From Dickens to Lawrence*, Paladin, St Albans.
—— 1974a, *Television: Technology and Cultural Form*, Fontana, Glasgow.
—— 1976, *Keywords: A Vocabulary of Culture and Society*, Fontana, Glasgow.
—— 1976a, *Communications*, 3rd edition. Penguin, Harmondsworth.
—— 1977, *Marxism and Literature*, Oxford University Press, Oxford.
—— 1979, *Politics & Letters: Interviews with New Left Review*, NLB, London.
—— 1980, *Problems in Materialism and Culture: Selected Essays*, New Left Books, London.

—— 1981, *Culture*, Fontana, Glasgow.
—— 1983, *Towards 2000*, Chatto & Windus, London.
—— 1989, *Resources of Hope: Culture, Democracy, Socialism*, (ed.) R. Gable, Verso, London.
—— 1989a, *The Politics of Modernism: Against the New Conformists*, (ed.) T. Pinkney, Verso, London.
—— 1989b, *What I Came To Say*, (eds) N. Belton, F. Mulhern and J. Taylor, Hutchinson Radius, London.
Wilson, S. 1995, *Cultural Materialism: Theory and Practice*, Blackwell, Oxford.
Wolff, J. 1990, *Feminine Sentences: Essays on Women and Culture*, Polity Press, Cambridge.
—— 1993, *The Social Production of Art*, Macmillan, London.
Wolfreys, J. 2000, 'In Perspective: Pierre Bourdieu', *International Socialism*, 2nd series, 87.
Wollstonecraft, M. 1975, *A Vindication of the Rights of Women*, Norton, New York.
Woolf, V. 1966, *Collected Essays*, 1, Hogarth Press, London.
—— 1979, *Women and Writing*, Women's Press, London.
Wright, E.O. 1997, *Class Counts: Comparative Studies in Class Analysis*, Cambridge University Press, Cambridge.
Yúdice, G. 1998, 'The Privatization of Culture', *Social Text*, 59, 2.
Zizek, S. 1989, *The Sublime Object of Ideology*, Verso, London.
—— 1991, *Looking Awry: an Introduction to Jacques Lacan through Popular Culture*, MIT Press, Cambridge, Mass.
—— 1992, *Everything You Always Wanted to Know about Lacan: (but were Afraid to Ask Hitchcock)*, Verso, London.
—— 1993, *Tarrying with the Negative*, Duke University Press, Durham.
—— 1994, 'Introduction: the Spectre of Ideology', in *Mapping Ideology*, (ed.) S. Zizek, Verso, London.
—— 1999, 'The Undergrowth of Enjoyment: How Popular Culture Can Serve as an Introduction to Lacan', in *The Zizek Reader*, (eds) E. Wright and E. Wright, Blackwell, Oxford.
—— 1999a, *The Ticklish Subject*, Verso, London.
—— 2001, 'Postface', in *A Defence of 'History and Class Consciousness': Tailism and the Dialectic*, G. Lukács, trans. E. Leslie, Verso, London.

Index

Page numbers in bold type, e.g. **89–91**, indicate where a topic is defined or discussed in detail.